SPREADING THE LIGHT:
WORK AND LABOUR REFORM IN
LATE-NINETEENTH-CENTURY TORONTO

This book explores new evidence on the gendered nature of working-class experience and on gender relations within the Toronto working class. Christina Burr presents case studies of the printing and garment industries to demonstrate how class, race, and especially gender were integral to the politics of work and labour reform in nineteenth-century Toronto.

One of the unique features of the study is Burr's use of workers' poetry, fiction, and political cartoons as source material. Language, symbols, and popular culture, in addition to economic factors, are examined to reveal how the working class experienced their world. Burr employs a deconstructionist cultural materialist approach to explain the strategies by which power relations were produced and reproduced by Toronto labour reformers.

In addition to being a valuable scholary contribution, *Spreading the Light* is a focused study that will prove to be a popular book in Canadian social history, women's history, and labour history courses.

(Studies in Gender and History)

CHRISTINA A. BURR is an assistant professor in the Department of History, University of Windsor.

STUDIES IN GENDER AND HISTORY

General editors: Franca Iacovetta and Karen Dubinsky

CHRISTINA BURR

Spreading the Light: Work and Labour Reform in Late-Nineteenth-Century Toronto

UNIVERSITY OF TORONTO PRESS
Toronto Buffalo London

© University of Toronto Press Incorporated 1999
Toronto Buffalo London
Printed in Canada

ISBN 0-8020-0940-9 (cloth)
ISBN 0-8020-7908-3 (paper)

∞

Printed on acid-free paper

Canadian Cataloguing in Publication Data

Burr, Christina Ann, 1959–
    Spreading the light : work and labour reform in late-nineteenth-century
    Toronto

    (Studies in gender and history series)
    Includes bibliographical references and index.
    ISBN 0-8020-0940-9 (bound)   ISBN 0-8020-7908-3 (pbk.)

    1. Labor movement – Ontario – Toronto – History – 19th century.
    2. Working class – Ontario – Toronto – Social conditions.   3. Working
    class – Ontario – Toronto – History – 19th century.   4. Sexual division of
    labor – Ontario – Toronto – History – 19th century.   I. Title.   II. Series.

    HD8110.T672B87 1999   331.8'09713'54109034   c98-932639-x

---

University of Toronto Press acknowledges the financial assistance to its publishing
program of the Canada Council for the Arts and the Ontario Arts Council.

This book has been published with the help of a grant from the Humanities and Social
Sciences Federation of Canada, using funds provided by the Social Sciences and
Humanities Research Council of Canada.

For my parents,
Frank and Barbara Burr

Contents

ACKNOWLEDGMENTS ix

1 Introduction 3
2 'The Other Side': The Rhetoric of Labour Reform 14
3 'Spread the Light': Phillips Thompson and the Politics of Labour Reform 32
4 'An Artist of Righteousness': J.W. Bengough's Comic Art and Labour and Working-Class Reform 56
5 'The Art Preservative': Gender, Skill, and Craft Sense in the Printing Trades 98
6 Beyond the Home Circle: Separate Spheres, Labour Reform, and Working-Class Women 126
7 'Bring the Girls into the Fold': Work, Family, and the Politics of Labour Reform in the Toronto Garment Trades 152
8 Conclusion 180

NOTES 185

BIBLIOGRAPHY 227

INDEX 247

Acknowledgments

This book could not have been completed without the support of family, friends, and colleagues, and it gives me great pleasure to thank them here.

I completed most of the work on the nineteenth-century Toronto printing trades as a Ph.D. candidate at Memorial University of Newfoundland. Greg Kealey supervised the thesis on which a chapter of this book is based. While comparisons will no doubt be made to his own research on the nineteenth-century Toronto working class, Greg generously shared his research notes, microfilm, and knowledge of the world of the nineteenth-century Toronto working class with me. In addition to intellectual stimulation, he also provided solid advice on how to negotiate the politics of academic life. Linda Kealey was also one of my mentors, and fuelled my feminist consciousness. Caitlin Kealey and Max provided welcome diversions during my years at Memorial. I can't begin to express my gratitude to the Kealey family for all they have done for me over the years.

During the time I lived in St John's, Robert Sweeny and Elizabeth-Anne Malischewski provided conversation, companionship, and many excellent meals. Gary Kinsman's intellectual input into the project has been invaluable. He willingly tolerated my many queries about feminist and poststructuralist theories. He also introduced me to Brian Conway, who provided accommodation on several occasions during my research trips to Toronto.

I benefited from the collective knowledge and support of many colleagues and friends who encouraged me as I worked on this book. In Toronto, Franca Iacovetta, Craig Heron, Bettina Bradbury, Ian Radforth, and Kate McPherson all provided invaluable input. At the University of Ottawa, Ed Montigny and Chad Gaffield encouraged me to keep at it.

I also thank the archivists at the Provincial Archives of Ontario and the National Archives of Canada. Sharon Shipley and Alain Lamarche at the

National Archives provided the illustrations for this book in record time. I acknowledge the financial support provided by the Social Sciences and Humanities Research Council of Canada, both for a postdoctoral fellowship that allowed me to complete the research and for funding to publish the book. At the University of Toronto Press, the labours of Franca Iacovetta, Karen Dubinsky, Gerry Hallowell, Emily Andrew, and John St James in guiding the manuscript through the many 'hoops' of publication is very much appreciated.

This book is dedicated with much love to my parents, Frank and Barbara Burr. They have taught me the lessons of twentieth-century working-class life, helped to finance three university degrees, and moved me from city to city. They made many sacrifices to provide me with a higher education, and I know that they are tremendously proud to see this work in print. Now that I have relocated to Windsor, I am delighted to see that our 'Home Circle' is together more often these days.

SPREADING THE LIGHT:
WORK AND LABOUR REFORM IN
LATE-NINETEENTH-CENTURY TORONTO

1

Introduction

In 1887 T. Phillips Thompson, a prominent Toronto journalist, radical intellectual, Knights of Labor member, and labour reformer, published his critique of the North American political-economic system, entitled *The Politics of Labor*.[1] The 1880s were an era of mounting public concern about conditions within the working class, and also of increasing unemployment and labour unrest, which culminated in widespread upheaval in 1886. 'Unless a thorough reconstruction of the industrial system arrests the tendency to demoralization by ensuring healthier conditions for the development of a higher standard of manhood and womanhood,' Thompson wrote, the same enfeeblement and degradation of the race which proved the ruin of the ancient civilizations based upon slavery and caste supremacy will assuredly sap the system reared by capitalism upon a like foundation of industrial serfdom.'[2] For Thompson, and for other late-nineteenth-century labour reformers, industrial-capitalist transformations could not be reduced simply to class structure, economic restructuring, and urban growth. These developments were interwoven with discourses about the detrimental impact of industrialization and urbanization on the sexual morality of working men and their families, and with concerns over nation-building and the preservation of the 'race,' which for most later-nineteenth-century Torontonians meant the hegemony of those of British-Protestant origins.

In *The Politics of Labor*, Thompson further pointed to the diversities and differences that existed within the working class. 'The forces of labor,' he indicated, 'have in the past been divided by countless lines of cleavage in all directions, by differences of party, nation, creed, of sex and color, of occupation and locality; by jealousies between skilled and unskilled brain and manual workers; and by finely-drawn grades and distinctions between those of the same trade.'[3] While some Canadian historians have lamented the fragmentation of their idea of Canadian consciousness in the writings of social historians, nineteenth-century labour reformers themselves, as Thompson's writings reveal, understood that industrial capitalism was simultaneously creating and dividing the working class along the lines of sex, race, skill, occupation, and nationality.[4] Within the field of Canadian labour history, however, there has been a tendency to privilege male workers over female workers, the workplace over the family, and English-Canadian workers over immigrant workers.

In the pages that follow, I investigate the ways in which class, gender, and race informed the politics of work and labour reform in late-nineteenth-century Toronto. By politics, I do not mean solely contests about formal participation in government, although these struggles certainly occurred, but contests over power and knowledge that took place in a variety of institutions, including the workplace, the trade union, and the family. The focus on Toronto, a leading nineteenth-century Canadian industrial city, allows historical study of an important formative moment during which local reformers and workers of both sexes struggled to interpret and transform the conditions of workers in industrializing society.[5] I argue that, in addition to class, gender and race also permeated the consciousness of Toronto's working men and working women in various and sometimes diverse ways. Although class sometimes emerges at the forefront of my narrative, and in other instances gender and race seem to take centre stage, I suggest that class, gender, and race had a distinct but interconnected existence among the nineteenth-century Toronto working class and in the rhetoric of labour reformers.

The line of enquiry pursued in the book stems from my engagement with feminist critiques of the writings completed by the 'new labour historians' over the last twenty-five years. When I first began studying labour history in the mid-1980s, I felt alienated as a white woman from a working-class-family background by the writings in labour history that did not consider gender as a category for analysis. Labour historians writing in the late 1970s and early 1980s, who were influenced by the late Edward Thompson's *The Making of the English Working Class*, called for the historical study of the 'totality' of working-class 'experience' including 'their cultural backgrounds and social relations, as well as their institutional memberships and economic and political behaviour.'[6] Emphasis was placed on the materiality of working-class culture and the emergence of a homogeneous working-class 'culture of control.'[7] The 'new labour history' produced a rich portrait of Canadian working-class movements, working-class culture and social networks, and labour processes. As feminist historians point out, however, labour history has 'remained a preserve of male workers,' and women are still marginalized in the narratives of labour historians.[8] This focus on class analysis has further precluded the effective integration of gender and race into the writing of labour history.

I found interpretations more congenial to my knowledge of working-class life in the writings of Canadian women's historians who criticized male labour historians for their masculinist view of class. They argued that the experience of class, and of class consciousness, was not the same for both sexes. Working-class immigrant women were the focus of study in a pioneering collective endeavour in the field of Canadian women's history entitled *Women at Work, Ontario 1850–1930*, which appeared in 1974.[9] The field developed during the 1970s in a dialogue with Marxism and the Left. A concern with working-class women was central to the feminist political agenda of the time, and to the writing of women's history.[10]

When I began my research in the late 1980s, I was influenced by the writings of Marxist feminists and socialist feminists, who argued that within the workplace skill classifications were socially organized to define men's work as skilled and women's work as unskilled or semi-skilled. *Spreading the Light* builds on the material experience of working-class life as conceived by this group of feminists during the 1980s, most notably, Anne Phillips, Barbara Taylor, and Cynthia Cockburn.[11] The case studies of the Toronto printing and garment industries, in chapters 5 and 7 respectively, show how masculinity and femininity shaped the division of labour during Toronto's industrial revolution as employers sought to replace skilled working men with cheaper women and child labour. In response, male artisans identified skill with manhood at the expense of fragmenting the working class. While I sympathize with the concerns of women's historians that studies of gender and masculinity must not dominate the field, with women's experiences taking second place to those of men, I agree with those working-class and women's historians who argue that masculinity has historically been a constitutive part of working men's identities.[12] Also, as the case studies of the printing and garment trades show, masculinity worked to confirm male privilege, power, and authority. As a result, as Barbara Taylor wrote more than a decade ago, 'the men are as bad as their masters.'[13]

The connections between work and family, as Joan Scott, Anna Clark, and Bettina Bradbury have remarked, were neglected in the writings in labour history, which 'portrayed working-class activists as rational heroes who forged a working-class consciousness' in the 'public sphere' of work and labour organizations.[14] The case study of the garment industry in chapter 7 shows how a discourse of domesticity forged links between work and family, and between family and work. Women garment workers, nevertheless, organized separate women's unions in Toronto and demanded equal pay with male workers. My study builds on the writings of women's labour historians who have argued that although women did not participate as fully as men in labour activism, the tension between women's militant activism and the rhetoric of domesticity was an important dynamic of the working-class movement. Women, as these studies further illustrated, also articulated their own set of interests as workers.[15] Thus, I explore the ways in which 'gender,' defined as the cultural meanings associated with sexual difference, forms the basis for inequalities in power, rights, and privileges.[16]

During the 1980s, the politics of sexual difference took on another different meaning as Third World women, women of colour, and working-class women criticized white, middle-class feminist theorizing for neglecting to consider differences in experience among women, and for its inability to effectively integrate an analysis of race.[17] In the writing of women's history, awareness of the difference between women's and men's history has been complemented, as Gisela Bock remarked, 'by an awareness and historical study of the otherness, the differences and inequalities among women themselves.'[18] This emphasis on diversity among women, and a questioning of whether historians can even know women's 'experience,' has posed a challenge to the notion of a universal Anglo middle-class ideal of masculinity and femininity that was imposed on the working-class from above.[19] Exposure to this body of feminist literature also made me attentive to the ways in which racism is essential to colonial and imperialist social relations.[20] By studying already used sources in new ways, particularly the vibrant nineteenth-century Toronto labour press and trade-union journals, I was able to locate gender and race in these sources where the previous generation of labour historians had thought they did not exist. Also, by casting the net wide to incorporate a variety of institutional sites, including the workplace, the family, the trade union, and the labour movement, I have been able to show the numerous and diverse ways in which class, gender, and race were integral to the nineteenth-century Toronto working-class experience and the politics of labour reform.

If we are to understand fully how class, gender, and race informed the nineteenth-century labour-reform movement we must also integrate language with institutional practice. An analysis of how these systems of meaning are contested politically and given form through discourse is central to understanding how Toronto labour reformers constructed discourses of working-class manliness counter to those of employers that disparaged working men. In doing so, labour reformers opened up a space for 'counter-identification' that empowered rather than victimized working men.[21]

While the tools of post-structuralism are useful for understanding how systems of meaning are put together, I do not want to suggest that 'discourse is all,' or that all social relations can be reduced to language, as some post-structuralist historians have claimed.[22] By combining the experiences of working men and women with the analysis of the rhetoric of labour reform, and by grounding an analysis of culture in the material, I go beyond the sterile debates about whether it is economics or language that determines class consciousness. In Canadian historiography the recent studies by Cecilia Morgan and Lynne Marks have illustrated that the material and the discursive need not be mutually exclusive approaches. The deconstructionist cultural-materialist approach used by Marks in her discussion of how the Knights of Labor used, and reinterpreted, the ideas associated with the dominant discourses of respectability, manliness, and Christianity to assert working people's rightful place in society influenced my discussion of the rhetoric of radical domesticity and woman's sphere in chapter 6.[23]

Workers' poetry, fiction, and political cartoons, sources that in more traditional historical circles are still considered peripheral to the project of writing 'real' labour history, are used extensively throughout the book. These sources allowed me to explore the ways in which language, symbols, and popular culture, in addition to the economic components of working-class life, were integral to an understanding of the ways in which working people experienced their world as organized, yet simultaneously divided, along the lines of class, gender, and race. Symbols, metaphors, and tropes were not merely interesting literary devices, or a reflection of social and economic changes, but rather were strategies by which power relations were produced and reproduced. Discourses of labour reform, furthermore, were grounded in political economy and material social relations, particularly the organization of the labour market, colonization, imperialism, and state intervention.

Materialist feminist and post-Marxist feminist theorizing has provided a reconceptualization of subjectivity and experience that takes into account that the subject is not always a force for domination in a particular discursive context. We are not passive acted-upon agents but, instead, 'active-while-acted-upon' agents.[24] Experience is given meaning and made comprehensible through discourse. Thus, consciousness of self, and of class, gender, and race, 'is interpreted or reconstructed by each of us within the horizon of meanings and knowledges available in the culture at given historical moments.'[25] This cultural-materialist and historical notion of self as a subject, which is not always a force for domination, validates direct agency and creates a space for resistance. This conceptualization of the self and agency informs my study of work and labour reform.

Chapter 2 opens with a discussion of the rhetoric of labour reform during the nine-hours movement of the early 1870s. Toronto Local 3 of the Coopers International Union provided the impetus for the organization of the Toronto Trades Assembly (TTA) in April 1871. The following spring the journeymen members of the TTA were embroiled in the province-wide struggle for shorter working hours, which became known as the nine-hours movement. The class dimension of the nine-hours campaign has already been documented in the writings of Canadian labour history.[26] The language of labour reformers, and the coded sets of representations by which they defended the morality of the working class and articulated their own definition of working-class manhood is explored in the chapter. In opposition to employers who negatively defined working men as a class to be feared, labour reformers and skilled craftsmen articulated a counter-discourse that emphasized worker independence and commitment to the collective goals of trades unionism. This was accomplished, at least in part, through the institutional framework of the Toronto Trades Assembly. Labour reformers also wrote poetry and fiction that was published in the labour press, and working people read and digested them as part of their cultural diet.

Although the gender rhetoric of Toronto's skilled white workmen was in many ways similar to that of the late-Victorian middle class, it sustained a unique working-class politic. Masculinity for a 'good' craftsman was organized around adherence to the principles of trades unionism, specifically loyalty to union brothers, and intellectual and moral elevation, which was associated with the ideals of citizenship. The body was invested as a political field during the nineteenth century, and the application of disciplinary power over the mind was crucial to the collective goals of labour reform. Among Toronto labour reformers, furthermore, masculine gender identity was not defined exclusively by workplace status, but also by a male worker's status in the family as father, husband, and breadwinner.

During the early 1870s, male trade unionists were as much concerned with constructing their own identities as skilled white working men as they were with categorizing those they defined as 'others,' notably Chinese and unskilled immigrant labourers. Their capacity to locate themselves in a position of authority vis-à-vis Chinese and immigrant labourers was an important aspect of the authority of skilled male British-Canadian trade unionists. In 1871, 44 per cent of the city's total population of 56,092 was British-born, and 51 per cent was Canadian-born, although the latter group was also largely of British stock.[27] British immigrants were an important source of the city's factory labour throughout the latter nineteenth century. This connection with Britain was an integral part of the discourse of labour reform articulated during the 1870s. It defined a select community of Canadian working men who retained ties to the 'Mother Country.' Local labour reformers simultaneously created and fragmented the working class by excluding certain groups by race and by articulating their own variant of national identity. Surprisingly, liberal, Anglo-Protestant reformer John Wilson Bengough, cartoonist, lecturer, poet, and editor of the popular comic paper *Grip*, was ambivalent about the Orange-Green sectarian conflicts that dominated nineteenth-century Toronto. While he suggested that the peaceable citizens paid dearly for sectarian strife, his comic art reinforced Irish racial stereotypes well known to his audience, particularly his

Toronto readers. The Irish-Catholic immigrants of Dummer Street were identified in the pages of *Grip* as a source of vice and urban degeneration.[28]

The term 'labour reformer' was never synonymous with 'trade-union official,' although the two were not necessarily mutually exclusive. In nineteenth-century North America, leadership for the nascent labour-reform movement was provided by a loose coalition of men and women, both middle class and working class, who devoted themselves to the interests of the labouring classes as they understood them.[29] Among them were journalists, lawyers, clergymen, pamphleteers, doctors, trade-union leaders, artisans, skilled mechanics, small entrepreneurs, and men and women heads of reform associations. In late-nineteenth-century Toronto, a small but colourful group of dissenters and radicals established a network of clubs and organizations for the transmission of their ideas for improving the conditions of the working class. By the early 1890s, Toronto's radical movement included labour reformers, single taxers, supporters of women's suffrage, Bellamyite nationalists, anti-monopolists, supporters of the Patrons of Industry, and members of the Irish Land League. Many radical reformers belonged to more than one organization. This diverse and often ambiguous radical legacy was characterized by a Christian and secular ethical appeal.[30] In contrast to their more moderate contemporaries, including William Howland, mayor of Toronto in 1886 and 1887, radicals agreed that fundamental changes had to be made to Canada's systems of government and ownership in order to alleviate the problems of unemployment, inadequate housing, and low wages among the working class.

Chapter 3 focuses on the rhetoric of labour reform in the writings of radical Phillips Thompson. His career has been described by historian Ramsay Cook as a 'kaleidoscope of late Victorian nonconformity.'[31] During the 1880s and 1890s, Thompson was at the forefront of virtually every social and labour reform movement in Toronto. He lectured and wrote extensively on labour reform, land monopoly, and landlordism in Ireland. He was active in a variety of reform organizations, including the Knights of Labor, the Single Tax Association, the Nationalist Club, the Anti-Poverty Society, the Trades and Labor Congress, the Patrons of Industry, the Theosophical Society, and the Toronto Suffrage Association.[32] While co-editing the Toronto daily *News* with Edmund E. Sheppard from 1883 to 1887, Thompson also wrote a regular column for the regional Knights of Labor organ, *The Palladium of Labor*, under the pseudonym 'Enjolras.' These articles formed the basis for his 1887 work *The Politics of Labor*.

As a journalist for the local labour press and various daily newspapers, and a central figure in the city's labour and social reform movements, Thompson was one of a handful of 'brainworkers,' who viewed their role as one of educating working people about the problems associated with industrial-capitalist growth.

This education would provide workers with the knowledge necessary to implement change. The various newspapers for which Thompson wrote, and sometimes organized and edited, were integral to the process by which the message of labour reform was transmitted to a wider audience. Through his often humorous lectures and clever songs and verses, Thompson was an active agent in the formation of a distinctive labour-reform discourse counter to that of the dominant bourgeois class.

In addition to his work as an activist, Thompson articulated a vision of political economy drawn from his experience as a labour reformer at the centre of Knights of Labor activity in Ontario during the 1880s. Unlike the exclusive craft-based unions, the Knights of Labor included unskilled labourers, women, and workers of non-Anglo ethnic backgrounds. In opposition to bourgeois liberal political economy and laissez-faire economics, the language of political economy in Thompson's writings combined the rhetoric of democratic republicanism and Christian moral economy.

While other historians, namely Gregory Kealey, Ramsay Cook, and Russell Hann, have studied Thompson's career as a labour reformer, their works focused primarily on the class dimension of Thompson's writings.[33] The contribution of the discussion presented here is to incorporate an analysis of the language of race and gender in addition to that of class. During the 1880s, Thompson presented his view of political economy from his position as a radical labour reformer at the forefront of Knights of Labor activity in Ontario. His political economy combined the ideals of democratic republicanism and Christian moral economy with the rhetoric of 'the solidarity of labor.' This construction of political economy, however, was incompatible with a set of racial prejudices that excluded outsiders who did not share them. Together with his contempories in the Knights of Labor and in the Toronto labour movement, Thompson targeted Chinese and immigrant labourers for exclusion. Also, while Thompson incorporated women workers into his discussion of political economy, his use of the language of 'equal rights' and 'separate spheres' was ambiguous. He was deeply sympathetic to the plight of women workers, and supported the organization of women operatives, but like other male Knights of Labor he too looked forward to the day when women workers might return to their 'sphere' in the home. According to Thompson, the role of educated labour reformers, or 'labour's intellectuals,' was to educate workers, through public addresses and the labour press, about the principles of labour reform. During the 1880s, the Knights of Labor provided the institutional support for Thompson's project of labour reform.

Unlike the radical Thompson, who would embrace the socialist solution by the early 1890s, John Wilson Bengough remained committed to the single-tax doctrines of American social critic Henry George as put forth in the 1879 book *Poverty and Progress*.[34] Bengough's comic art, as chapter 4 explains, relied on powerful symbols and institutional supports through which the project of labour and social reform was organized and conveyed to the public. The political vision laid out by Bengough in his cartoons and poetry was laden with metaphors and allegories that utilized images of class, gender, and race. His critique of the National Policy was represented in his cartoons through the gendered image of Miss Canada. Bengough used coded representations of gender and race in his comic art not only to encourage opposition to the Conservative government's National Policy tariff, but also to mobilize working-class support. The Protestant moralist Bengough held the 'Christian craftsman' in high esteem in his vision of social reform. Although both Bengough and Thompson advocated independence from Britain, they articulated their ideas about nation-building in terms of Anglo-Saxon absolutes and racial hierarchies organized around the notion of the superiority of the Anglo-Saxon race and their vision of a British-Canadian identity. Bengough saw the work of cartoonist and social critic as entirely compatible. Like Thompson, he too saw his role as primarily that of educator. My analysis of Bengough's cartoons and writings goes beyond existing historical writing by explicating how the language of gender, race, and class presented in *Grip* was an integral part of a social-reform discourse whereby existing power relations were challenged and sometimes reinforced.

Throughout the nineteenth century, male printing-trades workers were at the forefront of the local labour-reform movement. Many prominent Toronto labour reformers either apprenticed as printers, or continued to work in the printing trades. Chapter 5 is a case study of nineteenth-century Toronto printing-trades workers. How gender enters into trade unionism and the definition of skill is explored. A gender division of labour, combined with a masculine workplace culture and a predominantly male trade-union organization, contributed to the relegatation of women workers to low-paying, low-status jobs that were socially defined as unskilled or semi-skilled.

Skilled British immigrant printing-trades workers, including Toronto engraver Frederick Brigden Sr, brought with them a knowledge of the 'craftsman ideal' as espoused by John Ruskin and William Morris. The 'craftsman ideal' reasserted the power of the skilled working man by reuniting 'art' and 'labour,' using powerful masculine symbols rooted in the roughness and imperfections of Gothic architecture. The reunification of 'art' and 'labour,' was necessary to the reformers' project of curbing the fragmentation of social life brought about by industrial capitalism, thereby enabling the organization of a cooperative commonwealth.

Toronto's extensive commercial and industrial growth during the later nineteenth century provided new employment opportunities for women outside domestic service. By 1871, the garment industry was the leading sector of industrial production in Toronto. This sector was dependent on the sweated labour of immigrant women and children in the home, which was never reported in the census enumerations. Toronto's industrial revolution, furthermore, relied extensively on older family-based modes of production in addition to factory production. Women also found work in a variety of other industrial and commercial sectors, including boot and shoe factories, bookbinderies, cigar factories, box-making establishments, or as sales clerks in the city's retail stores.[35] While both working men and women were subjected to long hours, dangerous working conditions, low pay, and periods of unemployment, women workers were even more vulnerable.

Civic reformers and middle-class women reformers took up 'the girl problem.' They established rescue agencies and institutions for policing sexual danger. These reform initiatives, notably those by middle-class club women, who established a chapter of the YWCA in Toronto in 1878 or joined the local branch of the National Council of Women in the 1890s, have already received considerable scholarly attention in the writings by women's historians.[36] Toronto's labour reformers were also concerned about the plight of women workers. An initial attempt to organize women workers occurred during the period of initial labour-movement upsurge in the city with the organization of women shoe operatives into a branch of the Daughters of St Crispin in 1870. During the 1880s a concerted effort was made to organize women workers under the Knights of Labor.

Chapters 6 and 7 take up the question of women's wage work. The metaphor of 'separate spheres' is unpacked in chapter 6. While this metaphor has long been an organizational framework for the writing of both women's history and labour history, my research has been influenced by Linda Kerber and Sonya Rose's calls for a rigorous deconstruction of the binary oppositions surrounding separate spheres.[37] Thus, I show how the rhetoric of separate spheres was used for radical political purposes by male labour activists to protect their position of privilege in the workplace and in the family. The rhetoric of domesticity and woman's 'private sphere' in the home was also used during the 1880s to draw women into the 'public sphere' of the labour movement. Chapter 7 focuses on how men and women employed in the city's garment industry negotiated the reciprocal effects of work on family and family on work. Women's inferior position in the family reinforced sex segregation in the garment industry by allowing employers to reproduce severe forms of exploitation using the 'outside system.'[38]

Spreading the Light breaks new ground in the writing of the Canadian labour and working-class history by showing how class, gender, and race were integral to the politics of work and labour reform in nineteenth-century Toronto. In doing so it reveals the complexities of nineteenth-century working-class life and the possibilities for change. For the writing of gender history, it suggests that gender is constituted and reconstituted continually as various groups politically contest various notions of masculinity and femininity. As Toronto's labour reformers struggled to improve the lives of working men and women in the industrializing city they did so with optimism and an eye to a future world like that penned by Phillips Thompson in a song entitled 'In the Reign of Justice.'

There's a glorious future in store
　　When the toil-worn shall rise from the dust,
Then the poor shall be trampled no more
　　And mankind to each other be just.

　　　　　　Chorus
　　In the sweet by and by,
When the spirit of justice shall reign,
　　By and by.
　　In the sweet by and by,
When the spirit of justice shall reign.

Then the world with new life shall be blessed,
　　Oppression shall vanish away,
None shall toil at another's behest
　　In the light of the glorious day.
　　Chorus – In the sweet, etc.

In this weltering chaos of night,
　　Though the struggle be bitter and long,
Let us still turn our eyes to the light
　　And gain strength for the battle with wrong.
　　Chorus – In the sweet, etc.

In the fullness of time it will come
　　And our labor the way will prepare,
Though our hearts may be bold in the tomb
　　Yet our spirits that rapture will share.
　　Chorus – In the sweet, etc.[39]

2

'The Other Side':
The Rhetoric of Labour Reform

During the early 1870s, in a period of economic growth and industrialization in
Ontario, trade-union membership increased, new unions were organized, the
important struggle for shorter hours occurred, and the institutional framework
for the labour movement was put into place. In February 1871, the journeymen
members of the Coopers International Union (CIU) No. 3 of Toronto, on the
directive of international president Martin Foran, appointed a committee composed of John Hewitt, E.S. Gooch, and James Judge to consult with the various
organized societies of working men in the city for the purpose of forming a central body.[1] Twenty-eight-year-old Hewitt, a Irish-Protestant immigrant, had
already amassed considerable knowledge about labour reform while working in
New York for three years in the late 1860s. He would emerge as a leading
spokesman and idealogue during the nine-hours campaign of 1872.[2]

On 12 April 1871, delegates from the various trade organizations in the city
met in the Iron Moulders' Hall and formally organized the Toronto Trades
Assembly. Hewitt was elected president, John Dance of the Iron Moulders'
Union vice-president, and James S. Williams of the Typographical Union
recording secretary. Both Dance and Williams had been born in London,
England. The identification of Toronto labour reformers with the United States
and Britain, and their knowledge of the labour-reform movement in those countries, helped to shape the rhetoric of the nascent Toronto labour movement.[3]

In the midst of the nine-hours movement, which was launched by Hamilton
workers on 27 January 1872, Hewitt provided the impetus for the founding of a
labour newspaper in Toronto. Established as a cooperative newspaper, the first
issue of the *Ontario Workman* appeared on 18 April 1872, with James S. Williams as editor. The *Ontario Workman* was published weekly until 9 April
1874. The newspaper remained a cooperative venture for only six months, however. In September 1872, John A. Macdonald, in an effort to attract working-

class voters, secretly loaned Williams, and his partners Joseph C. McMillan and David Sleeth, the money to purchase the paper. All of the men were known Conservative party supporters.[4]

In response to the rhetoric of employers – most notably that of George Brown, editor of the *Globe* and Grit politician – which negatively defined working men as a class to be feared, labour reformers were confronted with the task of building a positive working-class identity. The language of labour reformers during the early 1870s created a positive image of working-class manhood for purposes of mobilizing working-class support and combatting the opponents of the nascent labour movement. Labour reformers presented a distinctive masculine subject organized around the honest, skilled, Anglo-Saxon working man who struggles against the evils of capitalist exploitation. The masculinity of the working man was not completely autonomous, however, and its content was influenced by the dominant middle-class culture.

The role of the nineteenth-century labour reformer was to educate working-class men, and to transform them into concerned citizens, workers, trade unionists, husbands, and fathers. A handful of intellectuals and reform-oriented journalists attempted to create an alternative 'serious' working-class fiction and labour press that was unlike the 'penny dreadfuls' or dime novels favoured by workers during their leisure hours. The representations of male workers in working-class fiction was counter to the images of working men presented in the writings of middle-class reformers.[5] In response to the subjection of workers in the factory and the workshop, working-class narratives reversed bourgeois discourses that disparaged workers, and trade unionism in particular. This portrayal opened up a space for counter-identification that empowered rather than victimized male workers.

Melodrama was used to educated workmen in the cause of labour reform. A novel entitled *The Other Side*, by American labour reformer Martin Foran, was published in the *Ontario Workman* in weekly instalments between 27 June 1872 and 27 February 1873. The working-man subject was partially constituted by the discourses of the state, the trade union, the workplace, and the family, but that subject was also less formally, perhaps, but no less effectively, constructed through literature.

Rethinking Labour Reform in Toronto during the Early 1870s

During the spring of 1872, George Brown, editor and owner of the *Globe*, played a prominent role in mobilizing employer resistance to the nine-hours movement through his editorials in that newspaper. He spearheaded the organization of an employers' association, named the Master Printers' Association.

Brown also had the striking printers in his employ prosecuted for conspiracy to combine.[6] A follower of Manchester liberalism, Brown reduced the issue to one of the simple operation of the economic law of supply and demand. 'It is a question of profit and loss as between the employer and the employed,' he argued. '[I]t is one that may well be discussed on social and moral grounds; but there is no law in morals or philosophy that makes eight or nine hours' labour right, and ten hours' wrong.' In his editorials, Brown suggested that workers had a right to bargain with employers for shorter hours and higher wages, but he further indicated that if employers decided to make a bargain for a ten-hour workday, there was no injustice in their position.[7]

Brown denounced the arguments in favour of a reduction in working hours made by labour reformers at nine-hour rallies held throughout southwestern Ontario in the spring of 1872. He classified the speakers who addressed the crowds gathered at these rallies as 'foreign agitators' or 'the agents of English trades' unions who make money out of labour agitation.' Another even more dangerous class, Brown further suggested, were those men 'of dreamy, imaginative character, who form exaggerated notions of the evils of manual labour and vague aspirations after a different and what they consider a much higher life.' He used Charles Kingsley's fictional character Alton Locke, which was loosely based on the life of Thomas Cooper, the Chartist poet and editor of *The Chartist Rushlight*, as a symbol of the danger he believed this group of workmen posed to society.[8]

Following a nine-hours demonstration held in the Music Hall on 15 March 1872, which was addressed by Richard Trevellick, president of the National Labor Union, Brown accused Trevellick of being 'profoundly ignorant of how the social fabric of Ontario is constituted.' In his editorial, Brown claimed a position of authority as an 'insider,' and utilized the consensual 'we' pronoun in order to claim that he spoke for 'the people.'[9] 'We all work,' he wrote. 'We all began with nothing. We have all got by hard work all we own – and the richest among us work on still, and like to do it.'[10] These 'agitators' were ignorant of conditions in Canada, where, according to Brown, no class distinctions existed.

In his editorials Brown challenged the credibility of the nine-hour activists. He asked, 'What is the ambition of every working man but himself to become one of those capitalists on whose hoards so many look with no little jealousy?'[11] He relied on the dominant middle-class discourse of self-help, and emphasized that a large proportion of the capitalists of this country began as artisans or workers for wages and by 'hard saving and self-reliance' became employers.[12] In opposition to the hard-saving and self-reliant 'capitalist,' Brown described the 'handicraftsman' as a worker who relied almost exclusively on brute strength and knew little of mental effort. In Brown's view, any man who refused to work ten hours a day was a 'loafer,' and did not properly carry out his 'manly' obligations in the public realm or provide adequately for his family. Brown did not agree that a reduction in working hours would necessarily be used for purposes of self-help, education, or a healthier home life. He further asserted that an increase in leisure time would only heighten the moral degeneration among the working class by giving them more time to frequent the tavern and the billiard hall.[13] Thus, Brown transformed the issue of a reduction in working hours into a problem of lack of moral fibre among working-class men.

During the early 1870s, Toronto labour reformers confronted the task of constructing a positive working-class masculine identity. In doing so, they emphasized that their efforts were not isolated, but were instead, as John Hewitt stated at the 15 February rally, 'on the heels of the noble working men of Great Britain and those in the United States.'[14] Later, at another demonstration held in the city's East Market Square, on the evening of 24 April, Hewitt referred to the 'cosmopolitan feeling' among working men, and suggested that 'they were losing that local and sectional feeling which used to characterize them.'[15]

Canada's colonial relationship with Britain was incorporated into labour-reform discourse, and was used to define a community that included Canadian working men. Rather than the 'foreign agitators' depicted by George Brown, Toronto labour reformers indicated that the nine-hours movement was derived from the 'Mother Country,' and as members of the 'great Anglo-Saxon race' working men should endeavour to align themselves with their 'brethren at home.' Toronto labour reformers promoted identification with the nine-hours movement as a 'duty' owed by workers to the Mother Country. In his speech to the rally in the East Market Square, Richard Nye, a cabinetmaker and British immigrant, used an allegory around the term 'Albion' to develop this colonial connection. The *Ontario Workman* reported:

Mr. Richard Nye, who, on coming forward, was greeted with loud cheers, said it afforded him much pleasure in again taking up the post of duty, and from which he did not nor would not flinch; but that England expected that every man would do his duty, and as he (the speaker) was from the shores of Old Albion he was highly gratified to be able from the balcony of the Albion Hotel, to advocate the rights and claims of his fellow-workingmen, whom, he was pleased to see, had met so numerously for such a noble purpose as for their own advancement, and to vindicate liberty and justice to which they, as British subjects owing allegiance to Her Majesty the Queen and the good old Union Jack, were rightly entitled to. (Applause).[16]

Poetry was also used by articulate workers to construct a working-class variant of patriotism. In the first issue of the *Ontario Workman* a poem entitled

'Canada' was published. Written especially for the *Ontario Workman*, it was
signed 'Canadian.' In the opening stanza the anonymous bard expressed the
patriotic and political ideals of Anglo-Canadian labour reformers:

> Canadian hearts, let us be loyal,
> And remain 'neath England's wing
> Till she can no longer guard us
> Then to Canada e'er cling.
> Patriot's love and heal inspire us
> To maintain our country's rights;
> Yield – no, never, to our formen,
> Though we come to bloody fights.
>
> May that time be ages distant –
> Ever here at peace remain!
> Never may Canadian freemen
> Fell the haughty tyrant's chain.
> Heaven smile upon our country –
> Guard it with thy righteous wand!
> Make it great as nations have been –
> Might as its Mother Land![17]

Patriotism, which embraced the notions of duty, obligation, and sacrifice for
Canada and the 'Mother Country,' was expected of male workers, but as the
above verse suggests, working men also had rights as citizens and as 'freemen.'
Contrary to the rhetoric of employers, notably George Brown, which excluded
or 'otherized' working-class men, Toronto labour reformers constructed their
own variant of national identity using a discourse that emphasized working
men's obligations to the British empire and their role as 'the mainstay of the
country.'

This construction of working men as vital to the project of nation-building
applied to 'white' workers only. In 1874, when the Mackenzie Liberal government announced that Chinese labourers were being considered to complete the
Canadian Pacific Railway, this particular group of workers was targeted for
exclusion by the TTA. The editor of the *Ontario Workman* stated outright that
the government should not use 'cheap Chinese labor,' and that a 'great injustice
would be done to the white population of the country.' Racist metaphors, such
as 'pig tail,' were used to define Chinese labourers as undesirable immigrant
workers.[18]

During the early 1870s labour reformers united working men around the demand for universal manhood suffrage so that they might eventually win their full rights as citizens. They drew both on the tradition of British constitutionalism and Painite egalitaritianism, and spoke of 'the universal rights of man.' J.S. Williams indicated that in politics the motto of labour reformers was 'first, Man, and then Property.'[19] The existing franchise based on property qualification was targeted as a relic of the feudal age, and independence became a powerful masculine ideal. Labour reformers rejected the rhetoric of liberal political economy that compared them to 'serfs.' In rejecting the qualification for the vote based on property, labour reformers spoke of themselves as 'free men' with a 'natural right' to the vote.

Power was reinvested in the individual in labour reformers' constructions of manliness. Qualification for the franchise, Hewitt suggested, should 'no longer be measured by that old dreg of feudalism,' but 'rather on the basis of intelligence, morality and worth, which alone constitute true manhood.' In another letter-to-the-editor of the *Ontario Workman*, Hewitt used satire to criticize the existing system of suffrage based on property. He wrote, 'Whether the man so admitted is a wise man or a fool it matters not; don't you see he is a man of property?' He continued, 'Whether he be a person of high moral character, or a profligate person, never mind; Don't you see the property; upon this the law has made him free, how dare you further question the man's respectability.'[20]

Toronto's male trade unionists applauded a bill introduced in the provincial legislature in January 1873 to extend the vote to every man who received an annual income from any calling of not less than $300 in any city or town, and of $200 in any village or township.[21] The measure, Williams wrote, 'will give votes to a large class of young men, clerks, students, professional men, mechanics and others, who have hitherto been excluded from voting because they are not on the assessment roll.'[22] Women, many of whom also worked for a wage, were omitted from the proposed suffrage amendments, and from labour reformers' comments on the proposed legislation.

Toronto labour reformers also confronted the employer-worker relationship. Their critique of the new industrial order was based on the labour theory of value.[23] 'Labor is both superior and prior to capital, and alone originally produces capital,' editor J.S. Williams stated in the *Ontario Workman*.[24] Elements of the older pre-industrial ideology of the mutuality of interests between worker and employer, and the skilled working man's property of skill and control over his labour, were retained, however. 'The interests of both classes are bound together,' Williams concluded. 'If either one is harmed, the other must ultimately suffer.' Toronto trade unionists stated at nine-hours rallies and in the *Ontario Workman* that they believed in 'a fair day's work for a fair day's pay.'[25]

Toronto labour reformers referred to the 'nobility of labour' and the 'dignity of labour,' in contradistinction to employers' efforts to 'master' the labour force. In pre-industrial social relations, the term 'master' meant a 'master of the craft,' who had also perhaps acquired his own shop. With industrial capitalism, the term 'master' was redefined to mean a 'master of men.' In a letter-to-the-editor of the *Ontario Workman*, journalist John McCormick ridiculed 'money-grubbers' who believed that 'We the employers of labor, are your masters, you are our servants, and we have the right to dictate to you the terms upon which you shall labor and live or exist.' For McCormick the very term 'master' was an abomination, as man was systematically robbed and held cheap by current social relations of production, and by laws that placed property first and man afterwards.[26] Another correspondent, who used the nom de plume 'Wood Worker,' wrote that he was highly amused to read in the *Globe* that carriage makers Messrs Hasson and Guy called themselves 'master' carriage makers. Neither of the manufacturers possessed the skills of a craftsman, yet, according to 'Wood Worker,' they cried out the loudest against benefitting skilled workmen. The correspondent concluded his letter with an evocation of workers' power as craftsmen: 'Let the mechanics of Ontario be true to each other, and we will teach those brainless, self-styled Masters, that the workmen of Ontario know their power, and are determined to use it.'[27]

During the early 1870s, the 'body politic' emerged as a site of political intervention for Toronto labour reformers.[28] In addition to investing power in the body through their articulation of labour as the source of all capital, labour reformers constructed a whole series of codes of discipline over the individual. Among nineteenth-century labour reformers few words enjoyed more popularity than 'manly,' with its connotations of dignity in labour, respectablility, and defiant egalitarianism. 'Self-help' and 'self-elevation' were consistently cited as crucial to the objectives of the labour movement. This ideal of manliness was reinforced in workers' poetry.[29] A stanza of 'A True Mechanic,' written for the *Ontario Workman* suggests that

> The man who polishes heart and mind,
> While he frames the window and shapes the blind,
> And utters his thoughts with an honest tongue,
> That is set as true as his hinges are hung,
> He is the nobleman among
>   The noble band of mechanics.[30]

The allegory mixes the images of the skill and precision required in the builder's craft with the building of the 'frame' of the 'noble' workman, which requires honesty and a pure heart. Another example of the use of the building trades as a metaphor for character development advised working men as follows:

There are as many master-workmen in you as there are separate faculties; and there are as many blows being struck as there are separate acts of emotion or volition. And this work is going on perpetually. Every single day these myriad forces are building, building, building ... It is a building of character. It is a building that must stand, and the work of inspiration warns you to take heed how you build it, to see to it that you have a foundation that shall endure; to make sure that you are building on it, not for the hour in which you live, but for that hour of revelation, when you shall be seen just as you are.[31]

Although the notion of 'self-help' articulated by labour reformers in the editorials, letters, poetry, and improving literature published in the *Ontario Workman* embraced many aspects of dominant middle-class constructions, including a Christian belief in the building of a moral character, humility, honour, and a commitment to honest hard work, there were important discrepancies between the classes. Labour reformers criticized the measurement of success as represented by the boy who rises from poverty to become a millionaire like American Jacob Astor. The fallacy of the middle-class ideal was in the manner of acquiring success. Labour reformers argued that under the prevailing social system wealth could not be acquired without chicanery in bargaining and disregard for workers. 'The standard of success is a false one,' Williams wrote. 'It is impossible for one man to get rich without causing others to suffer. It is proverbial that just and generous men do not get rich.'[32]

'Self-elevation,' incorporating both moral and intellectual improvement, was promoted as the way to a better life for working men. The rhetoric of progress and self-culture, not entirely unlike that of the late Victorian middle class, was used by Toronto labour reformers to sustain a radical critique of employers during the nine-hours campaign. At a nine-hours rally held in the Music Hall on 14 February 1872, Andrew Scott, a member of the Machinists' and Blacksmiths' Union, suggested that progress could only be made if workmen had the time to cultivate their intelligence. This goal of self-elevation, Scott observed, required a reduction in working hours in order to provide workers with the necessary leisure time.[33]

Labour reformers were confronted with how to reconcile self-elevation with the collective objectives of labour organization. They suggested that the growth of intelligence among workmen was needed to promote understanding of the importance of cooperation to the workers' cause. Cooperation among working-class men could only be furthered through the progress of intelligence. The short-lived Canadian Labor Protection and Mutual Improvement Association, organized by the leaders of the Nine-Hours League in April 1872, provided the institutional framework for the discourse of self-elevation. The intent of the organization was to elevate the intelligence of workmen, and to promote workers' common interests across local and trade boundaries.[34] Intelligent, sober, industrious, and, consequently, independent, mechanics would ultimately combine and save the country from monopolies and corrupt politicans.

The cooperative goals of Toronto labour reformers did not easily incorporate unskilled labourers, however. An 'Ex-Labourer' wrote that 'while the artisans and tradesmen of all classes are asserting the rights of labor and manhood, the laborers *par excellence* – the men of the pick and shovel, of the crowbar and hod – are, I regret to say, lying in a state of lethargy and supineness.' The 'Ex-Labourer' attributed the situation to a lack of organization.[35] A Labourers' Union was organized in Toronto in May 1873, but it apparently had a marginal presence in the TTA as its leadership was drawn from the ranks of skilled trade unionists.[36]

Among labour reformers individual elevation and self-education included a commitment to domesticity and sobriety. Opponents of a reduction in working hours argued that if workers were given more leisure time they would only spend it drinking and gambling. They targeted those male workers who spent their time away from home and in the pub. 'If the laborer thus released applies his leisure hour to his own domestic business, to his garden or his shop, to his needed rest or the education of his children ... to almost anything except dissipation, idleness and debauchery – it will prove a blessing,' J.S. Williams remarked.[37] In a subsequent editorial, Williams attributed the propensity to drink among workingmen to the monotony and drudgery of incessant labour, and for this reason he concluded that moral suasion could never succeed, and that a strict prohibitary law was necessary.[38] The rhetoric of domesticity was used to defend the morality of male workers in the larger political context, and was integral to the positive masculine identity for working men constructed by labour reformers.[39]

The nine-hours campaign of 1872 politicized the wives of working men, and a 'militant domesticity' evolved that differed from middle-class ideals of female domesticity. In a letter to the editor of the *Ontario Workman*, 'A Printer's Wife' responded to comments made by George Brown in the *Globe*. On 23 March, Brown wrote that 'the man who thinks ten hours hurtful or oppressive, is too lazy to earn his bread; and in the name of all the women of Canada, we protest against sending home such a fellow to pester his wife, loafing around for another hour daily.' The printer's wife indicated that she became indignant upon reading the 'lies' in the *Globe*, but that she thought it prudent to wait until the strike was over before commenting. No doubt she feared that her husband would lose his job had she responded before the strike was settled. In her letter the woman remarked: 'The extra hour is spent at home, 'tis true, but it is in the shape of gardening, fixing up things generally, or reading and writing, and miserable fellow – playing with the children.' She also urged the wives of working men to support trade unionism and not to 'rat it.' 'Don't let your men "go back" on the Union,' she advised; 'the extra will do good to all concerned, and will not, as some have said, be spent in the tavern or in idleness.'[40]

J.S. Williams suggested that reading the *Ontario Workman* by the home fire after a day of toil was a suitable way for working-class men to promote self-elevation and the cultivation of domesticity, although this remark was probably intended, at least in part, to increase subscriptions. He wrote: 'We want to help one another, as far lies in our power, to share more fully in the rich fund of edification, refinement and elevating enjoyment to be found in the literature of our age.'[41]

'The Other Side': Melodrama and Labour Reform

On 23 May 1872, editor Williams announced that CIU president Martin Foran had consented to the publication of his novel entitled *The Other Side* in serial instalments in the *Ontario Workman*. Williams pronounced enthusiastically:

Something of this kind is what we have long wanted, as the whole field of story writing has been occupied and controlled in class interests, and every workingman should hail with joy the advent of one of themselves into the literary world, who is not only well able to use his pen in the field of fiction, but willing to take up the cause of labor, and battle for its rights with literary ability against the acknowledged champions in this great and powerful range of thought.[42]

Foran was a familiar figure among the organized workers of Toronto. He corresponded on several occasions with the TTA, and was acquainted with John Hewitt through their respective involvement in the CIU. Earlier, in May 1871, the TTA had arranged for Foran to deliver a public lecture on education and labour reform.[43]

In the introduction to *The Other Side*, Foran provided two reasons for writing the novel. First, he shared with other labour reformers the belief 'that if the laboring class could be made a *reading* class, their social and political advancement and amelioration would be rapid and certain.' He pointed to the 'popular taste among the masses' for fiction, especially those whose education was limited and did not include 'a classical training.' Rather than disparage the love of fiction and dime novels among the working class, Foran used the novel to encourage workmen to develop their intellectual side. For nineteenth-century labour reformers intellectual development was essential to the attainment of complete manhood.[44]

Foran's second objective was to counter the anti-trade-union rhetoric used by the popular British novelist Charles Reade in an melodrama entitled 'Put Yourself in His Place,' which was published serially in *Cornhill Magazine*, in seventeen instalments beginning in March 1869.[45] Reade's novel portrayed the decay of the aristocracy and the rise of the manufacturing middle class in the fictional city of Hillsborough. The hero, Henry Little, a cutler and inventor of tools and machinery, is driven out of Hillsborough for neglecting to 'square' himself with the trade and join the Edge-Tool Forgers' Union. Reade characterizes trade unionists as blackguards and ruffians – 'skilled workmen at violence.' In the aftermath of a series of threats, beatings, warning letters, and explosions all secretly arranged by union leaders, Little sets up a small forge in an ancient, unused country church. Unemployed cutlers hired by union officials to drive Little away, or else kill him, are frustrated by the timely arrival of Squire Raby. The title of the novel is explained by another character, Dr Amboyne, a philanthropically inclined physician, who in treating Little's injuries urges him to 'put himself in his place.' Amboyne advises Little to consider all the angles of an issue, and to situate 'Life' before the relations of 'Labor and Capital.'

Reade's biographer, Malcolm Elwin, indicated that the novel was well received by its reviewers as 'none of their class loved trade unions in those days.'[46] Trade unionism, however, was given a dramatically different representation in Foran's novel. In his introductory remarks Foran admitted that many of the measures and means employed by workmen to redress grievances were 'neither born of justice nor wisdom.' Before these men were condemned, however, he urged that their side of the story be told. Foran criticized Reade for 'not delineating both sides of the subject, in not putting himself in the places of all the characters in his story.' *The Other Side*, therefore, was both instructional and defensive in its intent.[47]

The conventions of melodrama were followed quite closely by Foran in the novel. Melodrama was the dominant modality in the nineteenth century. As Martha Vicinus has argued, 'it was important as a psychological touchstone for the powerless, for those who perceived themselves as "the helpless and unfriended."' 'Social and economic conditions were unstable during much of the nineteenth century,' Vicinus writes; 'melodrama acknowledged this and seemed to demonstrate how difficult circumstances could be endured and even turned to victory.'[48] Melodrama was immensely popular among later-nineteenth-century working-class audiences who were seeking to comprehend the social transformations wrought by industrial capitalism.

In their fiction, labour reformers departed somewhat from the stereotypical characterization and plotting of melodrama, and emphasized the political implications of the situation. Working-class audiences identified with the tragedies suffered by the honest-hearted mechanic hero. This departure from the conventions of melodrama reinforced perceptions of working-class oppression. These writings, which focused on the manly and virtuous mechanic hero and his many misfortunes, were intended to mobilize workers to support the collective goals of the labour movement.[49]

Each literary genre employs certain textual strategies, which cue readers to expect a particular kind of discursive experience. Melodrama denotes the indulgence of excessive emotionalism, inflated rhetoric, overt villainy, persecution of the good and the final reward of virtue, exaggerated expressions of right and wrong, remarkable and improbable coincidences, dark plottings, suspense, and numerous plot twists.[50] Nineteenth-century melodrama was organized around a binary world of good and bad, rich and poor, male and female, and was bounded by faith in a universe ruled by morality. Evil drives the plot by unleashing a betrayal of the moral order. The hand of Providence ensures the triumph of good, but only after the virtuous hero or heroine was sorely tried. Romance and sexual desire were integral to this drama of persecuted innocence and virtue triumphant. Villains were always destroyed, thus providing the reader with catharsis and, finally, solace. A potent dogma of democracy assured equality among all men, but only if they retained a pure heart.

Domesticity was the cardinal virtue of nineteenth-century melodrama. The family was the setting for passion, sacrifice, and sympathy. Within the home women were both a symbol of purity and the focus of emotional tension and self-sacrifice. Home with its cornerstone of feminine purity was the most potent symbol of good. The focus on the family gave melodrama its power. In industrializing nineteenth-century society, melodrama provided a resolution of conflicts between home and the outside world through happy endings.[51]

Foran created a facsimile of himself in his manly worker hero, Richard Arbyght, a young farm-bred cooper.[52] As in all melodramas, a series of tragedies befall the young hero. Richard's father is robbed and murdered on a roadside as he journeys homeward. Completely devastated by the death of her husband, Irene Arbyght dies of a broken heart soon afterward. Orphaned at the age of nine, Richard is separated from his younger sister, Bertha, when a wealthy woman visiting a neighbour adopts the girl, and pledges to raise her respectably, give her an education, and make her a lady. A year later, Richard receives a letter from the woman informing him that Bertha has died from a severe attack of the croup.

Squire Stanly takes in the orphaned boy and raises him. The Squire is Foran's ideal of the sturdy, honest, intelligent farmer who existed before widespread urban and industrial development. Foran indicates that the Squire is of the 'old school of political economists,' who believe 'that our laws should be so framed and administered that they would tend to better advancement of the toiling masses, and the greater glory of the nation.' The Squire and the pure country life are associated with good, in contrast to the evils and dangers of the city for workmen and their families.

Richard excels in the village school, but he is quick to recognize that the teacher treats the children from socially prominent backgrounds with considerable deference. Foran's political message was clearly delineated for his audience: the educational system privileges one class, not necessarily the more intelligent one, while another class is kept in hopeless ignorance. The perceptive young hero concludes that, '[t]o preserve a republic like ours free and intact, it requires a grand national education.' Nineteenth-century labour reformers' broader demand for a national system of state-funded education to ensure that working-class children are educated about their duties as citizens was injected into the plot of the melodrama.

Deprived of the inheritance that would have allowed him to continue his education, Richard must learn a trade. He is apprenticed to a local cooper. Artisanal pride in craftsmanship is reinforced in the narrative. Richard 'was especially fond of excelling in skilled and superior workmanship.' At age twenty the hero is fully six feet tall, sinewy and strong, with 'a quick, elastic movement, and fiery, dark eye.' His countenance is 'open and expressive, his demeanor dignified and grave, his mind inquisitive, his heart brave and sympathetic.' His every look and movement 'gave assurance of the greatness and goodness of that noblest attribute of man – SOUL.' While Foran's worker hero was inflicted with some of the same signifiers as the hero of bourgeois fiction, specifically courage and a sympathetic heart, the 'mechanic accents' are different.[53] Manliness for the worker hero in Foran's melodrama incorporated craft skill and trade-union membership. The upper-case type of the word 'SOUL' in the copy published in the *Ontario Workman* reinforces the idea that for labour reformers manliness was not based on wealth.

Following a period of service in the army during the Civil War, which in true heroic fashion is marked by bravery, Richard relocates to Chicago. The villain, a tyrannous employer named Alvan Relvason, who was described by Foran as 'the typical employer,' is introduced. Throughout the novel Foran makes references to physiognomy, which was widely popular among North Americans during the latter part of the nineteenth century. Relvason, as the villain, and Foran's representation of most employers under industrial-capitalist social relations, is given physical features consistent with his character: 'His eyes were set far in his ponderous head and were black, restless and knavishly cunning. His complexion was of a yellowish dusky cast that never appeared clean or clear. His gait was awkward and ungainly.'[54]

Richard secures a position in Relvason's shop. A few days later, employer and worker confront one another in the shop. Annoyed by what he interprets as Richard's impudence, Relvason reminds him, 'You are the employed and I the employer.' Richard in turn responds, 'I would have you remember that I, too, am a MAN as well as you.' Richard tells Relvason that they are 'equals,' who meet as buyer and seller: 'I have a commodity which you desire to purchase and which I am willing to sell for a consideration which you are disposed to give in exchange for it.' In opposition to the dominant political economy, Foran uses a labour theory of value.

With the aid of two trusted workmen, Richard secretly organizes the journeymen coopers into a union. The villain, Relvason, discovers that a union has been organized, and he schemes to destroy it. He threatens to dismiss any worker who refuses to sign an ironclad agreement. In the binary world of melodrama, and consistent with the politics of labour reform, Relvason is the antithesis of virtue. He is an example of 'abnormal humanity,' and is described metaphorically as 'ghoulish,' a 'leviathan,' 'knavishly cunning,' and a 'monster.'

The workers, of course, refuse to abandon their union. In contrast to the representation of trade unionists presented by Reade, the mechanics who support the union in Foran's novel are classified as 'manly.' They also have a distinctive physical appearance from years of hardship and toil, 'a young old look,' Foran writes, 'a dull, oppressive, heavy expression, seen only on those who toil ten hours or more per day.' Commitment to family and nation are integral to Foran's construction of the manly and honest working man: 'the honest man who married and brought up a large family did more service than he who continued single and only talked of population.' Trade unionists were depicted by Foran as men who love their children, and for this reason they willingly, even cheerfully, endure lives of never-ending toil.

Relvason issues an ultimatum that Richard must abandon the union or else be fired. Concerned with the plight of his union brothers, and consistent with the heroic ideal of self-sacrifice typical of melodrama, Richard decides to leave the trade. 'He did not regard it good unionism for one man to throw a hundred men out of employment, and stop their children's supply of bread.' The hero's hardships mount. He is blacklisted by the employers, and is thus unable to secure another position.

Race and national identity are interwoven into the novel's overarching theme of the importance of union solidarity to the cause of labour reform. In searching for employment, Richard is told by one anti-union employer that if his men 'dare' to organize, he will discharge them all and fill their places with cheaper Chinese workers. The employer remarks that the men in his employ are of his own 'nationality' and he feels obligated to keep them on. Richard responds that these national ties would quickly deteriorate as soon as the men questioned his right to dictate to them what their labour is worth. Foran, however, excludes Chinese workers from his ideal of the unity of male workers under trade unionism.

Frustrated by the unwillingness of any employer to hire him, Richard returns to his boarding house, where he finds Alexander Fargood waiting for him. Fargood agrees to give Richard a job. Foran presents his conceptualization of the ideal employer in the character of Fargood: 'The bearing of the employer was never that of a *master*. 'In a word the relations existing between these two men were pre-eminently those that should ever exist between all employers and employees: MUTUAL OR RECIPROCAL INDEPENDENCE AND DEPENDENCE.'[55] Like other nineteenth-century writers of working-class fiction, Foran recreated a world of artisanal independence rather than developing a critique of proletarianization under industrial-capitalist social relations.[56]

A series of improbable plot twists occur, most of which are attributed by the author to 'Fate,' or an act of God. The worker hero undergoes more hardships, which elevates the emotional intensity for the novel's readers. Working-class readers would easily have identified with the hardships suffered by the hero.

In another incident that the author attributes to 'Fate,' a young woman, Grace, is driven from the home of her benefactor. She wanders the city until a woman, 'showily attired, middle-aged, with a forbidding, libidinous look,' tries to tempt her into prostitution. Once again, 'Fate' intervenes, and Richard, who happens to be walking along the street intuitively senses that something is amiss. He rescues the woman, and discovers that Grace is actually his sister Bertha, whom he had long believed to be dead. Foran's construction of working-class womanhood differs from middle-class representations of working-class femininity. For much of the nineteenth century the bourgeois class associated the single working woman with prostitution.[57] In Bertha, Foran creates a pure and virtuous working-class girl, whom he describes as 'slight, graceful, *spirituelle*.' Bertha earns her own living by giving music lessons and taking in sewing at home. Foran, however, never mentions the issue of the sexual morality of women who worked in factories.

While the political objectives of labour reform were at the forefront of Foran's narrative, the plot of *The Other Side* centres around the unresolved tragedy of the Arbyght family and the romance between Richard and Vida Geldamo – the daughter of a banker. In Vida, Foran presents what he suggests is the 'true woman.' Vida is described as having all of woman's spiritualized nature: 'She was all goodness, all loveliness – an angel.' This ideal of femininity is analogous to middle-class constructions of womanhood. Foran articulated an ideal of womanhood that values feminine purity above wealth. Vida in all her goodness of heart could never believe 'that the possession of money made the heart warmer ... or the soul purer.' In the conflict between marriage based on property and romantic love, Mr Geldamo favours property. He orders Vida to marry Mr Allsound, who, although not as morally worthy as Richard, is a man of property. In the spirit of heroic self-sacrifice characteristic of melodrama, Richard resolves not to see Vida again in view of the barrier erected between them 'by caste and wealth.' Vida becomes despondent, and then seriously ill from a broken heart. Her father relents and agrees to let her marry Richard, but the young hero must first prove himself capable of building a home.

As in all melodramas, moral virtue triumphs in *The Other Side*. The villain, Relvason, is destroyed. The hero, Richard, discovers that it was Relvason who murdered his father. He also wins the hand of Vida Geldamo. While it appears that romantic love has triumphed over the traditional idea of marriage based on property, their union is sanctioned only after her father loses all of his money in a business downturn. While sexuality based on heterosexual desire triumphs over property, Foran, in his narrative, was unable to overcome the class tensions emerging from the marriage of a working-class man to a woman from a wealthy family.[58] Arbyght and Geldamo establish their own business, and employ several men who are treated as 'social equals.' The novel concludes with trade unionism flourishing in the city. 'Through its agency,' Foran writes, 'workingmen are fast becoming more thoughtful, more industrious, more temperate, and are making fearful strides in mental and moral worth and social elevation.'

The Other Side thus becomes caught up in the central paradox of melodrama. While the domestic ideal is defended in Foran's melodrama against the evils of industrial-capitalist society under the belief that a universal moral order would prevail, the moral order championed in the melodrama is in fact a reflection of dominant middle-class gender and class values. Foran never proposed that the existing social order be overthrown, and for Foran the home remains the symbol of moral permanence and feminine purity. Also, the relationship between this literature and working-class and middle-class cultures remains ambiguous. In trying to create a work that measured up to the criteria of the bourgeois literary community, Foran neglected the ethnic variables in working-class culture. For instance, dialect was a major vehicle for literary expression among working-class writers in Britain during the nineteenth century, and was used to join older folk traditions with emerging industrial and urban values. Foran, however, rejects any ethnic identification and indicates that he cannot understand 'how our language is to be made purer or purged of crudities and become universally classical, by spreading before the rising generation our ideas and thoughts, clad in the garb of broken French or German, Irish idioms, broad Yorkshire cockneyisms or backwoods Yankeeisms.'[59]

By August 1872 the nine-hours movement had been defeated, and by the end of the decade labour reform's initial upsurge in Toronto had been crushed by a combination of economic recession, stifled militancy, trade-union isolation, and Tory domination.[60] During the early 1870s, however, Toronto labour reformers defined the social subjectivity of the honest working-class mechanic, which encompassed their own distinct class-based representation of manliness. While employers, most notably George Brown, sought deference from workers, the nascent labour movement through its central institution, the Toronto Trades Assembly, and its organ *The Ontario Workman*, constructed a counter-discourse that emphasized worker independence and the collective goals of trade unionism.

The masculine rhetoric of labour reformers, with its emphasis on progress, citizenship, and self-culture, was not entirely unlike that of the late Victorian middle class, but it was inscribed with a distinctively working-class politic. It sustained a radical critique of employer-worker relations under the prevailing social relations of production. To define their status as citizens, and make the case for universal male suffrage, Toronto labour reformers maintained that they held property in their labour. In this way, Toronto labour reformers, like their British counterparts, articulated a notion of class that excluded women and children.[61] Toronto labour reformers also drew on their colonial relationship with Britain to shape their notion of class. Patriotism, which embraced a sense of 'Britishness' stemming from Canada's colonial status, was incorporated into their discourse of working-class manhood.

Alongside the institutions of labour reform, working-class fiction, poetry, and improving literature guided workers in the collective goals of the labour movement, and provided instructions on how to be a 'good' trade unionist, worker, citizen, husband, and father. This rhetoric was an important part of the cultural world of Toronto workers, and the strategy used to challenge employers' incursions upon the long-established rights of skilled mechanics.

An emphasis on sobriety and domesticity was elaborated in the early 1870s. Domesticity functioned to defend the morality of working men against attacks from employers. The working-class man as father and husband was an integral part of the positive masculine identity constituted by Toronto labour reformers during this period. Yet, labour reformers never successfully resolved the tension between the private, and powerless, domestic sphere, and the public world of work. The ideal of domesticity, as found at the conclusion of working-class melodramas, never translated into a resolution of the problems created for working-class families by the growth of industrial capitalism. For most working-class families domesticity was an illusion, as few families were able to survive on the wage of a single male breadwinner. During the 1870s, furthermore, the plight of women workers was rarely mentioned. It was only in the 1880s, with the rise of the Knights of Labor in Toronto, that women workers were put onto the political agenda of the labour movement.

Although labour reformers constructed a national identity that outlined an imagined community incorporating all workers, unskilled and Chinese labourers were effectively excluded. The labour-reform movement of the early 1870s functioned to promote the social and political interests of one segment of the working class, namely, skilled, Anglo-Saxon working men, and ultimately fragmented, as much as it consolidated, the working class.

3

'Spread the Light': Phillips Thompson and the Politics of Labour Reform

During the late nineteenth century a small group of 'brainworkers' constructed a discourse oppositional to bourgeois political economy in their writings for the labour press. Although few workers could spare a few cents to buy an issue of a labour paper, and the illiteracy rate within the late-nineteenth-century working class remained high, there is no doubt that the papers were widely read among labour reformers and union activists. T. Phillips Thompson, who has been described as 'Canada's foremost late nineteenth-century labour intellectual,' was a direct producer of a revolutionary knowledge oriented towards radical social change.[1]

Thompson was born in 1843 at Newcastle-on-Tyne. At the age of fourteen he emigrated to Canada with his parents. The Thompson family took up residence briefly in Belleville and Lindsay, before settling in St Catharines. Thompson studied law, but he never practised. Instead, he chose journalism as his vocation. His career as a radical social critic began in 1864, when he published a commentary rejecting the position taken by D'Arcy McGee in support of a monarchical form of government. The dominance of an aristocracy was at the heart of Thompson's opposition to a monarchy. 'Already there are those amongst us who affect to despise the farmer and the mechanic, the "bone and sinew" of our country,' Thompson wrote, 'and it should be our aim to repress rather than encourage this feeling, which the establishment of an aristocracy would assuredly tend to strengthen and develop.'[2] He called for the creation of a 'British American Independent Republic.' He rejected Canada's colonial dependency on Britain, and suggested that Canada must develop the independence of a nation. Also, Lower Canada had to be thoroughly 'Anglicized,' which meant the exclusion of French-Canadian laws, language, and institutions.[3]

Thompson honed his journalistic skills as an unpaid worker on the St Catharines *Post* during the absence of the editor. In 1866 he covered the Fenian

Raids as a special correspondent for the Montreal *Herald*. After a brief sojourn in Montreal, where he edited a daily paper started by a Presbyterian clergyman, he returned to St Catharines and took a salaried position at the *Post*.[4] In 1867, Thompson moved to Toronto, where he went to work for John Ross Robertson at the *Telegraph* as a police court reporter.

Three years later, in 1870, Thompson switched over to the *Mail*, where he began writing a weekly column of witty political commentary under the nom de plume Jimuel Briggs, D.B., correspondent for the Coboconk *Irradiator*. His degree was that of 'Dead Beat' from the bogus Coboconk University. As Jimuel Briggs, Thompson criticized government policy, the partisan press, and the social customs of the privileged classes. George Brown, the Grits, and the *Globe* were the usual targets of Thompson's satire. Selections from Thompson's columns for the *Mail* were collected and reprinted as *The Political Experiences of Jimuel Briggs, D.B.*, which sold for the sum of five drinks. With tongue-in-cheek, he dedicated the pamphlet to George Brown, 'In recognition of his authority as DICTATOR FOR THE REFORM PARTY, whose favourable opinion is absolutely necessary in order to secure political advancement.'[5]

Thompson took up the cause of 'Canada First' in *The National*, his first venture in independent journalism, which he started with H.R. Smallpiece in 1874. *The National* was opposed to the partyism of the Grits and the Tories, which perpetuated sectional and racial differences, and made the formation of a unified Canadian nationality impossible. A protective tariff was viewed by the editors of *The National* as the key to increased prosperity for the manufacturer, the working man, and the farmer.

Not long after the inauguration of *The National*, Thompson split from William Foster, Goldwin Smith, William Howland, and other supporters of Canada First, who allied behind the elitist publication *The Nation*. Whereas the latter group settled into complacency around the exclusive National Club, Thompson wanted to transform 'Canada First' into a popular movement. He found the outlook of organized farmers under the Grange particularly attractive. Although Thompson did not yet acknowledge the need for a coherent working-class movement, he recognized the prevalence of class prejudice towards working-class men and women, and argued that all manual labourers should be treated with dignity.[6] Finally, on 8 July 1875, *The National* formally announced that it was withdrawing its connection with the 'Canada First' party.[7]

Meanwhile, Thompson's reputation as a humourist grew. He lectured in communities throughout southwestern Ontario as Jimuel Briggs. In August 1874, Briggs lectured to the Young Men's Christian Association of Toronto on 'The Experiences of a Bohemian.'[8] The old school of Bohemians was described as jovial, careless, and dissipated, not unlike the character of Jimuel Briggs

himself. In the fall and winter of 1875, Briggs delivered a series of lectures entitled 'Random Shots at Flying Follies,' in which he continued his satirical attack
upon the dominant Canadian social and political order.[9]

With *The National* on the verge of bankruptcy, Thompson moved in 1876 to
Boston, where he went to work as literary and assistant editor on the *Traveller*.
He also contributed to *American Punch* and the Boston *Courier*. He continued
to deliver his 'Random Shots at Flying Follies,' and he presented another public
lecture entitled 'Journalistic Ante-Types.' During his soujourn in the United
States, Thompson was exposed to the ideas of American radical social thinkers,
which were incorporated into his writings later during the 1880s.[10]

Thompson returned to Toronto in 1879. He was re-employed at the *Mail* for a
brief period, and then was hired by the *Globe* as a special correspondent. In
October 1881, the *Globe* sent him to Ireland to investigate land-holding regulations and living conditions. The series that appeared under the byline 'Troubled
Ireland' ran between 15 November 1881 and 10 January 1882. Thompson interviewed evicted tenants, landlords, officials from the Land Commission, and
members of the Land League. He also interviewed Henry George, whose book
Poverty and Progress was making inroads among the more prominent and educated members of the Irish Land League.[11]

Along with the transition to mature industrial capitalism in the 1880s, a
resurgence of labour-movement activity occurred in Toronto with the reorganization in August 1881 of a central labour organization subsequently named the
Toronto Trades and Labor Council (TTLC). During the 1880s the city also
became a focal point for Knights of Labor activity in Canada. The Noble and
Holy Order of the Knights of Labor was founded in Philadelphia in 1869 under
the leadership of Uriah Stephens. The Knights 'combined aspects of a religious
brotherhood, a political reform society, a fraternal order, and pure and simple
unionism.'[12] Unlike the exclusive craft-based unions of male Anglo-Saxon
skilled workers, the Knights of Labor had as its objective the organization of all
workers, including the unskilled, women, and workers of all races and ethnic
backgrounds. Workers joined Local Assemblies (LAs), organized either by
trade or by mixed occupational affiliations. In *Dreaming of What Might Be*, a
major study of the Knights of Labor in Ontario, Gregory Kealey and Bryan
Palmer argued that the Knights created an 'movement culture,' a labour-centred
cultural alternative to the burgeoning industrial-capitalist society.[13] The
Knights supported land nationalization, the prohibition of child labour,
currency reform, cooperation, the shortening of the hours of labour, weekly
payment, compulsory arbitration, the prohibition of foreign contract labour,
and, for both sexes, equal pay for equal work.

The education of working men and women about the objectives of the

Knights of Labor was crucial to the project of labour reformers in the 1880s. LAs were instructed to incorporate educational sessions into their regular meetings. Separate schools of instruction and Knights of Labor libraries were organized. Male workers were taught to cultivate self-improvement and cooperation as masculine ideals. Standards of behaviour were set that taught working-class men to fend off the temptations arising from the saloon, gambling, and the virus of 'Mammon-worship' instilled in the formal education system and in the popular press.

Upon its organization in Toronto in June 1886, Thompson joined Victor Hugo LA 7814 of the Knights of Labor. Although designated as a 'mixed' LA, Victor Hugo assembly consisted primarily of journalists. Well before the formation of the LA, however, Thompson was an active 'brainworker' for the Knights of Labor. In opposition to bourgeois political economy, which had rendered obscure the oppression of men and women workers under industrial capitalism, Thompson 're-presented' political economy from his vantage point as a radical labour reformer at the centre of working-class mobilization in the 1880s. Class, gender, and race were integral to Thompson's textual mediations, but they must also be considered in relation to the broader social anxiety surrounding nation-building, British imperialism, and the expansion of the labour market.

From 1883 to 1887, Thompson wrote for *The Palladium of Labor*, a Knights of Labor organ published weekly in Hamilton, while simultaneously working as assistant editor and chief editorial writer for the *News*, a Toronto daily owned and edited by Edmund E. Sheppard. In the *News*, Sheppard and Thompson presented a new, more radical discourse of democracy, one independent of party politics. The *News* embraced many of the planks already put forth by the Knights of Labor, as well as several that were specific to the unique Canadian context, including provisions for an elected Senate and a revision of the constitution to define more strictly the respective powers of the federal and provincial governments. By the summer of 1884, the *News* openly endorsed the Knights of Labor.[14]

Thompson's project during the 1880s was to 'Spread the Light.' Light as a symbol of truth is a recurring element in both Christian and Western culture. In nineteenth-century labour and social-reform discourse truth and knowledge were equated with light. Knowledge would ultimately bring about social regeneration and freedom for the working class. The metaphor was explained by Thompson in the lyrics to a song entitled 'Spread the Light,' which he wrote some time in the 1880s. The song, performed to the popular tune 'Hold the Front,' was included in his collection of songs entitled *The Labor Reform Songster*, published in 1892. The collection was intended for use at public gatherings and local Knights of Labor assembly meetings.[15]

Spread the Light

Fellow-toilers, pass the watchword!
  Would you know your powers?
Spread the light! and we shall conquer,
  Then the world is ours.

  Chorus
Spread the light! the world is waiting
  For the cheering ray,
Fraught with promise of the glories
  Of the coming day.

In the conflict of the ages,
  In this thrilling time,
Knowledge is the road to freedom,
  Ignorance is crime
  Chorus – Spread the light, etc.

Wolves and vampires in the darkness
  Prey on flesh and blood,
From the radiance of the sunlight
  Flee the hellish brood.
  Chorus – Spread the light, etc.

Light alone can save the nations,
  Long the spoilers' prey,
Bound and blinded in their prison
  Waiting for the day.
  Chorus – Spread the light, etc.

Men who know their rights as freemen
  Ne'er to tyrants cower,
Slaves will rise and burst their fetters
  When they feel their power.
  Chorus – Spread the light, etc.

What is important is not so much the equation of light with truth and knowledge, but the way in which specific groups were organized in relation to one another.[16] A collective body of workers who had experienced the oppressions of capitalism, but had been falsely educated by the capitalist press, and were unaware of the evils of the acquisition of wealth at the expense of others, had to be educated before social regeneration would occur. Vampires, wolves, and darkness symbolize the capitalist press and their circle of influence who 'prey' on the flesh and blood of workers to acquire wealth and position.

The role of labour's 'intellectuals' was to educate workers, through their public addresses and columns in the labour press, about the principles of the Knights of Labor. 'Men who understand these questions should spread the light so far as their opportunities permit, by speaking and writing upon them,' Thompson wrote in a column for *The Palladium of Labor*. He further indicated that because workers had not been educated about the objectives of labour reform, and were not self-reliant, they were not ready to made sacrifices for the cause of labour reform.[17] For too many working men the millionaire was an object, and they desired nothing so much as to be monopolists themselves. Education, therefore, would create a revolution in public opinion. 'The picture is merely a faint presentation of what might be,' Thompson remarked, 'but cannot be at present solely because of the blindness, ignorance and want of union among workingmen – but what I trust yet will be when the scales of error, of misleading education and of temporary self-interest have fallen from their eyes – so they can see the Light.'[18] Thompson was not only an active producer who shaped knowledge about labour reform, he was also an active 'doer' who disseminated this knowledge through his writings in *The Palladium of Labor* and the daily *News*, and through the numerous public speeches he delivered to Knights of Labor assemblies throughout Ontario during the 1880s.

'Spread the Light': Enjolras and the 'New' Political Economy

Thompson began writing for *The Palladium of Labor* in September 1883. He was probably the author of 'Our Social Club,' a narrative about a fictional social club that ran in twelve weekly instalments in *The Palladium* beginning on 8 September 1883.[19] The series focused on a diverse group of workmen who come together to discuss issues of concern to the working class, and was obviously didactic in its intent. The topics discussed at the weekly meetings of the social club include Henry George's *Poverty and Progress*, tariff protection versus free trade from the working man's standpoint, the solidarity of humanity, currency reform, woman's suffrage, the attitude of the churches towards labor reform, Canada's colonial relations with England, land speculation, and the meaning of 'collectivism.'[20]

Many of the topics discussed in 'Our Social Club' were revisited in Thompson's regular column for *The Palladium of Labor*, which he wrote under the pen name 'Enjolras,' borrowed from Victor Hugo's novel *Les Misérables*. In Hugo's novel the character Enjolras was a member of the ABC Society, whose purpose was the education of men. Enjolras symbolized Thompson's conceptualization of his role as a 'brainworker' and a labour reformer. Enjolras, like Thompson, 'was both thinker and man of action, a soldier of democracy in the short term and at the same time a priest of the ideal rising above the contemporary movement.'[21] Thompson's writings as Enjolras formed the basis for his book *The Politics of Labor*, published in 1887. In his columns for *The Palladium*, Thompson began to articulate a 'new' radical political economy counter to the dominant discourse of liberal, bourgeois political economists.

The *Politics of Labor* was influenced by Thompson's reading of American radical social theory. The argument of the book was made with American terms of reference, probably in an attempt to capture the larger American market. Thompson had at his command a plethora of other sources of inspiration, not all of which were congenial to the cause of labour reform, but from which he imputed meaning in constructing his version of political economy.[22] The authors cited in his 'Enjolras' columns, and subsequently in *The Politics of Labor*, include Henry George, Herbert Spencer, Harriet Beecher Stowe, Matthew Arnold, Victor Hugo, A.D. Swinburne, James Russell Lowell, Adam Smith, Wendell Phillips, Henry Thoreau, Walt Whitman, and many others. Thompson read widely in literature, history, and political economy, and he studied a wide range of British and North American periodicals and journals as well as the daily press. He also drew on his first-hand knowledge of the living conditions of workers and their families. As special correspondent for the *Globe* he had investigated landlordism in Ireland in 1881 and the conditions of cotton workers in Quebec and eastern Ontario in 1882.[23] Later, in the Spring of 1885, he investigated the labour struggles of the coal miners of Pennsylvania for the *Globe*.[24] Also important to a complete understanding of the political economy explicated by Thompson was the unique Canadian context of his writings, which were rooted in the struggles of the Canadian Knights of Labor and in Thompson's deep concern for Canadian affairs.[25] Implicated in Thompson's text, therefore, are a particular set of social and cultural practices from which he articulated his 'new' political economy.

In the introduction to *The Politics of Labor*, Thompson remarked that the task of educating workers in the principles of labour reform had been 'perverted by the inculcation of the untruths and half-truths of bourgeois political economy.' According to Thompson, one of the greatest difficulties in arriving at a solution to the 'labour problem' was the defective terminology of political economy, with its vague and imprecise terms, or the lack of words in the English language to express many of the ideas generated by the industrial agitation of the 1880s. These inadequacies in the language of political economy, Thompson maintained, were used by the upholders of the existing system to their own advantage. For instance, the term 'capital' had acquired a double meaning. 'Primarily it signifies those accummulations of the product of labor used for further production,' such as buildings, machinery, raw material, and money in the bank used to pay wages, Thompson indicated. The term as ordinarily used in politico-economical discussions had a quite different meaning. 'When men speak of the rights of capital, the conflict between capital and labor,' Thompson explained, 'they refer to the power which the possession or control of capital gives to a small minority of the community of regulating how much labor shall receive of what it produces – to the special interest of the accumulator of labor products in the result of further productive industry.' Thus, Thompson suggested, a distinction between 'capital' as an instrument and 'capitalism' as a force was necessary. 'Labour' could not possibly have any quarrel with the first, or 'material' definition of 'capital.' 'Capitalism,' or control by means, first, of monopolizing resources, and second, of competition among workers, was 'a usurpation, and a growing menace to popular freedom.'[26]

The term 'monopoly,' according to Thompson, was equally vague and imprecise. 'Monopoly' had previously meant the special privileges granted to a single person by the government. By the 1880s, the term was used to express the powers and privileges obtained by large classes under the ordinary working of business competition and the law of supply and demand. To speak of the 'monopoly' system misrepresented the ideas suggested by the social and industrial developments of the period. 'Political economy pretends to have spoken the last word as regards the relations between labor and capitalism,' Thompson remarked, 'yet its exponents have not even invented a term which in any way describes this process of grinding or crushing between the opposing forces of monopoly and competition.' The French word *exploitation* came nearest to representing the idea in a single word, but that it was still too vague and general for use in any discussion requiring precision.[27]

Thompson agreed with Henry George's premise that, of all the forms of monopoly, private land ownership was the most oppressive. George's *Poverty and Progress* was central to discussions of labour reform and exercised considerable influence over late-Victorian radicalism.[28] At the inaugural meeting of 'Our Social Club,' the members discuss *Poverty and Progress*. One of the fictional club members, Frank Harcourt, an English-born, Oxford-educated book canvasser, opposes George's ideas on land nationalization, but he accepts George's view that the accumulation of wealth in the hands of the few was the actual cause of poverty. Another character, Alfred Freeman, a carpenter by trade, an avid reader, and an enthusiastic supporter of the labour movement, states that a return to a pre-industrial order is not desirable. 'It is not machinery that is the cause of the trouble, it is a wrong system of distribution – it is monopoly of opportunities,' Freeman asserts.[29]

Thompson was deeply affected by the effects of landlordism he witnessed in Ireland. In his reports for the *Globe*, he described in some detail the suffering of evicted tenants and their families. After touring the slums of Galway he wrote, 'I sicken and shudder now at the memory of it, and the whole day I have been in a state of mental and physical depression from the effects, which almost incapacitated me for work.'[30] Irish Nationalism was a strong radical tendency in the Toronto working-class world during the 1880s. A branch of the Irish Land League was organized in Toronto in January 1881. Thompson joined the Toronto branch of the Land League, which also attracted other prominent local labour-movement leaders, including Daniel J. O'Donoghue, an Irish-Catholic printer and the first labour member of the Ontario legislature; Alfred Jury, an English tailor and Lib-Lab supporter; and A.W. Wright, a newspaper editor and Tory fixer, who rose to prominence in the Knights of Labor in the mid-1880s. From the outset, however, sectarian and political differences plagued the organization. At a meeting held in mid-May, Thompson pointed out that landlords and monopolists were not foolish enough to quarrel over differences of 'race,' and that the League might urge the abolition of land seizures for rent.[31]

Canada too had not escaped the evils of landlordism, as Thompson suggested in an 'Enjolras' column for *The Palladium of Labor*. In the aftermath of the uprising in the Northwest in 1885, he wrote,

The North-West during the last few years has become an Ireland on a large scale – a land of absentee proprietors and arbitrary government officials appointed by a distant power and wholly out of sympathy with the people they oppress – but an Ireland without representation in Parliament, tenant right, or compensation for improvements. The rule of Dublin Castle is no worse and no less detested than that of the thievish and incompetent Dewdney and his ring of pampered parasites.[32]

He later pronounced Riel's trial at Regina a 'Bloody Assize,' and urged his readers to 'put yourself in the place' of the 'half-breed' whose former resource of buffalo-hunting had been destroyed by colonization companies of speculators taking up land all around him.[33]

In *Progress and Poverty*, Henry George proposed that equal right to land was an inalienable right of every individual, and that land belonged to the whole community. He grounded his discussion of American social problems in Protestant ethical teachings. In doing so, George directed Christians away from theological concerns towards social criticism, and helped to lay the basis for the social gospel in the United States and in Canada.[34] George's cure for the prevailing state of affairs was a taxation policy that would give society the unearned increment currently pocketed by landlords. Not surprisingly, the Georgeite solution, which subsequently became known as the 'single tax,' attracted a large following among labour and social reformers. During the 1880s and 1890s, they banded together in societies and clubs, often sharing a common membership, all of which were to some degree influenced by Georgeite doctrine. In Toronto this group included the Knights of Labor, the Anti-Poverty Society, the Single-Tax Association, the Nationalist Clubs, and the Toronto Suffrage Association. Thompson was a member of the first four organizations, and was acquainted with the members of the Toronto Suffrage Association, whose cause he supported in his columns. By the time *The Politics of Labor* was published in 1887, however, Thompson was convinced that land monopoly was only part of the problem. In the book he identified the problem broadly as one of monopoly from above combined with competition among wage-earners from below.[35] At some point, in the early 1890s, Thompson left Georgeism behind and embraced Bellamyite socialism.

In *The Politics of Labor*, Thompson proposed that political economy be reconsidered from 'the standpoint of the Sermon on the Mount and the Declaration of Independence.'[36] Hitherto, political economy had concerned itself exclusively with the production of wealth and the promotion of the material interests of the nation. 'Labour' was looked upon as a raw material to be used in the manufacture of goods, and like other raw materials had to be acquired as cheaply as possible to keep down the costs of production. Bourgeois political economy, therefore, had no concern with the rights of the labourer as a 'man' and a 'citizen,' and had created a power relation that defined capitalism as natural and inevitable.

According to Thompson, the remedy for the existing abuses of workers required nothing less than a complete transformation of habits of thought. In May 1884, Thompson presented an outline of his ideas for a 'new' political economy to a meeting of the Toronto Secular Society. 'We must put Man before Mammon,' he declared, 'and regard that as the ideal social condition in which the general standard of comfort of the mass of the people was highest, without regard to the national prosperity or greatness.'[37] In opposition to liberal political economy, Thompson's political economy combined the ideals of democratic republicanism with a Christian moral economy that emphasized collective self-help. Its highest ideal was 'the greatest good to the greatest number.' This was also a guiding principle of the Knights of Labor. Religion was not only embedded in the rituals of the Order, it was used to legitimate the political objectives of the labour movement as its leaders claimed Christian morality for organized labour.[38]

Thompson was raised a Quaker. In the 1870s he participated in the free-thought movement. By the early 1890s he had turned to Theosophy. Despite his unorthodox religious beliefs, Thompson used Christian rhetoric in his writings, and he even suggested that Christianity had a place in the project of labour reform. He acknowledged that Christ, 'the son of the carpenter was the greatest social reformer that ever lived.'[39] Ramsay Cook has argued that Thompson was less critical of the churches' doctrines than he was of the Church as a social institution. As Enjolras, Thompson remarked: 'In every epoch of the world's history, there have been foul and hideous wrongs which have found their strongest defenders in a corrupt and hypocritical church.'[40]

'The Brotherhood of Man,' in nineteenth-century labour-reform discourse, also implied 'the solidarity of labor.' 'The forces of labor,' Thompson wrote in *The Politics of Labor*, 'have in the past been divided by countless lines of cleavage in all directions, by differences of party, nation, and creed, of sex and color, of occupation and locality; by jealousies between skilled and unskilled brain and manual workers; and by finely-drawn grades and distinctions between those of the same trade.'[41] The habit of defining social problems in the language of Christian duty and moral goodness, however, was incompatible with a set of racial prejudices about the need to lift up the lowly and despised peoples of the world. The emphasis on Anglo-Saxon absolutes excluded those outsiders who did not share them.[42] Nineteenth-century Canadian labour reformers targeted Chinese railway labourers, who presumably took jobs from white workers at lower wages.

In one instalment of 'Our Social Club,' the members debate the 'problem' of Chinese immigration. Dennis Mulready, an Irish immigrant porter, pronounces emphatically, 'We don't want the rat-eating heathens here at all.' Freeman and Harcourt criticize Mulready for his racism. Instead, they use economic justifications for the exclusion of Chinese labourers. Freeman asserts that economic conditions of supply and demand rendered necessary the exclusion of Chinese workers, 'in order to preserve some measure of comfort and independence for white labor.' He further states that 'it is not necessary that we should hate or malign the Chinaman.' 'The Chinese question is not a question of race nor of morals – it is simply an economical question,' Harcourt continues. 'I believe in the brotherhood of mankind.' The same economic argument was then applied to pauper immigrants from Britain who received assisted passage from the federal and Ontario governments. Freeman praises the Toronto Trades and Labor Council for its adoption of a resolution to cooperate with British trade unions to put a stop to assisted immigration.[43]

The type of social formation outlined by Thompson in *The Politics of Labor* was one that substituted 'universal co-operation' for the wage system. The final result was intended to be 'more or less socialistic' in character. Thompson confronted the different meanings of the word 'socialism' in popular usage. 'Socialism, in the legitimate sense of the word,' he wrote, 'relates solely to the system, and has not the slightest reference to the means employed for bringing it about.' He rejected any association of the term with violence, including the tendency of a capitalistic press to link socialism with anarchism.[44]

Thompson recognized the usefulness of state intervention to the project of labour reform. In *The Palladium of Labor* he criticized the nineteenth-century system of government whereby 'capitalism is king.' 'The real rulers are not the puppet princes and jumping jack statesmen who strut their little hour upon the world's stage,' he wrote, 'but the money kings, railroad presidents, and great international speculators and adventurers who control the money market and the highways of commerce.'[45] In contrast to rule by the interests of capital, Thompson proposed 'popular sovereignty,' where government is representative of all people, rather than controlled by 'the machinery of capitalism.' He highlighted several barriers that stood in the way of the realization of independent democracy in Canada.

Colonialism was one obstacle to the attainment of popular democratic government and labour reform. In an instalment of 'Our Social Club,' Canada's colonial relationship with Britian is debated. Freeman argues that subserviency to British opinions prevents the Canadian people from adopting legislation suitable to the distinctive needs of the country. He rejects the importation into Canada of any ideas and institutions of caste and class supremacy from England. The appointment of Lord Lansdowne as governor-general was cited in the narrative as an illustration of the 'worst phase' of the colonial system. The members of the fictional social club eventually conclude that Canada will never have a progressive government until it severs the British connection with 'its aristocratic governors, tinsel titles, civil service dues, and imported notions of social caste.'[46]

According to Thompson, government would never be truly democratic, and embody the ideas of all of the people, as long as Canada remained the dependency of a monarchy with a corrupt aristocracy. Independence would advance the cause of labour reform by reducing the tendency to imitate British models and opinions in fashioning Canadian institutions.[47] Thompson pronounced the British influence 'utterly and irredeemably bad,' although he claimed that he had no hostility towards Englishmen as individuals. He referred to the principle of the Knights of Labor that stipulated, '[L]abor is of no country, and race and national prejudices have no place in the labour movement.' The caste system imported from England exalted rank, but it degraded manhood, which Thompson defined as that 'nobility of character which might be found in the peasant as well as the prince consort.'[48] When the Canadian Senate rejected Charlton's seduction bill introduced in 1884, a measure that was strongly endorsed by the Ontario Knights of Labor, Thompson used this as an example of how the British spirit of caste had manifested itself in the country in such a manner that the pleasures of the wealthier classes had superseded female virtue. He also relocated vice in the upper classes, in contrast to the ruling-class discourse that equated immorality with working-class women.[49]

In his editorials for the *News*, Thompson drew on the popular Victorian metaphor of 'national manhood,' where the birth and development of a nation was compared to growth to manhood. Consistent with the labour-reform platform of the *News*, however, he altered the metaphor to bolster his argument for independence. Like the boy who attains manhood and assumes independence from parental authority, Canada had reached national manhood with respect to age, development, and resources. 'There is no more reason why we should cling to colonialism than why a man of mature years should remain as subject to the orders of his father as a boy of ten,' he declared.[50] Analogous to the independent man who commands respect, and is admired for his force of character and resolution, the independent nation never submits to foreign rule, and is thus respected. Thompson argued that colonialism was detrimental to the 'national character' of Canadians. 'We cannot be patriotic until we own our country,' he remarked. 'We cannot have national spirit until we are a nation.'[51]

This rhetoric of independence was counter to the discourse of imperial unity and the movement for Imperial Federation during the 1880s. Late-nineteenth-century Toronto was, as historian Carl Berger writes, 'the most imperialistic city in the country.' The major spokepersons for imperial unity in Canada were Colonel George Taylor Denison, a member of a wealthy and prominent Toronto Loyalist family, soldier, and police-court magistrate; Principal George Munro Grant of Queen's University; and Sir George Robert Parker, a teacher and writer. The Imperial Federation League founded in London in 1884 was based on three planks: the possibility of colonial representation in the Imperial Parliament, the construction of an imperial tariff, and, lastly, colonial contribution to imperial defence.[52] In Canada, the descendants of the United Empire Loyalists were the major supporters of the League. They constructed a British-Canadian national identity that credited the Loyalists with implanting in Canada the British constitution and the impulse towards imperial unity. The Loyalists symbolized the preservation of the Anglo-Saxon race in Canada. The Imperial Federationists attributed the capacity for self-government and political organization to the aptitudes for liberty and self-government they believed were inherent in the Anglo-Saxon race.[53]

As Enjolras, Thompson expressed his opposition to any scheme for Imperial

Federation. 'We want to have as little as possible connection with England as long as either the bourgeois money-making spirit or the Jingo bullying, chip-on-the-shoulder, who'll-tread-on-my-coat-tail sentiment is in the ascendancy there,' he pronounced emphatically. If Canada were federated with England, Enjolras hypothesized, landlordism and capitalistic exploitation would be placed on a firmer and more enduring basis by allowing the British aristocracy and men of wealth to use the colonies as a vast 'dumping ground' for paupers and superfluous labourers.[54] Both the TTLC and the Knights of Labor were opposed to assisted immigration. Enjolras further argued that the supporters of Imperial Federation merely viewed the colonies as recruiting grounds, which would provide the Empire with resources in men and money for wars in Afghanistan, India, Egypt, Zululand, or any other region they sought to annex. In the fall of 1884 he openly denounced the use of a Canadian contingent of raftsmen to accompany Wolsely's expedition up the Nile. 'It is intended as a response to the independence movement, and a declaration of the sovereignty of Britain and the subjection of Canada for all time.'[55]

For the supporters of Imperial Federation, however, independence was associated with the demise of militarism. In Victorian culture martial values were held in high esteem by all classes, including the working class. Thompson, however, categorized militarism as undemocratic, and declared that 'the military spirit should be strenuously deprecated by every Labor Reformer.' A step had already been made towards the establishment of a military aristocracy in Canada, Thompson disparaged, with the foundation of the Kingston Military College. In a *News* editorial he described the college as a 'nursery of snobs,' intended to 'cultivate habits of genteel loaferism and supercilious arrogance towards honest labour.'[56]

Another obstacle to Thompson's vision of democratic government was the restricted franchise. As part of its guiding policy the *News* asserted that in provincial elections every man has a right to vote, notwithstanding the fact that he may be neither a property holder nor a payer of income tax. However, significant qualifications along racial lines to what on the surface appeared to be support for universal male suffrage on the part of the *News* editorial staff soon surfaced. In March 1885, the Macdonald government proposed an amendment to the Elections Act whereby Native men possessing and occupying a tract of land on a reservation with improvements valued at $150 could vote in federal elections. On 28 May, the *News* declared that '[n]o Indian living on a reservation ought to be permitted to vote.' The *News* editorial continued: 'There are but few of them who are intelligent enough or have sufficient interest in the affairs of the general community to be admitted to the franchise even if there were no other objection. They are, like the Chinamen, aliens not merely by blood but by the permanency with which they cling to the habits, customs and ideas opposed to those of civilized Caucasians.'[57] Among Toronto labour reformers, therefore, there was a general acceptance of the idea that the Anglo-Saxon race had an aptitude for democratic government. Thus, while Thompson and his colleagues encouraged class solidarity, they simultaneously promoted the fragmentation of the working class using justifications articulated along the lines of race.

Thompson was also a supporter of the movement to extend women's suffrage. He was acquainted with Dr Emily Howard Stowe, the energetic leader of the Toronto Women's Literary Club, reorganized in March 1883 as the Toronto Women's Suffrage Association. In December, the *News* declared its support for the agitation of the Women's Suffrage Association, but cautioned against focusing demand for the ballot around justifications of women as unrepresented property-owners, rather than on the democratic ground of natural right and justice. At a time when women were defined legally as property, the *News* made its appeal for an extension of the female vote on the basis of sex. 'If woman is entitled to the suffrage at all, it is by reason of her womanhood, irrespective of whether she be a millionaire or a sewing-girl,' the *News* commented.[58]

In *The Palladium of Labor*, Enjolras took up the question of sex as a qualification for the vote, and suggested that woman's suffrage was important to labour reform. He explained that women have the right to be recognized in all matters of citizenship as the 'equals of man,' and indicated that distinctions on the basis of sex are just as oppressive as those founded upon race, creed, birth, or property, which have wrought so much injustice and misery in the world. Political power, he further asserted, would increase women workers' capacity for organization and self protection. 'To enfranchise woman would be a long step to conferring upon her industrial equality with man, and equal pay for equal work.' In the same column he used the rhetoric of 'woman's sphere' to argue for an extension of the franchise to include all women. The fact that woman's sphere is home, Enjolras remarked, 'rather than being a reason for refusing her political equality with man is an argument for putting into her hands the ballot as a means of protecting that home from the despoiler.' Whereas men are too easily swayed by party considerations, 'the addition to the electorate of a large body of voters who make the welfare of the house their chief consideration, will have a tendency to supply the stimulus to effective and progressive legislation that is now wanting.' Women voters, he argued, would focus their attention on questions of poverty and intemperance, all of which affected woman's sphere more directly.[59]

'Partyism' was identified by Thompson as yet another obstacle to the realization of his vision of independent democracy. In *The Palladium of Labor*, Enjolras categorized 'party heelers,' those professed labour reformers who do much work 'in spreading the light,' but who lower themselves by accepting the bribes of politicians, as actual enemies of labour. At election times, he indicated, they could be found on the stump, using the influence they had gained as leading labor reformers, to win over the votes of working men for the Grits or Tories.[60] 'He is perfectly well aware that both parties stand ready to sacrifice Labor's rights at the bidding of the monopolist, and yet he will take the stump with a lie in his mouth and an appeal to the workingmen as one who is identified with their interests to support one or the other set of rascally humbugs,' Enjolras remarked. The party heeler not only sells himself out for a temporary position that will maintain him for a year or two at the government expense, he also sells out the cause that he ought to hold sacred.[61]

Both the Reform and the Conservative parties, furthermore, were dominated by capitalism. Enjolras accused Macdonald of 'pandering to a horde of greedy, conscienceless speculators and extortioners ... He has enriched the Canada Pacific monopolists at the cost to the Dominion of about $120,000,000. He has carved up the North-west into grants to colonization companies, timber limits given to buy votes in parliament, valuable mining and ranching privileges trafficked away for a song to political favorites of English aristocrats.'[62] The federal Grits, moreover, were no different from the Tories. 'Mr. Blake, as a Chancery lawyer, is identified with heavy corporation and capitalistic interests,' Enjolras complained. 'Both he and Mr. Mackenzie are concerned in loan companies, and their intimate associations are all with the money grabbing, shystering, speculating class.'[63]

Thompson maintained that where politicians have used labour in the past, the time had come when labour must use the politicans. In the final instalment of 'Our Social Club' the members decide that the usefulness of the club had since passed and that it ought to disband. The members agree that their work might be more effectively carried out by joining the newly organized Labor Political Association. Freeman and Harcourt contend that labour reformers must hold their party ties loosely and when parties fail to look to the interests of labour, working men should turn their back on them, rather than vote for the 'old party.'[64] The narrative was rooted in the events of the 1880s, during which labour in Ontario pursued independent political action. Once again, Thompson was not only an 'active knower,' but an 'active doer.'

Preparations were under way for independent labour political activity in Toronto in late 1882, soon after the organization of the first local assemblies of the Knights of Labor, and not long after the organization of the TTLC. In the municipal elections of 1882, the TTLC campaigned successfully in the mayoralty race against J.J. Withrow, a master builder, who had opposed the nine-hours movement in 1872 and the carpenters in a recent strike. The following year, the TTLC nominated independent labour candidates for the first time to contest in the provincial election. Carpenter Samuel R. Heakes was the independent labour candidate for East Toronto, and painter John Carter ran in West Toronto, although both were defeated amidst extensive partyism behind the scenes.

In Toronto, working-class issues also dominated the federal election campaign of 1882. The *Globe* launched an attack on Macdonald's National Policy as detrimental to the interests of the working class. In the spring of 1882, the *Globe* hired Phillips Thompson to investigate the impact of the National Policy on the cotton industry and the conditions of the operatives. Thompson studied the cotton mills at Hochelaga, Valleyfield, and Cornwall, all of which were controlled by the 'cotton monopoly' located in Montreal. Using statistics from the annual reports compiled by the firms themselves, Thompson argued that cotton milling was already an extraordinarily profitable enterprise, even before the introduction of additional protection under the National Policy. Thompson countered assertions made by Tory Senator Donald McInnis, a founder of the Canada Cotton Company at Cornwall in 1873. McInnis stated that cotton prices had not increased under the National Policy tariff. Also, contrary to McInnis's claim that the wages of operatives had risen since the National Policy was implemented, Thompson found that wages had actually declined by as much as 20 per cent.[65]

In the last two instalments of the series, Thompson probed the living and working conditions of the female factory operatives. The operatives at the mills investigated were almost exclusively French Canadian, with the exception of the Stormont Mills at Cornwall, which attracted women from the surrounding countryside. Thompson discussed the home life of the mill girls. 'The unhealthfulness of their occupation, adds to the effect of incessant toil in stunting the mental and moral nature as well as in producing physical weaknesses,' he wrote. 'The homes of many can scarcely be called homes.'[66] Thompson, however, was sympathetic to the plight of the women operatives, and in their defence he remarked: 'There must be girls whose purity of life resists the tendencies around them; these deserve real and practical respect; their weaker sisters deserve sympathy, for under the conditions in which they live there is little of an elevating character.'[67]

This association of working-class womanhood with vice, which was not unlike the rhetoric of nineteenth-century middle-class social reformers, unleashed a storm of indignation from women operatives and employers, much of which was published in the pages of the *Globe*'s Tory rival, the *Mail*.[68] Employers of female workers from Preston, Galt, Campbellford, Strathroy,

Paris, Brantford, Berlin, and Almonte sent letters to the editor of the *Mail*. They expressed their opinion that the whole thing was 'a miserable fabrication, and an abominable and outrageous slander on a class of operatives who belong to respectable families.'[69] The Tory *Mail* accused the Grit *Globe* of slander intended to make a political statement against the Tory's National Policy, and sent their own correspondent to investigate. The *Mail* correspondent interviewed a series of allegedly 'knowledgable authorities,' namely the manager of the Hudon Mill, a priest from Hochelga, and a physician, all of whom denied the validity of Thompson's observations and attested to the virtuous character and physical well-being of the operatives.[70]

On 14 June, an estimated fifteen hundred Cornwall cotton mill operatives held a meeting to protest the assertions made by Thompson in the *Globe*. Senator McInnis addressed the gathering. The crowd also heard speeches from overseers, mill managers, and several clergymen. The following evening a procession of men and women workers marched through the streets of Cornwall led by a brass band and ending with an effigy 'supposed to represent the local informant of the *Globe*.' According to the *Mail* reporter, mud, stones, and eggs were showered upon the dummy. Banners made out of cotton produced in the mills displayed the following mottoes: 'The Workingman's Bogus Friends,' 'The Slanderer of Our Wives and Daughters,' and 'The Despoiler of Our Homes.' After the parade through the principal streets of Cornwall, the effigy was burned 'amid the jeers, howls, and yells of the indignant populace.'[71] A few days later, on 17 June, mill operatives in Paris held a meeting in the town hall at which a resolution was passed protesting against the remarks made in the *Globe* about the morality of women cotton-mill operatives.[72]

Ironically, given Thompson's opposition to partisan politics, the *Mail* used what was interpreted as an attack on the moral virtue of working-class women to secure another victory for the Tories. The effect of these partisan struggles in the press, which in addition to the attack on Thompson's series included allegations by the *Mail* that the Legislative Committee of the TTLC was composed of 'pronounced Reformers' and one 'ultra-grit,' was to move Toronto labour reformers to draft an independent labour platform. The platform delivered before the TTLC on 6 October 1882 asserted the need for working-class representation in parliament, and reiterated a series of legislative reforms long sought by labour reformers, including an extension of the franchise, restricted immigration, shorter hours, and a factory act.[73]

The major triumph of Toronto labour in politics came in January 1886 with the election of William H. Howland as mayor. Howland's candidacy was endorsed by the *News*, and by both the TTLC and the Knights of Labor. His victory was fortified by an alliance with temperance and moral reformers and by the votes of women. The *News* pronounced Howland's victory a 'Triumph of Democracy.' 'Throughout the contest,' the *News* declared, 'due prominence was given to the idea of popular rule, and to bring the sense of the people freely in favor of the thing, who for some reason or other, do not like the name, and yet, what is Democracy in its strict etymological sense but "the rule of the people?"'[74] Bolstered by its success in the municipal election, the labour movement turned to the forthcoming provincial and federal elections.

As the elections approached, the *News* reiterated that 'a wire-pulling match between Grit and Tory heelers professing to be Labour Reformers would do infinite harm to the cause.' Rather than elect a Grit or a Tory workman who would be subservient to his party, Thompson argued that it would be better to elect labour-reform candidates absolutely independent of any party connections. He referred to the success of the small, but powerful, group of Irish Nationalists under Parnell's leadership who succeeded in dictating the policy of the Liberal party in England and advancing the cause of Home Rule. In extending the comparison to Ontario, Enjolras explained, a half-dozen independent workmen in the legislature could force either side to support measures in favour of the work class simply by cooperating with either party as their interests dictate.[75]

On 30 November 1886, ninety representatives from sixty of the city's labour organizations and an estimated 10,000 workers gathered in Richmond Hall. In a marathon six-hour meeting they nominated four labour candidates, two each for the upcoming provincial and federal elections. Charles March and John Roney, both painters by trade, were selected as candidates for the provincial election.[76] E.E. Sheppard was declared the federal candidate for West Toronto, and tailor Alfred Jury was nominated for East Toronto. At a ratification meeting held on 6 December in Temperance Hall, Phillips Thompson told the crowd of working men gathered that what they had to do was to elect their candidates 'to be true to themselves.'[77]

Charges of sectarianism on the part of the Tories echoed throughout the campaign. The Tory *Mail* attacked the Mowat government for its supposed education concessions to Roman Catholics. The *News*, in turn, reminded its readers of how sectarian bigotry has in the past kept the country in turmoil and strife, and so engrossed the country as to prevent the consideration of real and important measure of reform.[78] Enjolras cautioned that a war of creeds, such as the *Mail* and Tory politicians sought to wage, could only be harmful to the labour-reform movement. He reiterated the cry of 'Labor Reform first,' and warned that the gains made in the education of workers would be lost if working men were drawn into bitter sectarian wrangling.[79]

The Toronto labour candidates were defeated in both the provincial and federal elections. In the aftermath of the elections, the *News* concluded that there was no reason for despondency, and that it was only 'a work of time to wean men from their old-time party affiliations and induce them to support the candidates of a new movement.' The *News* also suggested that in order to establish a firm basis for future labour campaigns, the Labor Reform Party must learn from their party adversaries, who derive their principal strength from the preservation of their political organization intact by participating in municipal elections.[80]

Although, in Thompson's opinion, party politics and industrial evolution had threatened democracy and degraded its citizens to the level of wage-slaves, he acknowledged that it had also created a system for the organization of production that was worth retaining. Thompson rejected any notion of a nostalgic return to a pre-industrial agrarian past or individualism in economic enterprise. Rather, he asserted, it was more desirable, and easier, 'to transfer from the organizing and directing force of capitalism to the community the disproportionate share of the advantages of the system which capitalism now retains.' This meant preserving the social benefits arising from the elaborate mechanism of production, while eliminating the injustice resulting from the control by and in the interests of individuals.[81]

While Thompson rejected Social Darwinism, and its view of evolution that justified laissez-faire as part of the preordained struggle for survival of the fittest, he was greatly influenced by the writings of philosopher Herbert Spencer. From Spencer he adopted the idea that the evolution of society did not imply blind acquiescence to a spirit of fatalism. Social institutions were continually modified by the influence of the law, public opinion, and the initiatives of organizations that make a lasting imprint upon the community. Thompson accepted the idea of progressive social evolution and believed that 'human nature' was susceptible to improvement.[82]

For the most part, however, Thompson was highly critical of Spencer's writings, and also of American adaptations of Spencer's ideas. While he could accept the idea of social evolution, Thompson was never attracted to that part of Spencer's theorizing that advocated laissez-faire economics and survival-of-the-fittest individualism. He rejected the argument made by Spencer in 'The Man vs. the State,' where government regulation, especially over the working class, was referred to as the 'New Toryism.' In opposition, Thompson argued that regulating legislation was the legitimate outcome of the working of social evolution, with the institutions and intervention of government being developed as the need arises.[83]

The 'survival of the fittest' doctrine was an obstacle to labour reform. Like other late-nineteenth-century labour reformers, Thompson was highly critical of the valuation of the 'self-made man' and the high regard for personal wealth, which permeated not only the upper classes but the working class as well. The possibility of becoming a self-made man was used by the apologists of capitalism to justify unrelenting competition. In *The Palladium*, however, Enjolras pointed out that the possibility of 'rising through the ranks,' and becoming a millionaire was remote, and that the self-made man was a fallacy. He used the official statistics compiled by the Ontario Bureau of Industries which revealed that the average wages of workers in 204 occupations were only $383 per year. Even upon the remote possibility that a worker could save $200 a year, after forty years this meant savings of only $8000 – 'a mere flea bite in comparison to the fortunes we are called upon to admire,' Enjolras observed.[84] The fallacy of the self-made man was not that wealth was acquired through original industry. According to Enjolras, the fallacy centred around of use these small acquirements to live off the labour power of others and acquire more wealth through rent, interest, and usury.

Education and public opinion encouraged ambitious boys to 'be somebody.' Professional and mercantile occupations were held in high regard, while productive labour was belittled. Thompson argued that this social system, which not only attached wealth, but professional 'respectability' and superior gentility, to non-manual labour was entirely false. The effect of this teaching was to foster a selfish individualism and a contempt for honest toil.[85] It ought not to be necessary for anyone to 'rise in the world,' in the sense of ceasing to be a wage-worker or a manual labourer, before he can hope to be recognized as worthy to fill an important representative position.

'In the modern industrial and commercial world,' Thompson wrote, 'the very qualities which go to constitute true manhood are often calculated to retard success in life.' He revealed that the ideal of masculinity advocated by labour reformers, one that included generosity, outspoken candor, and a free-independent bearing, would also keep a man in an inferior position under the prevailing industrial-capitalist social order. In contrast to the masculine ideal of labour reformers, 'the self-made man,' Thompson explained, was 'a grasping and sordid creature, the predominant traits of whose character are avarice and a domineering harshness of disposition.' Self-made men were mercenary, cunning, heartless, greedy, and overbearing – the antithesis of the manly ideal of labour reformers.[86]

In *The Politics of Labor*, Thompson suggested that if, instead of legal regulations being framed in the interests of the wealthy, laws were shaped according to the right of the 'strongest,' those defined by the ruling class as the 'fittest' would be the inferior and they would succumb to the superior physical strength of the starving masses. Thompson elaborated his critique of laissez-faire economics, Herbert Spencer, and survival of the fittest most eloquently in his satirical poem 'The Political Economist and the Tramp,' which originally appeared in *The National* in 1878, but which he included in *The Politics of Labor*.[87]

The Political Economist and the Tramp

Walking along a country road,
  While yet the morning air was damp,
As unreflecting on I strode,
  I marked approach the frequent tramp.

The haggard, ragged, careworn man,
  Accosted me in plaintive tone:
'I must have food' – he straight began;
  'Vile miscreant,' I cried, 'begone!'

'Tis contrary to every rule
  That I my fellows should assist;
I'm of the scientific school,
  Political economist.

'Do'st though not know, deluded one,
  That Adam Smith has clearly proved,
That 'tis self-interest alone
  By which the wheels of life are moved?

'That competition is the law
  By which we either live or die?
I've no demand thy labor for,
  Why, then, should I thy wants supply?

'And Herbert Spencer's active brain,
  Shows how the social struggle ends:
The weak die out – the strong remain;
  'Tis this that Nature's plan intends.

'Now, really, 'tis absurd of you
  To think I'd interfere at all;
Just grasp the scientific view –
  The weakest must go to the wall.'

My words impressed his dormant thought.
 'How wise,' he said, 'is nature's plan!
Henceforth I'll practice what you've taught,
 And be a scientific man.

'We are alone – no others near,
 Or even within hailing distance;
I've a good club, and now right here
 We'll have a 'struggle for existence.'

'The weak must die, the strong survive –
 Let's see who'll prove the harder hittist,
So, if you wish to keep alive,
 Prepare to prove yourself the fittest.

'If you decline the test to make,
 Doubting your chances of survival,
Your watch and pocketbook I'll take,
 As competition strips a rival.'

What could I do but yield the point,
 Though conscious of no logic blunder?
And as I quaked in every joint,
 The tramp departed with his plunder.

During the latter part of the nineteenth century Phillips Thompson worked to 'Spread the Light' about labour reform. He was one of a small group of radical intellectuals, or 'brainworkers,' whose role was to educate Toronto working men and women about the problems of capitalist accumulation at the expense of others, and thereby bring about social change. This task involved nothing less than a complete and radical change in sentiment and habits of thought among male workers who had been taught to 'exhalt money before manhood.' During the 1880s, the Knights of Labor established the institutional framework in Ontario for the dissemination of this knowledge about labour reform. The Knights organized an independent, but not completely autonomous, culture.

Thompson was not only active in the actual work of educating workers in his columns for *The Palladium of Labor* and the *News*, and through his witty lectures and songs, he was an active agent in the formation of a radical counter-discourse to the dominant bourgeois political economy of laissez-faire economics and survival-of-the-fittest individualism. In proposing that political economy be rewritten from the standpoint of the 'Sermon on the Mount' and the 'Declaration of Independence,' Thompson drew on a variety of influences, most notably perhaps Protestantism and Christian morality, the doctrine of Henry George, Irish Radicalism, and American critiques of the writings of Herbert Spencer. His textual mediations were constructed during a period when several key terms in political economy such as capitalism, monopoly, and socialism were being defined or redefined. Above all, Thompson's 'new' political economy was the product of his experiences in the Canadian Knights of Labor, and various other social clubs and reform organizations in Toronto. He was also influenced by the wider social and structural transformations brought about by industrial-capitalist growth, as well as concerns over nation-building, sexual impurity, and racial degeneration.

Gender, class, and race were interwoven throughout Thompson's discourse on political economy. Although Thompson viewed the racial divisions that permeated the labour-reform movement, and the wider working-class culture, with disdain, his idea of an independent Canadian national identity reinforced a racial hierarchy that privileged those workers of Anglo-Saxon origins over native peoples, and categorized Chinese labourers as 'alien' others.

4

'An Artist of Righteousness': J.W. Bengough's Comic Art and Labour and Working-Class Reform

John Wilson Bengough was one of a large number of latter-nineteenth-century English-Canadian liberal Protestants whose project was to 'regenerate' society by reforming it and building the foundations for a Christian republic.[1] Bengough's comic art and satiric verses in *Grip*, a weekly paper of comic art, satirical verse, and social and political commentary, relied on powerful symbols that were the vehicles by which the 'Truths' about social and moral reform were conveyed to the public. Complex metaphors and allegories, through which class, gender, and race were interwoven in visual images, organized and defined the work of political, social, and moral reform. A concern for labour and the conditions of the working class were incorporated into Bengough's reform discourse.

At its peak in the mid-1880s, the weekly circulation of *Grip*, according to its publishers, varied between 7000 and 10,000 copies, but the paper was reportedly purused by fully 50,000 readers every week.[2] Tracking the discursive formations and institutional supports of Bengough's comic art, one uncovers the interaction and collision of cultural worlds. As part of the expansion of mass-circulation magazines and journals in Canada during the late nineteenth century, *Grip* reached multiple reading publics. Politicians expounded their interpretations of Bengough's cartoons in official government institutions and on the stump, and intellectuals commented on his cartoons in competing periodicals. The cartoons, with the aid of the numerous public lectures, or 'chalk talks,' that Bengough conducted throughout the country, became part of the everyday culture of work and family in Victorian Canada. In his comic art Bengough delineated a masculinist, liberal-Protestant view of reform aimed at creating a Christian community and a new reformed social subjectivity. His discourse of labour and social reform relied for its meaning on the structural relations of class, gender, and race in nineteenth-century Canada, but also contributed to the shaping of these relations in specific ways.[3]

In contrast to the radical Phillips Thompson who, in the early 1890s, turned to Bellyamite socialism and theosophy for an answer to the 'labour question,' John Wilson Bengough, editor of *Grip*, lecturer, and poet, was committed to the doctrines of Henry George. In *Progress and Poverty*, Bengough found a message consistent with his evangelical Protestant conceptualization of the world, and anticipated social-gospel Christians with his contention that the implementation of a program of social action and practical charity was necessary for the church to make itself relevant again.[4] Predictably, Bengough's Protestant moralism led him to embrace prohibition and sabbatarianism, which he identified as distinctively working-class issues. What brought the Protestant-moralist Bengough together with the radical Thompson, and allowed them to work together at various times on the production of *Grip*, was a shared belief that monopoly and landlordism produced wealth for a handful and misery for the multitudes who actually laboured. Both men were highly critical of party politics, which they viewed as morally bankrupt. Also, both Thompson and Bengough were anti-imperialists. They shared a common anxiety about the future of the nation, and concerned themselves with the task of building a Canadian nationality.

The son of a Scottish immigrant cabinetmaker and his Irish wife, J.W. Bengough was born in Toronto on 7 April 1851. In the late 1850s and early 1860s, he attended grammar school in Whitby, where he displayed a talent for drawing.[5] He recalled many years later, however, that there was no attempt in those days at systematic art instruction: 'The tendency was perhaps rather to discourage it as a means of wasting time, except on special occasions.'[6] After his school days were over, Bengough worked briefly first in a photographer's studio, and them as a law clerk. Finding the law not at all to his liking, he became a printer's devil at the Whitby *Gazette*, owned and edited by George H. Ham, who subsequently became famous as a showman for the Canadian Pacific Railway. With aspirations towards an editorial career, Bengough seized upon the opportunity provided by the Franco-Prussian war, and accepted an offer from Ham to write a serial novel, which he entitled 'The Murderer's Scalp, or the Shrieking Ghost of the Bloody Den.'

Meanwhile, Bengough was attracted to the cartoons by Thomas Nast in *Harper's Weekly*. Nast exposed the group of corrupt officials under Tammany 'Boss' William Marcy Tweed, who had gained control of New York City and milked the treasury for millions of dollars while simultaneously running up a public debt of fifty million dollars. The Radical Republican Nast became Bengough's *beau idéal*, and stimulated in him an awareness of the power of the cartoonist as a social critic. Nast created, or popularized, several of the symbols that became mainstays of contemporary American political culture, including the Republican elephant, the Tammany tiger, the Democratic donkey, the work-ingman's paper cap and dinner pail, and the Rag Baby of inflationist sentiment. His influence on Bengough was enduring, and these symbols were a source of inspiration for a number of the cartoons he drew for *Grip*, as was the British paper *Punch*, especially the cartoons of its artist John Tenniel.[7]

Sometime in 1871, Bengough moved to Toronto, where he went to work as a reporter on the *Globe*, under managing editor George Brown. At that time, Bengough recalled, 'even the plain, purposeful cartoon, that is so well adapted to reinforce the editor's argument, had apparently not been thought of in daily journalism.' Bengough continued to nurture his artistic talent. He enrolled in evening classes conducted under the auspices of the Ontario Society of Artists, but found the copying of figures of Greek deities in plaster casts not at all to his liking, as he preferred to 'study from life.' The Hon. James Beaty, senator and owner of the *Leader*, a Conservative party organ, was an irresistible subject. Bengough showed his caricature of 'Old Jimmie' to Beaty's nephew Sam, who had it lithographed at nearby Rolph Brothers. Up to that time Bengough had been unfamiliar with lithography, but he had an idea: 'Why not start a weekly comic paper with lithographed cartoons?'[8]

Bengough was only twenty-two years old when he launched the first issue of *Grip* on 24 May 1873, with the backing of A.S. Irving, manager of the Toronto News Company. The name 'Grip' was borrowed from the talking raven in Charles Dickens's 1841 novel *Barnaby Rudge*. In Dickens's novel, Grip is the companion of the idiot Barnaby. Although he embodied all of the demonic impulses of the raven as an animalistic symbol in Victorian popular culture, Grip also provided comic relief. Grip, with his cry of 'I'm a devil,' accompanied by optimistic pronouncements such as 'Keep up your spirits' and 'Never say die,' had all of the wit. Barnaby declares that their relationship is one of master and man, and that Grip is the master.[9] In the inaugural issue of *Grip* Bengough mused:

Though the raven race have no enviable reputation, being traditionally stigmatised as bearers of ill-omen only, there is no reader but likes GRIP's company, for he is in all points an exceptional bird: there is, for instance, such a wholesome contrast between his glad and frequent, 'Never Say Die!' and the dismal *Nevermore!* of his dusky mate in literature – the despairing croaker that perched upon Mr. Edgar Poe's bust of PALLAS, and according to the latest account, –

> Still is sitting, still is
> sitting
> there.[10]

Throughout the twenty-year period that *Grip* was published, the raven Grip appeared on the masthead, or on the cover page, together with the motto: 'The gravest Beast is the Ass; the gravest Bird is the Owl; the gravest Fish is the Oyster; the gravest Man is the Fool.' In the early issues the editor was listed as Charles P. Hall. Bengough apparently did not want his actual name used as he was still on the staff of the *Globe*.[11] In the issues of *Grip* for the month of August 1873, Jimuel Briggs, D.B., Phillips Thompson's alter ego, was listed as editor. The following month, on 13 September, *Grip* announced that Mr Barnaby Rudge would henceforth carry the editorial burden. Until approximately two years before *Grip*'s demise in 1894, Bengough remained in control, providing much of the editorial text and the comic art. Part of the visual impact of Bengough's cartoons in *Grip* came from the size of his large full-page cartoons. The 'cut' in a woodblock was also a language of attack. The dark mass of a woodblock could, for example, accentuate the sombreness of a mood and sharpen the bite of a message.[12] For his less-informed readers, and for purposes of ensuring that his message was understood, Bengough labelled anything that might be unfamiliar using cut-lines and titles. Shortly after *Grip* first appeared, Bengough began to explain the message of his cartoons in lengthy editorial columns.[13]

Grip's Discourse on Political Morality

Although the first issue of *Grip* caused 'no great public furore,' success quickly followed on the heels of the Pacific Scandal. As Bengough later recalled, 'The whole country was at once aflame with interest and excitement, and an absorbing theme adapted to keep *Grip* going for many issues had thus been supplied at the right moment.'[14] In his comic art and satiric verses for *Grip*, Bengough used children's nursery rhymes and domestic metaphors to illuminate the corruption within the Macdonald government, and probably contributed to the Reformers' victory in the election of 1874.

For example, shortly after the collapse of the Macdonald government on 5 November 1873, Bengough suggested that 'The Liberal Programme' would initiate an 'era of purification.' In the cartoon, Alexander Mackenzie is clothed in the garb of a washerwoman, and is down on his hands and knees scrubbing away the 'dirt' of the Pacific Scandal and Conservative political corruption. Watching over the fumigation are Edward Blake, George Brown holding a copy of the *Globe*, and Oliver Mowat holding a coal scuttle in a bucket labelled 'Honesty.' In Victorian bourgeois constructions of class and gender, the responsibility for cleanliness and morality was with women in the private sphere of the home. The use of the domestic metaphor in the cartoon symbolized the antici-

THE LIBERAL PROGRAMME;
OR, THE ERA OF PURIFICATION.

Grip, 6 December 1873

pated cleansing or moral purification of government should the Grits be elected. Blake, Brown, and Mowat, on the other hand, appear as respectable middle-class gentlemen, and represent the middle-class masculine virtue of account-ability in the public realm.[15]

Bengough's comic art, and his discursive construction of political morality, quickly became a component of the political culture of the new Dominion. In his acceptance speech for the Liberal nomination in Sarnia on 25 November 1873, Prime Minister Alexander Mackenzie referred specifically to a cartoon

THE POLITICAL MOTHER HUBBARD
AND JOHN A.'S "DYING INIQUITY."

Grip, 15 November 1873

that had appeared in *Grip*, in which he was represented as Old Mother Hubbard, from the popular nursery rhyme. Rumours had been circulating in the press that the Reform government would soon appoint George Brown to the position of lieutenant-governor of Ontario. In Bengough's visual image, when Mackenzie, as the 'good' Mother Hubbard went to the cupboard to get her poor dog, George Brown, a political 'bone,' he/she discovered John A. Macdonald sneaking out the back door with one hundred patronage appointments in his pocket. In the cartoon, John Crawford, sketched in the shape of a little dog, is carrying away the political 'bone' of the lieutenant-governorship of Ontario, the appointment having been made in the dying days of the Macdonald ministry. 'There is no little significance in that picture,' Mackenzie remarked to the gathering of his loyal supporters.[16]

Despite his Grit sympathies and admiration for Alexander Mackenzie and Wilfrid Laurier, Bengough repeatedly emphasized that *Grip* was 'entirely independent' of the two political parties. This course, Bengough explained, was not one of 'pseudo-independence' that involved steering the middle ground between the two opposing parties, but one of 'true' independence, 'by upholding that party which is in the right, on each particular question as it arises.'[17] In *Flapdoodle: A Political Encyclopedia and Manual for Public Men*, he stated that the political party 'exercises the same fatal fascination over the minds and morals of its votaries that liquor does over the senses of a drunkard.' A politician was defined as '[a] person of small means but great assurance, who, declining or failing to make a living by honest industry, takes up the profession of politics as a quack doctor takes up that of medicine, with a view to making money out of the credulity of his fellow-men.'[18]

After he became prime minister, Alexander Mackenzie declared that the guiding principles of his administration would be 'Electoral Purity' and 'Independence of Parliament.' In 'The Premier's Model' Bengough created an allegory using Mackenzie's previous vocation of stonemason. He indicated that the 'virtuous' politican had all of the character traits of the skilled honest workman. The paper hat and apron worn by Mackenzie in the cartoon are symbolic of the honest artisan. Bengough frequently used headgear and clothing to identify the class, employment, and moral worthiness of the characters depicted in his comic art. For Bengough, therefore, Alexander Mackenzie was the ideal 'Christian craftsman,' as represented by 'Christ the carpenter.' Upon Mackenzie's death on 17 April 1892 Bengough wrote in tribute:

He was a Christian of that old-time sort –
Unfashionable now and growing rare –
Who knew no sacred barr'd from secular,
But worshipped God by doing honest work,
Whether with mason's tools as artisan,
Or in high place of State.
His amplest service to the land was this –
Beyond, above the toils he undertook,
And those he finished – be not one forgot! –
He gave the world an answer in his life
To that smug lie of this degenerate age –
'An honest politican cannot be,' –

THE PREMIER'S MODEL;
OR, "IMPLEMENTS TO THOSE WHO CAN USE THEM."

CANADA—"WELL AND BRAVELY DONE, MACKENZIE; NOW STAND BY THAT POLICY, AND I'M WITH YOU ALWAYS!"

Grip, 29 November 1873

A lie that has so much to feed upon
In scandal garbage of our public life
That it seems grown into a monstrous truth –
But 'tis not truth – 'tis still a cynic lie,
That for all time must cower away and hide
At mention of MACKENZIE'S stainless name.[19]

Through a common gender, Christian craftsmen shared a set of common responsibilities. Work was a 'calling,' not to be despised. Instead it was seen as a way of doing God's work in the everyday world. In the evangelical culture of

Victorian Canada, thrift, diligence, sobriety, and public service were all incorporated into the code of manly conduct.[20] A slippage between gender and race occurs in Bengough's discursive formation, however. Mackenzie's rugged physical features and character traits of honesty, truthfulness, and thrift were not only the attributes of the Christian craftsman. They were also associated with the Scots as a race. Bengough's memorial tribute to Mackenzie continues:

> Upon the shaft that marks his resting-place
> Engrave these words: 'Here lies a Patriot.'
> And let it be a four-square, honest shaft
> Of close-knit Scottish granite,
> With no vain floriture of art adorned,
> But sternly upright, fronting all the world,
> To match the man we knew.

Elsewhere in the poem, he remarked: 'His Scottish tongue could speak unvarnished truth.'[21]

In contrast to the visual images of Mackenzie as the Christian craftsman and the dour, upright, respectable Scot, John A. Macdonald seldom appeared in *Grip* as anything but a trickster, symbolized by the popular masculine representation categorized variously as the swell, the gent, the dude, the dandy, the masher, or the rake. This social type, as Judith Walkowitz and Peter Bailey have explained in the context of Victorian Britain, has a long and complicated class geneology. From its roots as a literary satire of pretentious upstarts, the image by the middle of the nineteenth century had been appropriated by popular entertainers as well as by aspiring young clerks and skilled artisans. The immaculately dressed, champagne-consuming swell was roguish, flamboyant, and self-conscious about dress. In Britain, he was made popular in A.J. Milliken's stories in the comic paper *Punch* of 'Arry,' a lower-class rake, and later in the weekly comic paper *Ally Sloper's Half-Holiday*, which appeared from 1884 to 1923.[22] For Bengough, the gent or the swell was anything but a model of respectable masculinity, although for some young working-class men and lower-middle-class clerks who strolled Toronto's Yonge Street in the evenings it was an attractive persona. More important, the swell was a popular cultural type that Bengough's readers could identify with. He could draw on this cultural stereotype to create the desired perception of Macdonald as a manipulator.

John A. Macdonald was fifty-eight years old when the first issue of *Grip* appeared in May 1873. In Bengough's cartoons, however, Macdonald was almost always represented as a young man.[23] Only nearer to Macdonald's death, in 1891, did Bengough sketch him as a thin and haggard old man. Macdonald's

MISS DOMINION,

TWENTY YEARS OF AGE, AND GROWING MORE LIKE HER "PA" EVERY DAY !

Grip, 2 July 1887

appearance, with his long thin nose and mass of curly hair, was particularly well suited to the social type classified as the gent or the swell. In Bengough's Dominion Day cartoon for 1887, marking the twentieth anniversary of Confederation, the visual image of the swell was used to represent Macdonald's mismanagement of Canadian government. Although the dress of the 'swell' demanded 'dash,' the exaggerated neck collar, oversized monacle, and clash of stripes and checks in Bengough's visual image is a catalogue of errors in taste intended to highlight Macdonald's misguided policies for *Grip*'s readers.

In the cartoon, Macdonald holds the hand of 'Miss Dominion.' At the bottom of the page the caption states: 'Twenty Years of Age, and Growing More Like

Her "Pa" Every Day!' Another nineteenth-century gender classification associated with the working class, namely the 'brazen courtezan,' or 'problem girl,' who is the antithesis of respectable femininity, was used to represent Miss Dominion.[24] Bengough wrote:

Since she got into her 'teens Miss Dominion has *not* been a modest, prudent, thoughtful damsel at all; but a giddy gusher, whose notions of the proprieties have been very queer indeed. She has winked at scandals that would have shocked any properly balanced young lady, and has bestowed her especial favors on those who have most richly deserved her censure. By this course she has so impaired her moral judgment, that it is now somewhat doubtful whether she knows the difference between right and wrong.[25]

Miss Dominion, Bengough further remarked, mismanaged domestic affairs, by living beyond her means and neglecting to pay her bills. As a result, she found herself holding the handbag of a debt of $285,000,000.

The image of Miss Canada in Bengough's comic art illustrates how ideas about gender and sexuality could be used to provoke reaction to the political issues of the late nineteenth century, and the project of nation-building in particular. Bengough explained that 'when we conjure up the typical figure of Canada, she appears to us as a beautiful wholesome, hopeful maiden.' Miss Canada was 'a type of the country and its untold possibilities; a land which was designed by nature to literally flow with milk and honey.'[26] In Bengough's construction of nation, as has too often been the case in male nationalisms, woman appears as the guardian, protector, and mother, but the roles assigned to her were conceived as passive rather than active. Women have been construed as the symbolic bearers of the nation, but were typically denied any direct relation to national agency. As historians George Mosse and Catharine Hall have argued in the European context, the theme of nation as female, which implies the gendering of the citizen as male, serves to set limits on the forms of national belonging available to women, and thus confers agency and power upon men to set the limits of national difference.[27] Bengough used the image of the 'problem girl' and the 'fallen woman' when he perceived that the project of nation-building was not being carried out properly.

In the lead cartoon in the 2 February 1889 issue of *Grip*, Bengough again used the familiar figure of the maiden Miss Canada, and suggests that 'She's Outgrown Her Dress.' Miss Canada appears as a girl about to enter womanhood. The skirt of 'colonial status' no longer fits her, and she is window-shopping at 'National Dressmaking' for a new dress, a more 'mature' dress. The dilemma for Miss Canada is which gown to select. Should she select 'the gown' of independence from Britain, Imperial Federation with Britain and the

SHE'S OUTGROWN HER DRESS.

MISS CANADA.—"I wouldn't have that Stars and Stripes dress on any account; that Federation affair wouldn't fit me, and besides, I don't like the cut of it; but I just dote on that Independence outfit! One thing is certain, I'm getting too big a girl to continue wearing THIS dress!

Grip, 2 February 1889

other colonies, or annexation with the United States. Miss Canada declares her preference for 'that Independence outfit.' Bengough uses the symbolism of dress, and its association with ideas of mature respectable womanhood, to indicate his preference for independence from Britain and the formation of a separate Anglo-Saxon community severed from 'the gentle ties of red tape' that constituted the existing 'connection.'[28] The chaste and modest young woman was used by Bengough to demonstrate the virtues of his idea of national identity for Canada. Bengough's idea of 'nation-ness,' therefore, was defined against the backdrop of the anti-colonial struggle.

AN INTERESTING INFANT.

Mr. Grip—" Don't you think, Foster, that she's about big enough now to wear grown-up clothes, and to enjoy a little freedom of trade ? "
Our Finance Minister—" Grown-up clothes ?   Nonsense, Mr Grip !   Why, she's only twenty-three past ! "

Grip, 12 July 1890

A decade later, Bengough was perhaps less optimistic about the future of the nation. While he remarked that the emergence of 'homemade' Canadian songs signified a growing sentiment of nationality, 'a spirit which had been slow in finding adequate expression in Canada,' the restrictive protective tariff under the Conservative's National Policy prevented Miss Canada from maturing into womanhood. In the cartoon, the raven Mr Grip appears in the dress of a gent. He asks the Conservative Finance Minister, George E. Foster, to remove the shackles of the tariff currently bound around the ankles of Miss Canada. Miss Canada is depicted as a grossly enlarged infant in the clothes of a child, and not in the dress suitable for a mature woman of twenty-three years. She had not only been prevented from growing up under the Conservative's tariff policy, but the gender of Miss Canada is represented as 'abnormal,' or a contrast to the ideal of respectable womanhood. She appears in the cartoon as an androgyne. 'She has been thwarted and mannacled and made a guy of by "statesmanship,"' Bengough commented.[29] This departure from dominant middle-class constructions of femininity, together with the widespread fear of androgony in the latter nineteenth-century, was intended to heighten reader awareness about the evils of statesmanship and the Conservative government's nation-building policies. According to Bengough, the only remedy was free trade and the elimination of partisan politics.

The National Policy and the Workingman

Following the Conservative victory in the federal election of 1878, a cartoon appeared in *Grip* in which Macdonald and his Ministers were sketched 'Riding into Power' on the back of the National Policy elephant. Animal metaphors and symbols were widely used by nineteenth-century artists and writers to convey various moral and spiritual messages. Thomas Nast's Republican elephant provided the inspiration for Bengough's National Policy elephant. For Nast, the elephant symbolized his belief in the vital need for a true republic, and the close relationship between morals and politics that would necessarily lead a man to support the Republican party.[30] The elephant took on a second different meaning in some of Bengough's cartoons. In his 1886 *Caricature History of Canadian Politics*, Bengough recalled that opponents of the National Policy tariff anticipated the difficulty the Macdonald ministry would have in reconciling the various trade interests. Consequently, they believed that the National Policy was a 'White Elephant,' or impossible to implement.[31]

During the election campaign R.W. Phipps, a journalist and contributor to *Grip* and *The National*, was the leading popular progagandist for protection. Together with William Weir, Alexander Whyte Wright, John Maclean, and Phillips Thompson, among others, they cultivated the protectionist and soft-money wing of the Conservative party. Leading the group was Hamilton merchant Isaac Buchanan. In the late 1870s they forged a Tory-Labour alliance out of the nine-hours movement called the Workingmen's Liberal Conservative Union (WLCU). Phipps's pamplet entitled *Free Trade and Protection* was widely distributed during the 1878 election campaign.[32] In Bengough's cartoon he is situated on the shoulders of Macdonald, with a cut-line that states, 'This elephant belongs to Phipps: He imported it, and no one else knows how to manage it.' A month later Phipps defected, apparently disappointed that Macdonald did not make him finance minister, making no secret of his conviction that neither Sir John nor his colleagues really understood the principles of political economy.[33]

RIDING INTO POWER.

Grip, 28 September 1878

A few months later, in April 1879, *Grip* announced that a '(Rag) Baby Elephant' had been born. Isaac Buchanan and A.W. Wright, editor of *The National*, who later in the 1880s would rise to prominence in the Knights of Labor as Master Workman Terence Powderly's Canadian adviser, promoted a scheme to imbue the WLCU with the ideas of currency reform and government ownership. Together they reorganized the Financial Reform League of Canada as the Currency Reform League. Wright was secretary of the new organization, and Tory MP William Wallace was elected chair. The advocates of currency reform in the Conservative government, led by Wallace, saw currency reform as a possible 'annex' to the National Policy, and thus potentially useful for political purposes. Hence the symbolic significance of the baby elephant in the cartoon. As editor of the *National*, A.W. Wright promoted a scheme to have the Canadian Pacific Railway built publicly through a complicated financial scheme that included currency reform. In an 1880 federal by-election in Toronto West, Wright tried to use the WLCU to win support for the 'Beaverback' cause. A variation of the American Greenback movement, the Beaverback was an amalgam of protection for native industry, resumption by the government of the right to issue monetary notes that had been given over to banking institutions, and the adoption of a system of paper money based solely on the credit of the Dominion, which would serve as legal tender for all debts, both public and private. Also incorporated into the Beaverback platform were planks excluding Chinese immigrants and favouring temperance. Wright won only 1.2 per cent of the vote, but by 1880 working-class opposition to Tory dominance was beginning to escalate. Wright's independent stand in the by-election prefigured the challenge by Toronto labour reformers to Tory hegemony later in the decade.[34]

Bengough opposed the scheme of the Canadian soft-currency advocates. From Nast, he appropriated the flaccid rag-baby that came to symbolize opposition to the Greenback movement in the United States.[35] In the spring of 1879, when Captain Wynne, a Greenbacker originally from Ohio, established a branch of the National Currency League in St Catharines, Bengough used the symbol of the rag-baby woven into a complex allegory about its birth in a foundling hospital. The birth of the rag-baby in the 'Financial Foundling Hospital, and Refuge for Worn-Out Ideas' in St Catharines was reported in *Grip* on 5 April. Architecturally, the foundling hospital was 'typical of the financial views of its founder, being composed entirely of paper and having no foundation.' The rag-baby, *Grip* continued, has every appearance of 'ill-usage,' and no wonder, 'for ever since its birth it has been dragged about by demagogues, and kicked from one State to another by sensible people.' In its effort to mould public opinion against the Beaverback, *Grip* further described the rag-baby as 'a pestilent little wretch, infected with a financial disease called Repudiation.'[36]

In '*Goods* Prohibited, but *Evils* Admitted,' Bengough suggested that while the National Policy tariff excluded American 'goods' of various kinds, American ideas that he classified as 'evils,' specifically, the rag-baby and the anti-Chinese politics of the California workingmen's party leader Dennis Kearney, should be excluded from entering this country. Miss Canada, portrayed as a wholesome maiden, informs John A. Macdonald that she will not allow the country to be made a 'slaughter-market' for these American evils. Bengough's position is stated clearly in the backdrop of the cartoon, where he suggests that the future strength of the nation depends upon 'A Permanent Civil Service, Honest Money, [and] Equal Rights to All Regardless of Colour.'

GOODS PROHIBITED, BUT *EVILS* ADMITTED.

MISS CANADA.—"NOW, MR. PREMIER, I DON'T PROPOSE TO ALLOW THIS COUNTRY TO BE MADE A SLAUGHTER MARKET FOR AMERICAN IDEAS, ANY MORE THAN FOR AMERICAN GOODS."

Grip, 26 April 1879

The issue of Chinese immigrant labour created a conflict for Bengough that he could not resolve. In January 1882, *Grip* lamented that a Chinese laundry-man had fled to Toronto after he was stoned and driven out of London, Ontario, for attempting to establish his business in that community. This was an affront to Christian brotherhood in Bengough's opinion, and he hoped that in Toronto, 'the city of churches and missions,' the Chinese immigrant would 'be protected with the strong arm of Christian justice in his humble endeavours to earn a living.'[37] Later, in 'The Real Chinese Giant,' Bengough used a representation of Chang, 'the celebrated Chinese giant' who visited Toronto in September 1885, as an allegory for the influx of Chinese immigrants into the Pacific slope. The

THE REAL CHINESE GIANT.

Grip, 12 September 1885

oversized, dark image of the Chinese giant with long claw-like fingers is omi-
nous. In the background, an army of Chinese immigrants marching into Canada
appear – a condition that, Bengough commented, '*may* shortly be nearer
home.'[38] During the 1880s, the Macdonald government faced growing pressure
from labour organizations, including the Knights of Labor and the Toronto
Trades and Labor Council, to place restrictions on the importation of Chinese
labour, since unrestricted immigration meant lower wages and job losses for
white workers. Bengough, however, was unable to resolve the contradiction
between the plight of the white male worker, and the misery that unrestricted
Chinese immigration caused the working class, and his Protestant religious

Grip, 3 November 1883

belief in the idea of a Christian community where all were equal regardless of race.[39]

By the early 1880s, Bengough realized that the Tory's campaign promises of prosperity for the working class under the National Policy had not occurred. Overproduction had resulted in factory closures and wage reductions, while a handful of monopolists accumulated more wealth. In several cartoons published in *Grip* throughout the 1880s, Bengough illustrated the negative effects of the National Policy on the working man and his family. 'Thou Shalt Not Kill!' appeared in *Grip* on 3 November 1883. The biblical reference was meant to provide the viewer with a text-based frame of reference for the visual allusions within the cartoon. Bengough's intent was to illuminate the negative effects of the National Policy on the 'average' male worker trying to provide for a family of eight on wages of only $1.25 per day. Bengough also made generous use of cross-hatching and shading in the cartoon in order to convey his message that the National Policy was destroying the working man and his family, and that their prospects, moreover, were dismal. In contrast to the working-class family, which is depicted as thin, dressed in rags, and suffering, the greedy monopolist is exceedingly well nourished, dressed in finery, and enjoying a cigar. The monopolist has his back turned to the workman and his family, unconcerned with their plight. Bengough was appalled that in a Christian community manu-

THE WORKINGMAN'S DELICATE POSITION.

Grip, 19 July 1884

facturers could be found that would allow one segment of humanity to starve so that their profits might increase. 'We fail to see any real difference between these greedy cormorants and the more vulgar description of murderers,' Bengough remarked.[40]

In 'The Workingman's Delicate Position,' the workman is crushed by the National Policy elephant of high taxes on consumer goods, whereas the monopolist riding on the back of the elephant profited from the protective tariffs and cheap imported labour from England and China. 'Protecting the Workingman' was perhaps even more graphic in conveying Bengough's message about the negative effects of the National Policy on the working man. The shield in Macdonald's hands symbolizes the home industries that benefited from the protec-

Grip, 27 October 1888

tive tariff. In the other arm Macdonald holds Canadian labour in a stranglehold. Because of the unrestricted immigration policy, cheaper foreign labour was able to sneak into the country. This influx, in turn, drove the wages of Canadian workers downwards. 'Everybody knows that wages are regulated by the number of persons seeking employment,' Bengough asserted, 'and if this law of political economy has been in any way modified, it is owing to combinations among the workers themselves, such as trades unions, Knights of Labor, etc.'[41]

On the heels of Macdonald's speech to the Toronto Board of Trade in Janu-

FACTS AND FANCIES.

CANADIAN LABOR.—" Sir John, what do you propose to do about these hard facts, discovered after careful investigation by the Legislative Committee of the Trades and Labor Council ? „Oversupply of men under free immigration, reduction of wages as a consequence, and hard times generally—and all under the N. P. that was to protect Labor, mind you ! "
    SIR JOHN.—" My dear horny-handed friend, what are facts to me ?   You can't have read my late banquet speech or you would know that everything is lovely in Canada under our beneficent Protection policy."
    MONOPOLIST.—" 'Course it is ! Just examine my bank account if you don't believe it ! "

Grip, 19 January 1889

ary 1889, in which he declared that Canada was revelling in prosperity, the Legislative Committee of the Toronto Trades and Labor Council released a report indicating that conditions for workers under the National Policy had deteriorated. Bengough sided with the TTLC in a cartoon entitled 'Facts and Fancies.' Bengough represented the 'hard facts' of the suffering of workmen in opposition to the 'fancies' presented by the prime minister in his speech. Bengough advised wage-earners that they alone had the power to rectify the situation by using their ballots 'in the face of Sir John.'[42]

Bengough used his comic art to mobilize labour-movement opposition to the National Policy. He viewed the National Policy as a piece of class legislation. Politicans pandered to greedy monopolists to garner Conservative party campaign funds, while workers with families struggled unsuccessfully to earn a breadwinner wage. *Grip* never masked its disdain for monopoly, partisan politics, or the National Policy, which it further tied to patriotism and the project of nation-building. 'Loyalty' was defined by Bengough as 'allegiance first and last to our own land, with cordial good-will toward all the rest of the world.' He continued, 'It involves the notion of a free country, with free institutions and free men. What we mean by free men is men having the liberty to exercise their natural and inalienable rights to breathe, speak, write, think, and trade with a freedom bounded only by the equal rights of others. We want the British flag to float over this land; or a flag of our own in alliance with the Imperial colors.' Bengough's idea of a free, independent Anglo-Saxon nation with Imperial ties to Britain was articulated in opposition to what he identified as loyalty of the 'N.P. variety,' where the 'old flag' is prized as 'a blanket under which scallawags and monopolists may continue to pick the pockets of Canadian consumers.'[43]

The 'Whole-Hog' Solution: Free Trade plus the Single Tax

In the Dominion Day issue for 1890, *Grip* declared that 'Miss Canada is fiscally a pretty sick young woman.' Miss Canada appears in the cartoon as a middle-class woman in austere dress. She is apparently suffering from the 'vapours.' Here Miss Canada symbolizes the decline of the country after more than a decade of the National Policy. Building on the allegory of middle-class feminine malaise, Bengough wrote: 'She has been for years indulging in tariff tight-lacing, and destroying her system with the poisonous stimulants of "Protectionism."'[44] Richard Cartwright, the former finance minister in the Mackenzie ministry is Miss Canada's doctor. The elixir, or the only 'safe cure,' is free trade and direct taxation.

Sometime in the early 1880s, Bengough became an advocate of Henry George's solution to 'the Labour Question.' He described George's formula of free trade plus the single tax as the 'whole hog remedy.' Unlike Phillips Thompson, who turned to socialism in the early 1890s, Bengough remained committed to the Georgeite solution, although he also became an active Liberal party supporter. Where Henry George and Phillips Thompson turned away from the established churches, Bengough remained a life-long Presbyterian.

THE ONLY "SAFE CURE."

Miss Canada—" Oh, Doctor, I feel so Faint and Depressed—just as if I were going into an Industrial Decline!"
Dr. Cartwright—"Stop your Tariff tight-lacing and throw away your Protection stimulants. Free Trade and Direct Taxation is the only safe cure for you!"

Grip, 5 July 1890

Some of his sharpest barbs, however, were directed at self-serving Protestant churches who pandered to the wealthy.[45]

Following Henry George, Bengough's critique of liberal political economy was rooted in the 'Truths' of Enlightenment faith in natural law and of evangelical Protestantism. He believed that nature and man both have their origins in the Will of God and are dependent upon each other. Man in his use of nature was bound by the laws of God, which are the rules of right. In 1896, Bengough published *The Up-to-Date Primer: A First Book of Lessons for Little Political Economists*. The pamphlet, which he composed in easy one-syllable words, subdivided into a series of 'lessons' with simple illustrations like that found in

VERY MUCH ALIKE.

Henry George— I DON'T SEE ANY DIFFERENCE BETWEEN SLAVERY AND—SLAVERY.

Grip, 23 July 1887

grade-school lesson books, ridiculed the liberal political economy taught in universities. Instead, Bengough presented free trade plus the single tax as a solution to the labour question. In Lesson IX, he asked: 'Who Owns the Man?' 'God, who made him, Owns him, but he gives Man a Free Will,' he wrote. 'Man has a Right to Life, and to be Free, and to seek Joy in this world.'[46]

The rhetoric of freedom in Bengough's writings – 'free,' 'God-given,' 'freedom of trade,' 'free land' – illustrates the fusion of the religious and the secular.[47] Like other labour reformers in North America and in Britain, Bengough struggled with the conflict between his desire to assert a belief in human free will and a benign Providence and his recognition of the helplessness of workers

THE ORIGIN OF LANDLORDISM.

Grip, 1 October 1887

under industrial capitalism.[48] The worker-slave metaphor was widely used by nineteenth-century labour reformers to challenge the idea of a free, unregulated labor market found in traditional political economy. As Bengough suggested in one cartoon, chattel slavery and wage slavery were 'Very Much Alike.' Under the industrial system, Bengough explained, labour cannot hope to secure anything more than the bare necessaries of life – food, clothing, and shelter. 'These things are what Slavery guaranteed to the Slave in exchange for his toil,' Bengough observed, 'and it follows therefore that, so far as the comforts and pleasures of this life are concerned, the laborer is literally in a state of bondage.'[49] His use of the metaphor focused on the conditions of white workers, thus revealing a well-developed sense of 'whiteness' rather than any concern for racial equality. Henry George is situated in the centre of the cartoon holding a banner that states, 'Every Man Has a Right to the Whole Results of His Own Toil.'

In 'The Origin of Landlordism,' Bengough declared, following George, that it is the labourer who comes out short. Under existing laws, land 'owners' charge rent on the use of land and the expenses of the community are defrayed by taxes levied on 'private' property, including houses, incomes, food, clothing. 'Capital' and 'Labor' in Bengough's discourse of labour reform are both forms of 'Toil.' Capital provides the implements that allow Labor to do more work in less time, and increase the fruits of 'Toil,' which Capital and Labor enjoy together. According to Bengough, Capital and Labor are not foes, as some nineteenth-century theorists, including Karl Marx and Phillips Thompson, had posited. Rather, the true foe of *both* Capital and Labor is the landlord.[50]

The characters in 'The Origin of Landlordism' are in blackface. Blackface minstrels were a popular form of entertainment in late-nineteenth-century America, and in Toronto as well. They contributed to the development of a popular idea of whiteness among workers that crossed lines of race, religion, and skill, and were widely used to criticize an industrial system that exploited white workers.[51] Thus, Bengough was not only criticizing landlordism in general, he was also criticizing a system that was detrimental to the interests of white Anglo-Saxon working men.

In Bengough's discourse of labour reform, the invention of land monopoly brought about 'The Eclipse of Human Rights.' Protestant reformers shared the belief that God created the planet for the equal use of all. Landlordism, which benefited only a few, and unjustly burdened those who laboured on the land with rent and taxes, was represented as a dark shadow over the earth, or an 'eclipse' over what God created for the use of all mankind. In his 'chalk talk' on free trade, and in his other polemical writings, Bengough denounced the 'High Tax plan,' or the 'Protectionist Tariff,' as 'anti-humanitarian,' 'anti-christian,' and 'unnatural.' He asked, 'Don't you think, now, this thing of walls and bars is more like a scheme which man has got up, and has no base in any law of God?'[52] In another 'chalk talk' on 'the Social Question,' Bengough stated that there is a 'natural law of revenue' for every nation: 'Providence which cares for ravens and lambs has not overlooked the needs of human communities.'[53]

Bengough divided the values that exist in any country into public values that ought to be reserved for the community and private values for the private individuals who justly own them. The public values of the community, namely, land values, franchise values, and the value of natural resources, rightly belong to the community for community use. Instead, through 'shortsighted and stupid statesmanship,' laws had been enacted under which the natural public revenue does not go to the public, but into the private coffers of citizens. Furthermore, the fruits of labour, or private value, ought to be tax-free.[54] The 'Eclipse of Human Rights' and the 'dark shadow' of landlordism would pass only with the implementation of free trade plus the single tax.

In Bengough's opinion free trade, and the tearing down of the tariff wall, while necessary, was not enough since land still would not be free. He referred to the situation in England, where, despite the fact that most goods entered the country tax-free, a staggering amount of poverty was found because land was not free. In addition to the removal of the protective tariff on industries, Bengough proposed the abolition of taxation on individual industry. To that end

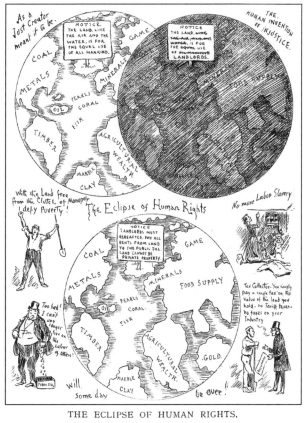

THE ECLIPSE OF HUMAN RIGHTS.

WITH A VIEW OF THE SIGN-BOARD AS IT WILL BE AFTER THE DARK SHADOW OF LANDLORDISM HAS PASSED OFF.

Grip, 19 May 1888

he adopted George's 'One-Tax Plan,' widely known as the single tax.[55] The single tax, Bengough explained, could be implemented by replacing existing tax schemes with one tax on ground rent – the sum each year that each piece of land, as 'bare land,' is worth. The individual worker would retain the fruits of his toil, and the single tax would eliminate public speculation in land. It would no longer be possible for a landlord to live in luxury and idleness on land rent.

Bengough promoted the free-trade and single-tax solution to the 'Labour Question' in his comic art and writings, and in numerous 'chalk talks' throughout Canada, the United States, Britain, and Australia. He was a long-time member of the Toronto Branch of the Single Tax Association, and he served as president of that organization for several years in the early 1900s. Later, in 1907, Bengough was elected alderman for Ward 3 on a single-tax and social-reform platform. The project of labour reform relied on powerful symbols and complex allegories that provided detailed instructions about how the work of labour reform ought to be organized.[56] Like Phillips Thompson, Bengough defined the role of the labour reformer as incorporating the work of education. In the conclusion to the *Up-to-date Primer*, Bengough wrote: '"A tax on Land Rent will make us Free." I have Shown you how it will Do this, my Child, and Now I bid you Good-By. Go thou and Spread the Light.'[57] The way in which Bengough organizes the images, with the labour reformer as teacher and the worker as a 'child'-like student, reveals organizational prescriptions for the project of labour reform.

The Single Tax Association, as it was called after 1890, was a reorganization of the Anti-Poverty Society founded in May 1887 in the aftermath of Henry George's visit to Toronto. The Single Taxers' instructions as to how the work of labour reform ought to be organized differed from those of the Toronto Nationalist Association, which was organized in Toronto in July 1890. The Toronto Nationalist Association was modelled after the nationalist clubs established in Boston in the aftermath of the publication of Edward Bellamy's *Looking Backward*.[58] There was, however, some overlap in membership between the two organizations. Phillips Thompson, for example, belonged to both the Toronto Nationalist Association and the Single Tax Association. Late-nineteenth-century Toronto contained a curious mixture of social reformers and radicals, who, in the words of 'Uncle Thomas,' shared the common project of social 'regeneration.'[59]

The discrepancies between the Nationalists and the Single Taxers were delineated by Phillips Thompson in *The Labor Advocate*. Partially financed by its publisher the Grip Printing and Publishing Company, *The Labor Advocate* existed for only ten months, from 5 December 1890 to 25 September 1891. During this period Thompson was also associate editor of *Grip*. Single Taxers, Thompson explained, 'hold that the land question underlies all other reforms, and that the first thing to be done is to shift all taxation upon land values alone,' whereas socialists maintain that land reform is inadequate. Socialists, Thompson wrote, hold that 'the ultimate end to be sought is the overthrow of the competitive system, the abolition of private ownership of the means of production ... and the organization of an industrial commonwealth under which the Government will control production.' Thompson encouraged his readers to send in their opinions about the respective merits of socialism and the single tax.[60]

J.W. Bengough's response to Thompson's editorial appeared in the next issue of *The Labor Advocate*. He agreed with Thompson that socialism would 'serve the interests of labor' more fully than the single tax, but expressed considerable doubt that such an elaborate scheme could be implemented all at once. Rather, Bengough proposed that the 'journey' be taken step-by-step: 'First, the abolition of protective tariffs, next the abolition of all tariffs and the imposition of the Single Tax on land values for revenue, next the Single Tax unlimited.'[61]

The Single Tax Association provided an institutional support for labour reform. The regular weekly meetings of the Single Tax Association were educational. Association members and guest speakers delivered papers on various schemes for social reform and the members debated their merits. The Single Taxers also lobbied the local and provincial governments for tax reforms and responded to critiques of the single tax. Although they had the support of several well-known Toronto clergymen who were active radicals and labour reformers, including Rev. William Oliver of St Simon's Church and Rev. Charles Street, founder of the Christie Street Anglican Church, the Single Taxers devoted considerable attention to trying to convert Church opinion. The target of Single Taxers, and of several sharp barbs from *Grip*, was the Ministerial Association. *Grip* criticized the Association for 'leaving the Single Tax subject on the shelf, while subjects of comparatively trifling importance are debated.' The Single Tax Association issued an address to the Ministerial Association in which it lamented that '[o]ur laws are now framed on the assumption that men are not all equally heirs to the common bounties of a common Father; but that one portion of society can rightfully claim this earth with its potentialities as their possession.' The Single Taxers' manifesto was endorsed by the Toronto Trades and Labor Council and several local unions.[62]

The wrath of Toronto social reformers was provoked further by a speech made by Principal Grant at Trinity College in January 1891. The eminent Queen's College theologian, normally a friend of reformers, and admired by Bengough, delivered a critique of Henry George's *Progress and Poverty*, in which he concluded that George was wrong 'from first to last.' Grant stated that there was no truth to George's premise that poverty was increasing in proportion to material progress and the accumulation of wealth.[63] In response, Bengough sketched 'The Schoolmaster Schoolmastered.' Henry George is depicted punishing the Presbyterian cleric for his 'errors' of interpretation, which Bengough spelled out for his readers in two captions situated in the backdrop of the cartoon. *Grip* further ridiculed Grant in a satirical verse entitled 'A Principle Granted':

Principal Grant, deeply versed in divinity,
In a lecture delivered not long since at Trinity,
Endeavored to show that the Single Tax scheme

THE SCHOOLMASTER SCHOOLMASTERED.

HENRY GEORGE (*to Principal Grant*)—" I'll teach you to criticize ' Progress and Poverty ' before you know the first thing about its contents !"

Grip, 31 January 1891

Is merely a wild and impractical dream,
Though strongly denouncing the Single Tax movement,
He says, 'Tax the land and exempt each improvement.'
Say the Single Tax men, 'That is just what is wanted,
And Principal Grant has our principle granted.'[64]

The Single Tax Association responded to Grant's critique of George. They focused on a comment made by Grant that '[i]t would be immoral to confiscate land after it had passed through many owners, and all the time treated like other commodities, would be to steal it.' The Single Taxers emphasized that their society was formed for the purpose of advocating that which Grant denounced as stealing. In their opinion, the present land system was in direct opposition to the teachings of morality.[65]

During the 1890s, the Single Tax Association lobbied the local and provincial governments for tax reduction, city management of the street railway, and the regulation of wage rates and hours for female telephone operators at Bell Telephone. Although the centrepiece of Bengough's reform program in the 1890s was free trade and the single tax, there were several additional planks to *Grip*'s reform platform, including state control of monopolistic business, abolition of the liqour traffic, female suffrage, complete manhood suffrage, the eight-hour workday, equal rights before the law, national independence, and one official language, that being English.[66] Unlike Thompson, however, Bengough acknowledged the importance of political parties in bringing about social and moral reform.

The 'Rake' and the Respectable Workingman: Prohibition, Sabbath Observance, and the Street Railway

As one of a loose coalition of Protestant reformers who undertook to 'regenerate' both society and the human soul, Bengough also participated in the creation of 'Toronto the Good,' a fiction that social and moral reformers consciously constructed during the late nineteenth century. The project involved a concerted civic effort to ward off the evils of urban life, particularly in working-class neighbourhoods.[67] While Toronto, with a total population of 144,023 in 1891, was nowhere near the urban metropolises of Paris, London, or New York, the fact and fantasy of urban exploration informed Bengough's comic art and verses in *Grip*. Bengough enjoyed the privileges of a male middle-class urban spectator, or *flaneur*, who could stroll across the divided spaces of the metropolis to experience the city as a whole.[68] In the manner of other mid-Victorian social investigators, Bengough represented the urban topography of 'Toronto by Gaslight' as a series of juxtapositions of 'high' and 'low' life. Like these observers, Bengough also reproduced a Dickensian cityscape of crowded and dirty streets, open sewers, and drunkenness among the poor and unemployed. Immigrant working-class men and women, in particular, were objects of classification and surveillance.

Women in public were presumed to be both endangered by, or a source of danger to, those men who congregated in the streets.[69] In the fall of 1879, *Grip* applauded both the *Mail* and the *Globe* for their attacks on the York Street dens and the streetwalkers on Yonge and King Streets. Mayor Beaty and the police commissioners were sharply criticized by Bengough for their failure to regulate the situation, and *Grip* issued a reminder that the civic election would soon be occurring.[70] The other category of women in public comprised virtuous women who walked along Yonge and King Streets as they shopped and young working

Grip, 2 May 1874

women returning home. They were forced to walk 'the Gauntlet' of men who sexually harassed them. *Grip* targeted this 'large and despicable class of ragga-muffins,' who 'infested' the street corners and insulted women. He sided with the 'respectable public of Toronto,' proclaiming that 'these persons are an unmitigated nuisance, and should not be tolerated any more than stagnant water or putrid offal.'[71]

The male 'rowdies' who frequented the street corners on Yonge and King Streets were the antithesis of the Protestant Anglo-Saxon ideal of manhood, with its emphasis on self-control, self-discipline, and hard work. Bengough's cartoons reveal that the public landscape of the urban *flaneur* in the 1870s and 1880s was an unstable construct. The notion of masculinity idealized by reformers was constantly challenged. Certain groups of immigrants were blamed for this 'degeneration.' Like the majority of nineteenth-century Anglo-Saxon Protestant reformers who were exponents of the Spencerian concept of racial hierarchy, Bengough believed that Anglo-Saxon Canadians were the vanguard of the race.[72] Vice and urban degeneration were frequently attributed to Irish-Catholic immigrants in Bengough's commentaries, and they were at times objects for satire both in *Grip* and in his 'Chalk Talks.'[73] The Irish were represented in Bengough's comic art using familiar racial stereotypes, including an ape-like physique with a protruding lower jaw and a quarrelsome character. On occasion, however, Bengough was sympathetic to the plight of the city's Irish pauper immigrants. In one *Grip* cartoon he criticized both the Canadian and British immigration policies. He urged 'Mrs. Britannia' to quit 'dumping' pauper immigrants on Canada without adequate resources, thereby forcing local charitable organizations to support them. Bengough suggested that Toronto adopt the 'New York policy of shipping paupers back to the Imperial authorities.'[74]

Alongside the 'degenerate' unemployed Irish-Catholic immigrant vagrant, the lower-class rake of urban vulgarity in Bengough's cartoons, known variously as the dude, the dandy, or the swell, joined Bengough's 'Sunday Promenade' on Yonge Street. Skilled male workers and lower middle-class clerks, tradesmen, and shopkeepers were attracted to the fantasy of the urban swell manufactured in the popular culture of the period, notably in the music hall and in comic art. The antithesis of the Christian craftsman held in high esteem by Bengough, the gin-swilling swell was distinguished by his flamboyant dress and rakishness. While Bengough, in his role as social reformer, described the swell as 'the Common Ninny' and the 'Ignoramus Scalliwagibus,' he may also have inadvertently encouraged a type of working-class masculine self-representation he wished to eradicate. The image of the swell, with its emphasis on masculine display and prowess, may have served as a compensatory fantasy for a working-class masculinity that was being defined, or redefined, with the decline of apprenticeship and the unreliable status of the male breadwinner in the late nineteenth century.[75]

Intemperance was also a hallmark of the lower-class rake. Following eighteenth-century English artist William Hogarth's famous illustrations of *Gin Lane*, Bengough sketched 'The Rake's Progress' in a series of frames contained in a dense full-page cartoon filled with visual allusions to the problems of alcohol. The garden rake becomes more decrepit in each successive frame of the cartoon, and symbolizes the demise of man from the evils of alcohol. Unlike Hogarth, who in a subsequent work entitled *Beer Street* provided a positive

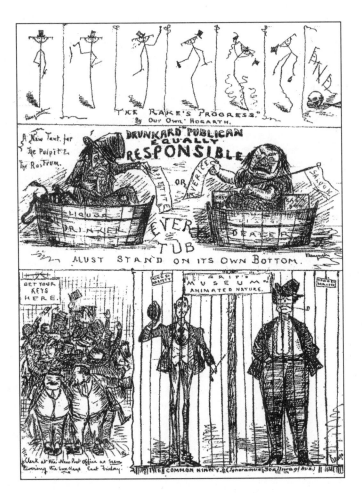

Grip, 25 April 1874

model in opposition to the negative values portrayed in *Gin Lane*, or, more generally, the temperance advocates, who used the thermometer as a symbol, with good living and water or milk at the top of the thermometer and evil and gin at the base (and beer in the mid-range), the prohibitionist Bengough saw the effects of alcohol as entirely evil. In the next line of the cartoon, Bengough visually represents the remarks made by the American preacher Thomas K. Beecher, in which he indicated that the drunkard is just as culpable for his

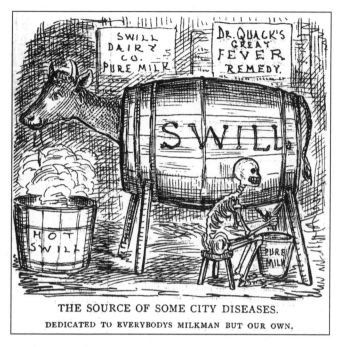

THE SOURCE OF SOME CITY DISEASES.

DEDICATED TO EVERYBODYS MILKMAN BUT OUR OWN,

Grip, 27 March 1880

own debasement as the saloon-keeper, for 'every tub must stand on its own bottom.'[76]

As in the rhetoric of the social-purity activists of the 1880s, pure milk and water for Bengough were both physically and symbolically pure.[77] Entire families turned to consuming beer for the very reason that it was more readily available and purer than the adulterated milk supply or the polluted Toronto water system. Bengough, however, associated disease and alcoholism among the labouring and destitute classes with the adulterated milk and impure water of the unsanitary city. In 'The Source of Some City Diseases,' a human skeleton, symbolizing the evils of alcohol consumption, is shown milking a cow at the 'Swill Dairy Co.,' where hot swill replaces pure milk.[78]

Bengough was a life-long prohibition activist. He delivered 'chalk talks' advocating total prohibition to the Woman's Christian Temperance Union, the Sons of Temperance, and the Royal Templars. He produced two pamplets: *The Prohibition Aesop: A Book of Fables*, for the Royal Templars, and *The Gin Mill*

Primer, published in 1898, in support of the Dominion Alliance for the Total Suppression of the Liquor Traffic.[79] In a 'chalk talk' to schoolchildren Bengough stated that 'character' is the essence of man or woman, and that it requires conscious effort to form 'good habits.' Using an allegory of a coasting game, Bengough sketched a boy on a sled at the top of a steep hill. 'It is a hill of bad-habit,' he stated, 'such as drink, the end of the course is a ruined character that may be represented by the figure of the typical sot.'[80] Drunken 'sots,' also referred to as 'topers,' were made, not born, according to Bengough. In his 'chalk talks,' Bengough began with a bright, hopeful, intelligent, youth in his finery at the dawn of his manhood, who when exposed to the atmosphere created by the liqour licence system came under the destructive influence of the habit-forming beverage. A change in the finery and physical appearance of the young man who drinks symbolizes the evils of alcohol. The 'sot' is depicted as dirty, unshaven, clothed in 'rags,' with a red, bulbous nose – all emblematic of the physical ravages of drink.

In an 1887 *Grip* cartoon entitled 'Miss Canada, Barmaid,' the evils of alcohol were symbolized by the representation of the male bartender as the devil, while Miss Canada is characterized as a seductive barmaid. From the mid-1880s the campaign for prohibition was part of the more general movement for social purity in which the barmaid was seen as a serious problem of physical and moral welfare. As Peter Bailey writes, 'Reformers conceded that the women drawn to bar work were not themselves necessarily of a low character, but maintained that the pub environment was inevitably corrupting.'[81] While the liquor trade regulated the flow of drink, so too did the trade manage the flow of sexuality and encourage vice. Government, Bengough indicated, catered to the liquor interests. The working class, moreover, was doubly injured by the liquor business. The liquor trade employed fewer skilled workers than any other trade in proportion to capital, while the liquor interests profited with the assistance of the Canadian state; but its product was drunkards, crime, misery, and even death amongst the working class.[82]

According to Bengough, the liquor traffic not only promoted vice and crime, it was also the cause of poverty and family ruin. The 'gin mill,' he argued, robbed the working man of his wages. In *The Gin Mill Primer*, Bengough suggested that the home is built on the heart and brain of man, and that drink makes a dire wreck of these. First, the male household head becomes a slave of drink, and his wife and even children quickly follow. The good state is built on the home, Bengough continued, and to have a 'good, free, pure, State, we must have Homes of the same kind.' He concluded, therefore, that '[d]rink must be the one great Foe of the State.'[83]

Woman, because of her sex, had a special role to play in making drink the

MISS CANADA, BARMAID.

WHEN WILL THE COUNTRY BE "RIPE" TO GET CUT OF THIS PARTNERSHIP?

Grip, 9 July 1887

enemy of the state. Following the defeat in March 1889 of the Waters' Bill to extend the provincial franchise to a select group of women, Bengough rejected the assertions by some statesmen that women should remain in the domestic sphere. 'The domestic realm is, of course, woman's special charge,' Bengough wrote, 'but there are babies in the political world, too, that required looking after in a motherly fashion, for there are wrongs in the political world which have a most intimate influence on the home.' Bengough referred specifically to the liqour traffic and the injury it did to 'woman's sphere' in the home. 'Should woman, the chief sufferer, have nothing to say upon this question? And what can she say effectively without the ballot in her hand?' Bengough remarked.[84]

Thus, prohibition was linked discursively to the campaign for women's suffrage.

A distinction was made between 'high' gin mills, or the grand bars frequented by the upper classes, and the 'low' gin mills, or backstreet dives of the working classes and unemployed poor. Bengough argued that the work done by both 'high' and 'low' gin mills was the same; both tended 'to Pull Down all that is Good in Man.' He used *Grip* to promote the regulation of drinking establishments frequented by the poor and labouring classes. On 5 September 1874 *Grip* reported that a row of buildings recently erected on Queen Street West was to be devoted exclusively to stores. 'There is not a single saloon under the roof, and the nearest establishment of that character is at least ten yards away,' *Grip* announced. He then accused the Inspector of Licences, Ogle Gowan, of being negligent in his job, and suggested, with tongue in cheek, that the number of licences could be increased even more if Gowan and the police commissioners would go personally in search of 'loose characters and little rookeries to license.'[85] Bengough endorsed the passage of a by-law to eliminate whisky groceries, and he supported the Canada Temperance Act of 1878, widely known as the Scott Act, which allowed for prohibition by local option.[86] Licensing restrictions and Toronto's water supply were perennial issues in local municipal politics. In the mid-1880s Bengough endorsed the reform platform of Mayor William H. Howland, which included sponsorship of Alderman Robert Fleming's by-law eliminating taverns, an allocation for a trunk sewer, and reform of municipal offices to eliminate pandering to ward heelers by politicans.[87]

When Senator Frank Smith's lease for monopoly control of the street-railway company came up for renegotiation in 1891, *Grip* supported the cause of municipal ownership, using the rhetoric of prohibition, civic reform, and Sabbatarianism. Strict Sabbath observance was integral to the nineteenth-century construction of 'Toronto the Good.' As the end of the street-railway charter approached, the issue of Sunday cars surfaced again. The Toronto *World* argued in August 1889 that Sunday service would allow the labouring poor to attend church. *Grip* countered with 'The Workingman's Position [o]n the Sunday Street Car Question.' At the bottom of the cartoon, the caption 'Here I Stand and Here I Rest' appears, attesting to *Grip*'s opposition to Sunday cars. Once again Bengough uses a biblical reference to make his point. In this instance the fourth commandment appears in bold lettering. The working man and his family in their Sunday finery occupy a central position on top of a pedestal. They represent the respectable Christian craftsman accompanied by his wife and helpmate, who manages the household and instils Christian values in the children. According to Bengough, Sunday cars would mean that Sunday newspapers, Sunday saloons, and Sunday business and labour of all kinds

THE WORKINGMAN'S POSITION

(On the Sunday Street Car Question).

"HERE I STAND AND HERE I REST!"

Grip, 10 August 1889

would quickly follow. Sunday cars would bring about the 'Chicagoizing of Toronto' and open the door for greedy monopolists seeking 'seven days' work for six days' pay.'[88]

In the fall of 1890 *Grip* and the *Labor Advocate* were integral to the mobilization of a combined initiative by Single Taxers, Nationalists, the TTLC, and suffragettes for public ownership of the street railway.[89] The bitter railway struggles of 1886 had not been forgotten, and Thompson and Bengough reminded workers that it was Frank Smith who had turned hundreds of labourers out onto the streets for exercising their rights as citizens by joining a labour organization. With its trademark wit, *Grip* even invited readers to sign a petition calling on Smith to take control of the whole municipal government since it had run the street railway so effectively.[90] The virtues of public ownership, specifically, efficiency, economy, and public accountability, were emphasized on numerous occasions in the pages of both *Grip* and the *Labor Advocate*.[91] When the campaign was lost, and the street-railway franchise was awarded to the Kiely-Everett syndicate in August 1891 by a narrow margin of nine votes to seven, *Grip* commented with considerable disappointment: 'We advocated the keeping of the franchise under municipal control, because we believe, as a matter of principle, that all business enterprises which are necessarily monopolistic should belong to and be worked in the interest of the public.' He continued, 'Perhaps, thirty years from now, this sound doctrine will have more influence than it at present possesses, and the railway may be the property of the city.'[92]

In an 1897 essay Rev. W.W. Withrow, editor of the *Canadian Methodist Magazine*, described J.W. Bengough as 'An Artist of Righteousness.' He referred to the moral effect of satire in Bengough's comic art and verses. 'Often where argument and logical demonstration have no effect,' Withrow wrote, 'the carved and polished arrows of ridicule find entrance between the joints of the armour.'[93] *Grip* was not only a successful commercial enterprise, but a medium through which Bengough, in his role as comic artist and Protestant moralist, articulated his discourse of labour reform and social regeneration. Like Phillips Thompson, Bengough saw his work as educational, or 'shining the light of truth.'

Bengough's use of allegories and symbols in his cartoons was integral to the building of a reformed social subjectivity. In his comic art Bengough turned out organizational prescriptions for social 'regeneration.' Unlike his friend Thompson, however, Bengough never embraced socialism as a solution to the labour question. He remained committed to the doctrines of Henry George. Bengough's labour-reform discourse was grounded in networks of institutional support. This was most evident, perhaps, during the controversy over public ownership of the Toronto Street Railway in 1890–91.

The representations of Miss Canada in Bengough's comic art illustrate how bourgeois ideals of respectable femininity were invoked to shape his discourse of national identity. While women were the symbolic bearers of the nation, they were denied agency in his discourse of gender, sexuality, and nationalism. Although Bengough supported suffrage for women, and bolstered his position using the rhetoric of equal rights, he denied women full citizenship and any real power in shaping policy beyond the domestic realm.

Class, gender, and race had an autonomous but interconnected existence in Bengough's social-reform discourse, and helped to shape that discourse in specific ways. *Grip*'s 'solid platform,' presented in April 1891 after Phillips Thompson had joined the staff again, this time as associate editor, embraced independent republican government with English as an official language, an alliance of Anglo-Saxon nations, public control of all monopolies for the benefit of the whole community, free trade with all the world, abolition of the liqour traffic, women's suffrage, and equal rights before the law.[94] Much of Bengough's reform discourse was based on pre-existing power relations. While, like Thompson, he was sympathetic to Native rights and the plight of Chinese labourers, Bengough saw himself as something of a missionary whose work was essentially that of creating a white, Anglo-Saxon, Protestant nation and a Christian community. This vision, moreover, was inspired and shaped by Bengough's interaction with the late-nineteenth-century Toronto cultural and social world.

5

'The Art Preservative': Gender, Skill, and Craft Sense in the Printing Trades

We lead the van in war for Liberty
And guard the precious boon Equality,
So let us not forget Fraternity
For Universal Brotherhood we strive,
And keep the grace of Charity alive,
Another era dawns upon the world,
The rings and money kings will soon be hurled
From self-elected thrones – their mills shall cease
To grind up flesh and blood for chariot grease.
May capital and labor join and say:
'A fair day's labor for a fair day's pay,'
So said the MAN whose Word our laws inspire
'The laborer is worthy of his hire.'[1]

The above stanza from a poem penned by International Typographical Union, Local 91 member William Taylor, welcoming delegates to the annual convention of the ITU in Toronto in 1905, suggests that by the turn of the century printers had articulated a version of masculinity that embraced transformations within the culture of production associated with industrial-capitalist growth. 'Efforts to define a fair day's work,' Ava Baron writes, 'became a battle over identifying manly workers.'[2] Within the nineteenth-century Toronto printing trades, the fraternity among men rooted in craft tradition and a well-developed trade-union structure, allowed skilled workmen to marginalize women both at work and in the home.

During the nineteenth century, confrontations between employers and skilled male printing-trades workers over the labour process and wages incorporated gender. Male journeymen's ideas of masculinity and femininity shaped the ways in which they dealt with questions of skill, managerial and technological innovations, and workers' control of production. From the 1830s through the early twentieth century, employers attempted to displace journeymen and replace them with boy apprentices and women workers who worked below the union scale. Apprenticeship relations between men and boys reveal the ways in which gender shaped their conception of what it meant to be a working man. Rather than pose a 'crisis' in masculinity, the outcome of the widespread struggles between the typographical union and employers over the use of typesetting machines was a redefinition of masculinity, and a reassertion of male domination of the typographical union.[3]

By 1871, Toronto was already the leading producer in the Canadian printing industry. Segmentation occurred within the printing industry in the latter half of the nineteenth century with the emergence of the daily press, technological innovations, the subdivision of the labour process into composition and presswork, and the additional separation of newspaper publishing from the book, magazine, and job sectors. Although intensive capitalization, mechanization, and vigorous competition occurred in the city's newspaper sector, many of the city's book, magazine, and job printing establishments retained old artisanal methods of production and relatively low levels of capital investment.[4]

Contrary to previous interpretations by modernization theorists, industrial-capitalist transformations in the Toronto printing industry involved no 'withering away' of small handicraft producers. Rather than constituting 'a declining pre-industrial sector,' small producers played a vital role in the industrialization process.[5] The practice of subcontracting jobs to small firms by large manufacturers attests to the continued viability of the small producer in the development of the printing industry. Technological innovations within the industry, including machine typesetting, stereotyping, and photo-engraving, created a 'service function' for petit-bourgeois producers in relation to the larger firms. For example, in the 1870s George Brown, proprietor of the daily *Globe*, contracted out engraving work to Frederick Brigden.[6] The subcontracting of illustrative work was a way for larger establishments to avoid high labour costs and additional capital investment in machinery.

Most Toronto printing-trades establishments continued to provide a variety of services. The Grip Printing and Publishing Company, incorporated in 1882, not only produced the comic paper *Grip*, it also carried out a variety of commercial printing, engraving, lithographic, bookbinding, and other publishing work, including the printing for the Ontario Legislature from 1884 to 1886.[7] Towards the end of the century there was a tendency to more specialization.

From 1893 the Grip Printing and Publishing Company was an engraving business only, and advertised that it had one of 'the most modern and up-to-date establishments in the Dominion.'[8]

In late-nineteenth-century Toronto, therefore, large factories existed alongside a multitude of small establishments operated by petit-bourgeois proprietors, who typically laboured alongside one or two journeymen and an apprentice. Printing-trades establishments, however, were also among the city's largest employers. Hunter, Rose & Co., the largest single printing-trades employer enumerated in the 1871 industrial census, employed a total of 173 workers – 70 men, 100 women, and 3 boys. A total of 126 workers were employed at Campbell's bindery, 90 of whom were women. The three daily newspapers were among the largest employers in the city's printing industry. In 1871, the *Telegraph* employed 75 men and 20 boys. The *Leader* and *Globe* newspaper and job printing shops employed a total of 80 workers each.[9]

By contrast, Charles Beale appears in the 1871 industrial census as the proprietor of an engraving business employing one adult male.[10] Charles and Henry Beale, the deaf sons of a wealthy Gloustershire family, both of whom apprenticed in the London shop of Chartist radical W.J. Linton, settled in Toronto sometime in 1868 or 1869. Their firm, Beale Bros., located at 48 King Street East, was listed in the city directory by 1871. Frederick Brigden, who had apprenticed with the Beale brothers in Linton's shop, and who was also deaf as a result of a childhood bout of scarlet fever, accepted their invitation to go into partnership. Brigden arrived in Toronto with his wife and two sons in October 1872. Several months later, Brigden wrote in his diary: 'Work is now getting slack, there is a prospect of none before long for sometime.' He continued, 'I fear the slack season is long. From June to November.'[11] The seasonality that characterized wage labour in the late nineteenth century among both men and women workers was perhaps more severe in the case of printing-trades workers. The weeks just before Christmas were a peak period in the local printing trades. The late spring and summer were described in the trade journals as a period of low activity.[12]

At some point in the early 1870s Brigden took over the management of Beale Bros., and invested his savings in the business. In 1876, after a brief period as Beale and Brigden, the business was renamed the Toronto Engraving Company. During the next decade Brigden, who possessed keen entrepreneurial abilities, put the company on sound financial ground.[13] A characteristic of nineteenth-century petit-bourgeois proprietors as a group was that their livelihood was derived both from their capital investment and their own labour.[14] Frederick H. Brigden recalled that during the 1870s his father did engraving work for the *Globe*. 'It took him all week to engrave a block for the weekly edition, and sometimes when a more elaborate subject such as a city view was called for he and his partner, the late Henry Beale, worked in two shifts of twelve hours, throughout the week.'[15]

Gender, Skill, the Culture of Production, and Trade Unionism

On 12 October 1832, twenty-four journeymen printers, primarily of British origin, met in the York Hotel to discuss 'the many innovations which have been made upon the long-established wages of the profession of the art of printing, and those of a kind highly detrimental of their interests.' The outcome of the meeting was the organization of the York Typographical Society. The first article of the constitution drafted by the society defined their objective as the protection of 'mutual interest of the employer and employed.' Also included in the constitution adopted by the typographical society was a standard wage scale of £1, 15s per week, a ten-hour workday, payment for overtime, apprentice restrictions, and travel assistance for members wishing to seek employment elsewhere. The York Typographical Society was short-lived. It collapsed in 1836 in the aftermath of a failed attempt by the journeymen to achieve wage parity with New York printers and the political turmoil of the pre-rebellion period. Following an eight-year lapse, the union was reorganized on 9 February 1844, in response to an attempt by the master printers to implement a wage reduction.[16] The Toronto Typographical Union has existed continuously since 1844.

The strength of the male compositor's position in his relations with employers throughout much of the nineteenth century lies in the fact that printing was not a 'beleaguered craft,' and 'the mechanization which ravaged the integrity of so many artisanal trades was not as brutal in the case of printing.'[17] Hand composition or setting type had not changed since the invention of the process by Gutenberg in the fifteenth century, and remained fundamentally unchanged until the widespread implementation of machine typesetting in the 1890s. Holding the composing stick in the left hand, the compositor selected lead alloy type characters of different fonts and designs from a wooden case using the right hand, and inserted the type upside down and from left to right on the stick. Each line of type then had to be justified using blank slugs to ensure that a line of text fit properly. When the stick was filled, the composed line was transferred to a shallow three-sided tray called a 'galley.' The nineteenth-century compositor's basic skill 'lay partly in speed and accuracy and partly in devising acceptable spacing for each line by judicious use of thick or thin spaces, so that the line of type fitted tightly into the pre-set stick.'[18]

With the division of the labour process into composition and presswork, and the separation of newspaper publishing from the book, magazine, and job sectors in the latter half of the nineteenth century, not all compositors did identical work. While all types of composition required literacy and basic technical skill, specifically, the ability to set a line of type by hand, the requirements of the trade required a second level of skill that compositors described as 'art.' For book compositors an artistic sensibility was required to make books look inviting and subject matter attractive. 'A badly-arranged title page, a profuse peppering of italics or capitals, or a neglect to proportion blanks, spaces, and margins, will repel an ordinary reader quite as effectually as dullness in the subject matter itself,' the *Printer's Miscellany* advised its compositor readers.[19] The job printer was required to display taste and execute unique designs. Tastefulness and innovation, together with experience, time, and habit, were incorporated into the 'art' of composition.

Specialty work, including work in a language other than English, typesetting music, or fancy display work in commercial advertisements, was time-consuming. Thus, the typographical union negotiated both a piece-rate scale and a time scale with employers. In 1872, time workers on daily newspapers earned $11 per week of 54 hours. Union piece workers on newspapers setting advertisements received $0.28 per 1000 ems for a week of 54 hours, with the provision that all work be carried out between 7 am and 6 pm, after which an overtime rate of $0.25 was paid.[20] Piece-rate workers on book and job composition earned $33\frac{1}{3}$ cents per 1000 ems. A higher rate was payed to compositors setting difficult items including tables, foreign-language material, and music. Foreign-language copy in Latin, Spanish, Italian, German, or French was charged $0.10 per 1000 ems extra, and Irish, Gaelic, or Native-language copy an additional $0.15 per 1000 ems. The scale for the composition of music was $0.60 per 1000 ems.[21]

While literacy and general intelligence were required of all compositors, the hallmarks of a superior compositor, namely, speed, accuracy, and craft sense, could only be acquired with practice and experience. Trade journals recommended that apprentices who wanted to learn the 'art and mysteries of printing' properly be instructed to set one line of type under the guidance of a journeyman who would point out the errors in the line, such as inaccurate spacing between words or errors in punctuation and hypenation. 'Handlers of the stick' took considerable pride in emphasizing that their trade was not like any other trade. 'Not a mechanic nor a professionalist, he is a compound of both, but affiliates with neither.'[22]

Part of the compositors' power lay in their intellectual superiority and control over the dissemination of the printed word. Printers composed verses, such as the following excerpt from the 'Song of the Printer,' in which their political power was associated with the unique requirements of the craft.

O, where is the man with such simple tools
   Can govern the world as I?
With a printing press, an iron stick,
   And a little leaden die,
With paper of white, and ink of black,
I support the Right, and the Wrong attack.

Say, where is he, or who may he be,
   That can rival the printer's power?
To no monarchs that live the wall doth he give
   Their sway lasts only an hour;
While the printer still grows, and God only knows
   When his might shall cease to tower![23]

Among nineteenth-century printers, the requirements of the craft were associated with what printers identified as their 'unique' character traits. Compositors were unconventional, eccentric, whimsical, clever, witty, melancholy, independent, self-indulgent, cynical, and improvident. Their moodiness and cynicism was also attributed, at least in part, to exhaustive labour, irregular employment, and night work, particularly among newspaper compositors. In English Canada, these distinctive character traits were sometimes linked to ideals of Anglo-Saxon manhood. As one printer wrote, 'They have all the Anglo-Saxon hatred of showing emotion; they would much rather be thought heartless than sentimental.' North American printers, furthermore, were more independent and radical than their European counterparts. The 'typographical temperament' manifested itself in the journeyman's tendency to champion the unpopular view and sympathize with the oppressed. These traits also made printers ideal labour reformers. Printers defined themselves as 'naturally' sympathetic to radical republicanism. They believed in the rights of working men as citizens, and rejected the privileges of the monarchy and the established Church.[24]

A distinctive masculine workplace culture, with its own rites, language, and rules, had evolved over the centuries. For apprentices an aspect of acquiring knowledge of the craft included learning this specialized semiotic repertoire. In keeping with craft tradition, the nineteenth-century printing office was called a 'chapel.'[25] Journeymen printers referred to the trade as the 'art preservative.' They took great pride in their knowledge of the 'mysteries of the craft,' which they guarded in a veil of secrecy. 'A properly conducted printing office,' the *Printer's Miscellany* reported in 1876, 'is as much a secret society as a masonic lodge.'[26] Fraternity, however, 'gave compositors the organised power to marginalize women at work and the cultural dynamism to subdue them at home.'[27]

The National Typographical Union (NTU) raised the issue of incorporating women into the organization shortly after its formation at the 1854 convention. A resolution was passed which stipulated 'that this union will not encourage, by its acts, the employment of females as compositors.' In 1869, the international union, reorganized as the International Typographical Union (ITU) in recognition of its Canadian members, amended its constitution to permit the granting of separate charters to women's unions in any city where the application was approved 'by the subordinate union of male members.'[28] During a strike by New York printers in January 1869, Susan B. Anthony, head of the Working Women's Association, encouraged employers to establish a school for training women as typesetters. Contrary to the male unionists, middle-class reformers and feminists viewed typesetting as an ideal employment opportunity for educated working-class girls. In the aftermath of the New York printers' strike, Women's Typographical Union No. 1 was chartered.[29] This experiment in trade unionism by New York women printers was not a success. The organization of women compositors met with the hostility of male union members. The men viewed the employment of women compositors as an attempt by employers to replace them with cheaper labour, and also to undermine masculine competence in the trade, which could only be attained through the completion of an apprenticeship. At the 1873 convention of the ITU in Montreal, a motion was passed that no more charters be granted to unions made up of women only, although women were permitted to join men's locals.[30]

In 1889, Local 91 reported that 35 women and 595 men were employed as compositors in Toronto. Twenty-eight of the women worked in the *Truth* office, a non-union weekly newspaper and job-printing establishment. Of the remaining women compositors, four were employed at the Central Press Agency, a boiler-plate concern owned by the *World* newspaper company; two set type at Dudley & Burns, a printer and magazine publisher; and one was employed at Timms, Moore and Co., a printer and publisher specializing in music printing. The latter two firms were not union shops. The women, with experience in the trade ranging from one to four years, were classified as 'learners,' and were paid wages well below those of skilled journeymen compositors.[31] None had completed an apprenticeship, which symbolized 'competency' in the trade and passage to 'skilled' worker status. The women worked on 'straight matter,' or typesetting lines of text. During the 1870s and 1880s the dearth of women compositors in Toronto probably meant that they posed little real threat to the wage-earning capabilities of journeymen compositors. Male unionists, however, constructed a gender discourse in which women compositors were ultimately defined as a threat to their position in the trade.

When asked if the union had any objection to taking in women compositors as members, John Lumsden, a Toronto newspaper compositor and vice-president of ITU Local 91, testified before the Royal Commission on the Relations of Capital and Labour in November 1887 that the union had no objections to women belonging to the union as long as they came in on 'equal terms' with the men, completed the term of apprenticeship, and received the union scale. [32]

Testimony by Stewart L. Dunlop, also a journeyman printer and member of Local 91, although not employed as a printer at the time, revealed that women practically never entered the trade on 'equal terms' with male compositors. Dunlop was responding to questions posed by A.T. Freed, Tory editor of the Hamilton *Spectator*, which might perhaps account for the ambiguity in some of his responses.

Q. Do female compositors work by the day or week, or by the piece?
A. They work, I believe, by the piece.
Q. If they do the same class of work as male compositors, are they paid the same rate?
A. Well, not usually.
Q. Is it your experience that they do their work as well as male compositors?
A. No it is not.
Q. In what respect are they inferior?
A. Almost invariably they do their work in a very inferior manner. I daresay there may be several reasons for it and it is partly on account of their getting such small pay – smaller pay than the men are getting.
Q. Do these female compositors begin in the same manner that boys do and work up to the position we would call journey work in the same manner?
A. No; they are put on case immediately, and are given copy and told to proceed.
Q. And if they continue at case four or five years do you think they become as expert compositors as boys would in the same time?
A. Some do, but there are fewer swift ones in proportion to the number among female compositors than there are among male compositors.
Q. Do employing printers prefer female labor at the lower wages to journeymen at the higher wages?
A. Some do.
Q. Then there is an advantage to the employer in getting females at the lower wages?
A. There must be in some cases, but of course, those who do first-class work and are competing for first-class work scarcely employ female labor at all except for feeding presses.

Women by virtue of their sex were never defined as 'first-class' workers in the printing trades. Among compositors, craft sense, which was the hallmark of a skilled compositor, was defined as masculine. Later in the questioning, Dunlop stated that women compositors were generally paid from $4 to $6 per week less than male compositors, who earned between $13 and $16 dollars per week. According to the final report of the Labour Commission, the rate paid to the city's women compositors was 20¢ per 1000 ems of type set. Union men working at piece rates were paid 33⅓¢ per 1000 ems in book offices, 30¢ on morning papers, and 28¢ on evening papers.[33] For women workers these wages were higher, or at least comparable, to the average wage of between $5 and $7 per week received by dressmakers, and the $6 to $8 per week received by sales clerks.

The 'equal terms' rhetoric performed a specific political function for the male typographical unionists. As 'learners' women never entered the printing trades on the same terms as men. Their work was viewed by the male unionists as 'inferior' to the work of male journeymen compositors. This discourse about women's work was used by Dunlop and his brothers in the typographical union to justify their position of dominance in the trade and to marginalize women workers.

Dunlop's testimony before the Labour Commission suggests that journeymen printers used male-breadwinner rhetoric and the concept of women's sphere of domesticity to exclude women from the trade and to reinforce their position of power in the family.

Q. Is it a fact that as a rule women who do go to work at the printing business consider it a temporary occupation; consider their business in life to get married and become the heads of families, while the men consider it their life occupation?
A. Certainly, it is a life occupation to the men.
Q. How is it with the woman?
A. Well, it is only a temporary occupation; it helps her to get her clothing, and perhaps she is obliged to pay for her board?[34]

The notion that women workers constituted a casual labour force was an exclusionary strategy used by nineteenth-century male unionists to protect their gender identities as skilled journeymen in the labour market and breadwinners in the family. Representations of gender and family entered into male unionists' understandings of the organization of work.[35]

Women who worked as typesetters were never accepted as the equals of skilled journeymen printers either in the workplace or in the typographical union. Rhetorical tropes and metaphors about heterosexual relations between men and women typesetters were used to solidify women's marginal position in the trade. Through the suggestion that the woman compositors never desired to make a career of the trade, male dominance in the workplace and in the family was augmented. In the specialized rhetoric of the trade, the *Printers' Miscellany* quipped, 'A bashful compositor refused to accept a situation in an office where girls were employed, saying he never *set up* with a girl in his life.'[36] On another occasion the trade journal stated: 'Female compositors are continually setting their CAPS for the editor.'[37] The inference was clear. A woman working as a compositor during the latter nineteenth century was perceived by journeymen as searching for a husband so that she might eventually lead a life of domesticity. The use of humour around courting reinforced heterosexuality and male dominance within marriage.

In the 1880s technological innovations in machine typesetting, notably the invention of the linotype by Otto Mergenthaler, together with the expansion of and extensive capital investment in the daily press, made machine typesetting a viable alternative to hand composition in the newspaper sector. The linotype had a keyboard similar to a typewriter's. When the machine operator depressed a key, a hollow brass matrix was released. When enough matrices were collected to form a line, the margins were justified and the operator pushed a lever to start the casting machine, which poured molten lead into the mould, thereby creating a 'line o' type.'[38] The 'Mergs' were designed for straight-matter composition, and though ideally suited for newspaper production, the machines were inappropriate for commercial job printing. The skills of the experienced hand compositor remained essential for book and job printing requiring fancy display work, and also for 'high quality' composition.

Newspaper publishers defined typesetting as analogous to the work of women typists in the clerical sector, and argued that women's physical attributes made them ideally suited for work at composition. In May 1894, the *Canadian Printer and Publisher* stated that women's 'delicate fingers are peculiarly suited to the setting of fine type.' Employers constructed this gender discourse with the intent of designating the operation of the machines as semi-skilled work suitable for women and boy apprentices.[39]

Fearing displacement by women and boy-apprentice operators, the ITU quickly moved to establish control over the operation of the machines. In 1889 the international union adopted a resolution stipulating that, in 'all offices within its jurisdication where type-setting machines are used, practical printers shall be employed to run them; and also that subordinate Unions regulate the scale of wages on such machines.'[40] The ITU appointed a committee to consider the need for additional legislation to govern the operation of typesetting machines. The committee's report emphasized the physical demands of operating the machines: 'That the work upon machines, being of a more exhaustive character, both physically and mentally, than hand composition, that the hours of labor upon them be reduced to the lowest possible number – eight hours being the maximum.'[41] The male unionists emphasized that the work of type-setting was physically demanding, and thus could only be carried out by men, and not by boys or women. This was contrary to the rhetoric of employers, which emphasized that the physical attributes of women made them ideally suited for the work.

The first typesetting machine in Toronto was installed in the *Globe* office in 1891. By August of the following year the widespread use of machines in news-paper composition was reported in the *Canadian Printer and Publisher*. Two kinds of typesetting machines were found in the city: the Mergenthaler Lino-type and the Rogers Typograph. Six linotype machines were already in use at the *Globe* office. Ten typograph machines were found in the city, distributed as follows: three at the *Globe*, three at the *Mail*, three at the *Empire*, and one at the J.B. McLean Co.[42] By 1893 typesetting machines were also in use at the Meth-odist Book Room in the production of the *Christian Guardian*.[43]

Initially, the employers were not satisfied with the performance of either the machines or the machine operators. The early typesetting machines broke down almost constantly and the efficiency of the operators was below employers' expectations. Throughout the early 1890s, the *Canadian Printer and Publisher* published detailed reviews of the performance of the machines, and their opera-tors, in various Toronto printing offices. For instance, in its review of the record of the typograph machine in the J.B. McLean Publishing Co. over a three-week period in August 1893, the *Canadian Printer and Publisher* noted that 'a fair quantity of matter was set, but the appearance was unsatisfactory.' The letters were 'zig zag,' and fins appeared between the letters and at the ends of lines. The Murray Printing Co. removed a linotype from their shop in December 1895 when the machine failed to meet the expectations of the proprietor 'for the class of work done in his establishment.'[44] Although publishers frequently com-plained about the poor quality of type produced by machine composition, sav-ings were found in the overall cost of composition. In an article entitled 'Union Wages Help Machines,' the *Canadian Printer and Publisher* observed that 'in Toronto in consequence of costly composition, the machines have displaced a large number of compositors.'[45]

The fear among male hand compositors of being displaced by women and boy machine operators was not entirely unfounded. In January 1892 the com-positors at the *Globe* complained to Local 91 that boy apprentices were being used on the typograph machine, and at rates below those received by journey-men. Not only were class relations between employers and journeymen strained, but the masculine prerogatives of journeymen who had attained 'com-petency' in the trade by completing an apprenticeship were endangered. Local 91 immediately attempted to establish control over the terms of the use of the typesetting machines. The union announced that a scale would be introduced in the hope of avoiding speed-ups in the operation of the machines. The employers, however, refused to agree to any scale. They claimed that they had not yet established the 'utility' of the machines and that they were still in the experimental stages.[46]

In September 1892, Local 91 unilaterally declared a time rate of $15 per week. The following month the *News* office announced that the Rogers Typograph was to be installed in the composing room, and that the men learning to operate the machines would be paid a sliding piece-rate scale from $0.25 per 1000 ems the first week, decreasing to $0.14 per 1000 ems after ten weeks. This was intended to compensate for any slow-downs during the initial learning phase. The *Canadian Printer and Publisher* estimated that a compositor learning to operate a typograph machine could not set more than 1500 ems per hour. 'This average at the rate offered by the *News* would allow the men to earn about 20¢ per hour or $1.60 for a day of eight hours; a reduction in their wages of at least 50¢ per day.'[47]

On 26 October 1892, the compositors at the *News* were locked out and replaced by non-union machine operators – many of them women. A subcommittee appointed by the union failed to reach an agreement with manager Darby.[48] In a letter to the editor of the *Globe*, H.C. Hocken, foreman at the *News* and a member of Local 91, wrote: 'This is not a fight against machinery. It is a struggle against a lower rate of wages than is paid to any other office in Toronto.' Hocken further disclosed that Charles Riordan, the proprietor of the paper was determined to eradicate the union from the office and had no intention of accepting the union's offer.[49] Subsequently, the compositors locked out at the *News* launched another daily newspaper, the *Star*.[50]

The lockout at the *News* was eventually resolved in favour of the union. Under the terms of the settlement the *News* became a union office. Local 91 also secured control of the operation of the typesetting machines for its male membership and a time rate scale. The News Printing Company was to nominate union men as students to learn to operate the machines at a rate of $12 per week for six weeks. At the end of the six-week period an operator demonstrating proficiency, which was defined as the ability to set 2000 ems per hour or 100,000 ems per week, would be remunerated at a rate of $14 per week. These union operators were to replace the non-union operators, many of whom were women. E.F. Clarke, a former practical printer, MPP from 1886 to 1894, and mayor of Toronto from 1887 to 1891, was appointed the sole arbitrator to settle any differences that might arise between Local 91 and the News Printing Co.[51]

On 19 December 1892, ten men were locked out at a local boiler-plate factory, the Ontario Stereotype Co., to make room for what Local 91's official correspondent to the *Typographical Journal* described as 'that coming curse – the incompetent compositress.' The locked-out journeymen were replaced by women compositors, employed at a lower piece rate of $0.23 per 1000 ems.[52] Concurrent with the events at the Ontario Stereotype Co., C.B. Robinson, the proprietor of a weekly religious newspaper, the *Canada Presbyterian*, announced that his combined newspaper and job printing office was an open shop, and as such he could operate the machines as he saw fit. The operation of many late-nineteenth-century Toronto printing offices as open shops, where union and non-union men worked side by side, clearly weakened the position of Local 91 in its negotiations with employers. Robinson also employed women 'learners' as machine operators at rates below the union scale. On 10 January 1893, twenty-two union men, two non-union men, and six boy apprentices walked off the job. The management of the *Presbyterian* replaced the compositors with non-union workers, most of them women and boys.[53] The office was declared closed to typographical-union members and the union men found employment elsewhere. The conflict at the Ontario Stereotype Co. was, however, resolved on terms that gave Local 91 control of the shop. On 5 June 1893, Local 91 passed a resolution declaring the boiler-plate establishment a union shop.[54]

No figures have been found specifying the number of women machine operators taken into the typographical union with the settlement of the disputes at the Ontario Stereotype Co. At the regular monthly meeting of the union on 8 July 1893, Allie Roy and Maggie Adair, both from the *Presbyterian* office, were initiated into the union. The women compositors from the Ontario Stereotype Co. made application for union membership in June 1893. There is no mention in the union minutes of the women ever being formally initiated into Local 91, although their applications were accepted.[55]

Slightly less than two years later, the issue of the employment of non-union women on typesetting machines at rates below the union scale surfaced again. In April 1895, the chapel from the Toronto Type Foundry, a local boiler-plate concern, brought a grievance before the union that the firm's manager was using 'girls' on the typesetting machines, and was paying them at rates below the union scale. When interviewed by a committee from Local 91, the treasurer of the Toronto Type Foundry Co. responded that the object of the introduction of cheap female labour was to remain competitive with the *Truth* in the manufacture of ready prints.[56] On 27 April the union instructed the chairman of the chapel to enfore the constitution and the scale of prices. The management of the Toronto Type Foundry refused to comply with the union's terms and a strike ensued.[57]

The result of the strike was another victory for ITU Local 91. In August the management of the Toronto Type Foundry agreed to hire members of Local 91 at the union scale. The outcome was less satisfactory for Margaret Aitken, an employee at the Toronto Type Foundry, and one of the few women members of the typographical union. In the fall of 1895, Aitken was brought before the union on charges of 'ratting,' or strike-breaking. At the regular monthly meeting of Local 91 on 5 October the Trial Committee reported: 'Miss Aitken said in her defence that she had lost money on the Stereo Plate Co., and also was liable for more losses, and also that she being a female she could not get back so easily and as quick as a male so she stayed in.'[58] The members of Local 91 voted to expel Aitken from the union. While in this instance the woman compositor certainly betrayed the interests of male union members, Aitken's testimony further attests to the gender inequalities in the late-nineteenth-century Toronto printing trades that denied women the same opportunities as men and neglected the concerns of the women as workers. A report submitted by Local 91 to the ITU on 30 April 1895 listed only two women machine operators, in contrast to forty-two male union machine operators.[59] It would seem, therefore, that the male unionists had effectively excluded women from the Toronto Typographical Union.

The latter decades of the nineteenth century were also a period of considerable tension between compositors and pressmen. The uneven process of industrialization left the skills of the hand compositor essentially untouched until the 1890s, whereas the earlier mechanization of presswork had forced pressmen to become machine tenders. Compositors were 'artists' who turned the form over to a pressman much as 'the sculptor hands his mould to the marble cutter.' 'But where the first is governed by rules of art, the latter is very largely controlled by those of mechanics.'[60] This metaphor located the compositor in a position of creative authority over pressman who, in the opinion of the compositors, were merely machine operators and not artists. Pressmen, however, countered using gender rhetoric which emphasized that the operation of the newer, more complex presses required more skill than previously. They reasserted their masculine authority in the trade by comparing the machines to women. The *American Pressman* advised journeymen that '[p]resses get cranky too ... and when they do, the true pressman speedily finds there is something wrong, and humors as he would woman in her moods.'[61]

Until the 1880s journeymen pressmen were included under the umbrella of the ITU. The pressmen members of the ITU, however, felt increasingly oppressed by the domination of the international union by its compositor members. 'Now, in their determination to be heard as craftsmen in their own right,' argued Elizabeth Baker, the historian of the pressmen's international union, 'they had come to feel more and more conscious of their value to employing printers and less and less dependent upon the compositors for strength.'[62] In Toronto, this resentment on the part of pressmen, stemming from a perceived neglect of their interests by the typographical union, resulted in the chartering of Toronto Printing Pressman's Union, Local 10 in October 1882, albeit initially under the ITU. The Toronto pressmen's union experienced organizational difficulties during its formative years. At the monthly meeting of Local 10 on 13 February 1885, a motion was carried that 'a circular be sent to every member of this Union stating the fact that the Union is to be reorganized in every shape.'[63] Later in the decade a shortage of pressmen in the city further hindered the pressmen's efforts to attract members. Employers attempted to take advantage of the situation by using cheaper apprentice labour. Relations between the local typographical union and the pressmen's union further deteriorated in October 1887 when Local 91 refused to recognize a strike by the pressmen for an increase in wages to $12 per week. The strike ended in defeat for the pressmen.[64]

Immediately following the organization of the International Printing Pressmen's Union of North America (IPPU) in October 1889, press feeders voiced their concern over the irregular enforcement of IPPU recommendations regarding the recruitment of apprentices. The IPPU recommended a ratio of one apprentice to four journeymen, and that pressmen's unions admit to membership apprentices who had completed three years of presswork either as an assistant or as a press feeder. Local unions, however, were given the authority to decide how many apprentices could be taken and at what stage they should be transferred. The assistants and press feeders felt that the recommendations denied many of the best assistants and feeders the opportunity to rise to journeymen status in the trade. As a result, the Toronto Printing Press Assistants' and Feeders' Union was organized in June 1890.[65]

The conflict between the pressmen and the press feeders and assistants was partially resolved at the annual convention of the IPPU in 1896, where concessions were made to the press feeders and assistants. The IPPU passed a resolution that when a member of an assistants' or feeders' union received the pressmen's scale, he should apply for membership in the local pressmen's union. Feeders and assistants were also given formal recognition in the international. The organization was renamed the International Printing Pressmen and Assistants' Union (IPP&AU).[66]

Beginning in the late 1890s, the IPP&AU attempted to redefine the work of press feeding as skilled men's work. The press feeder of the mid-nineteenth century was typically a young unmarried woman, or a boy just out of school, who had 'probably commenced his career in a printing office as an errand boy or sweeper and in spare moments learned to kick a jobber.' The IPP&AU,

through its organ *The American Pressman*, began to emphasize the skill and manliness required to operate the larger and more sophisticated presses. 'Instead of the boy or youth,' the journal observed, 'we find in the average feeder of the present time a matured young man, in numerous instances married and with a family to support.'[67]

In redefining the work of the press feeder as skilled men's work, the male press feeders, like the compositors, also used male-breadwinner discourse. Unlike the earlier period, when press feeding was unskilled work for apprentices or 'temporary' work for young women previous to marriage, 'the tendencies of the times have conspired to make his calling more of a permanency by lessening opportunities for advancement,' the *American Pressman* observed. Thus, the commentary concluded, '[a] feeder is a skilled workman and as such should at least be paid living wages and not a standard lower than that of a common laborer.'[68]

In a critique of women's employment in the pressroom, the *American Pressman* suggested that the employment of women in pressrooms was 'to the detriment of the rising generation of males as bread winners.' 'The female never aspires to be a pressman as the work is not adapted to their sex.' Pressrooms were usually located in the basements of buildings and were notorious for their dirty, damp, and dark working environment. According to the male unionists, women abandoned the pressroom as soon as they saw 'an opening for marriage or [found] a place congenial to their tastes.'[69]

The majority of women employed in the printing trades during the nineteenth century were confined to a narrow range of occupations in bookbinding and stationery manufacture. Women had a clearly defined role in the production process in the artisan bookbinder's family workshop, unlike the social relations in the male-dominated printers' chapel. In early-nineteenth-century Britain, Felicity Hunt writes, 'women had strictly demarcated areas of skill for they worked in the "forwarding" or early stages of the binding process.'[70] Women did preparatory jobs in the binding process, specifically, folding, collating, and sewing. All of the tasks between sewing and the actual 'finishing,' or the ornamenting of the cover, including trimming, rounding and backing, lining-up, and gluing and gilding the edges, were carried out by journeymen bookbinders who had completed an apprenticeship in the trade.

Table 5.1 displays a division by gender, and by sector, of the Toronto printing industry derived from the 1871, 1881, and 1891 decennial censuses. At all three census periods male workers dominated the local printing trades. The pattern of gender segregation, with the majority of women and girls working in binderies, is consistent with the trend in women's work in the printing trades in Britain and the United States. Although no statistics were compiled for individ-

TABLE 5.1 Divisions by sector, occupation, and gender in the Toronto printing industry, 1871–1891

		Number of employees				Total number of employees	Percentage of total city printing industry	Percentage of sector male	Percentage of sector female
		Adult		Child					
Year	Sector	M	F	M	F				
1871	Printing offices	274	7	70	2	353	40.3	97.4	2.6
	Bookbinding	162	252	13	25	452	51.5	38.7	61.3
	Engraving & lithographing	54	10	4	2	70	8.0	82.9	17.1
	Stereotyping	2				2	0.2	100.0	0.0
	Total	492	269	87	29	877	100.0	66.0	34.0
1881	Printing offices	862	116	233	24	1235	72.0	88.7	11.3
	Bookbinding	135	190	16	22	363	21.1	41.6	58.4
	Engraving & lithographing	91	7	20		118	6.9	94.1	5.9
	Total	1088	313	269	46	1716	100.0	79.1	20.9
1891	Printing & publishing	1790	441	147	6	2384	74.8	81.3	18.7
	Bookbinding	225	254	8	1	488	15.3	47.7	52.3
	Engraving & lithographing	248	15	12	1	488	8.7	94.2	5.8
	Electro-stereotyping	25	15			40	1.2	62.5	37.5
	Total	2288	725	167	8	3188	100.0	77.0	23.0

Sources: Ontario Census Returns 1871, City of Toronto, District 46, Schedule 6, Census of 1871, National Archives of Canada, RG 31, vol. 801; Canada, Census of Canada 1881, vol. 3, 420–1, 434–5, 460–1; Canada, Census of Canada 1891, vol. 3, 40–1, 142–5, 268–9.

ual communities for women workers, in 1889 the Ontario Bureau of Industries calculated that the province's women bookfolders worked, on average, 277 days a year and earned $173.82. Women press feeders worked an average of 271 days per year and earned $142. The wages of women bindery workers were approximately one-third to one-half those of journeymen in the printing trades. The cost of living for the women bookfolders surveyed was estimated at $178.71, thus indicating a small deficit.[71] Statistics were compiled by community for male workers. Toronto printers (probably compositors) worked, on average, 228.8 days per year, and earned $444.79. In comparison, pressmen worked an average of 290.9 days per year and earned $440.20. Journeymen bookbinders worked an average of 265.7 days per year and earned $462.96. The Bureau of Industries calculated that the cost of living for men with dependents and renting a home was $493.46. For men with dependents and owning a home, the cost of living was $547.80.[72] It was unlikely, therefore, that a breadwinner wage was realized in the households of most of the city's male printing-trades workers with families.

Between 1871 and 1891, the proportion of women employed in bookbinding decreased, although the actual number of women employed in this sector increased. Depending on the type of binding required, some of the forwarding work was performed by machine by the 1880s. Cheap editions, pamphlets, and catalogues were sewn by machine with wire instead of thread. The operation of the wire stitchers was described in an 1880 instructional manual: 'The machine is fed with wire from spools by small steel rollers, which at each revolution supply exactly the length of wire required to form little staples with two legs.'[73] The operation of wire stitchers and sewing machines in the bindery, according to the contemporary literature, was defined as women's work. British Labour Party leader J. Ramsay MacDonald stated in his 1904 study of women's involvement in the printing trades that 'convention determines that in these trades sewing machines and women go together. Sewing machines are domestic implements in men's eyes.'[74]

Folding machines were available after the middle of the century. In the case of the nineteenth-century London bookbinding trade, although men operated the folding machines, there was virtually no displacement of women hand folders by men machine operators. Because it was cheaper for employers to hire women hand folders, the operation of the machines was confined to overtime and night work when the employment of women was restricted by law. The Ontario Factories Act, amended in 1889, restricted overtime work by women and children to nine o'clock pm on thirty-six nights over twelve months subject to the approval of the provincial Inspector of Factories.[75] It is likely that large Toronto bookbinders also used their folding machines primarily during overtime hours and that no actual displacement of women hand folders occurred. In June 1892, the *Canadian Printer and Publisher* remarked that '[f]olding machines had been on the market for about 25 years, but were so slow in operation and so expensive they had little advantage over hand folding.'[76]

Middle-class labour reformers indicated that, in contrast to the strong trade-union organization among male printing-trades workers, efforts to organize women bindery workers had not been successful. Ramsay MacDonald commented that 'woman having an eye to marriage is not equally wedded to her trade.' The custom of the trade was for women to leave the bindery upon marriage.[77] During the 1880s women bindery workers were organized by the Knights of Labor. On 25 February 1886, the Toronto Bookbinders' Benevolent Society became Local Assembly 5743 of the Knights of Labor, and was named 'Hand in Hand.' Women bindery workers were taken into LA 5743 as members.[78]

Toronto bookbinders' LA 5743 collapsed in 1894 in the midst of the widespread demise of the Knights of Labor in Ontario. Earlier, in May 1892, the International Brotherhood of Bookbinders (IBB) was formed in Philadelphia with the amalgamation of National Trades Assembly No. 230 of the Knights of Labor and the International Bookbinders Union. Women bindery workers were included under the umbrella of the IBB from the outset.[79]

Toronto Local 28 of the IBB, chartered in June 1893, incorporated journeymen bookbinders previously affiliated with the Knights of Labor.[80] Two prominent Toronto labour reformers and journeyman bookbinders, brothers Robert and William Glockling, joined Local 28. Robert Glockling had previously served several terms as president of the Bookbinders' Benevolent Society, and had been prominent in District Assembly (DA) 125 of the Knights of Labor. At the annual convention of the IBB in 1898 he was elected first vice-president. Later, in 1905, he was elected president – a position he held until his death in 1913. Robert Glockling was also president of the Toronto Trades and Labor Council in 1889–90, and again in 1895–6. From 1900 to 1906 he was secretary of the Ontario Bureau of Labour.[81] His brother William was secretary of Bookbinders' LA 5743 in the early 1890s, and later secretary of Local 28 in the early 1900s. In 1916 he was elected first vice-president of the IBB.[82]

In his annual report to the IBB convention in Toronto in May 1898, President Bodin stated that he was dissatisfied with the efforts made thus far by the officers of local unions to organize bindery women. The laws of the IBB were modified in 1899 to provide for the chartering of separate locals of women bindery workers, using the designation 'Bindery Women's Local Union.'[83] On 26 June 1901 Bindery Women's Union No. 34 was chartered in Toronto. The bindery women at the Methodist Book and Publishing House were at the forefront of the organization of the women's local. Charles Goldsmith, an organizer for the IBB and a bookbinder at the establishment, assisted in the organization of the union.[84]

Although Toronto Bindery Women's Union No. 34 was founded with a membership of 150, and initially showed much promise, only half of the estimated city total of 500 women bindery workers had joined the union by the following year. In 1902 Bindery Women's Union No. 34 made an unsuccessful bid for a 50 per cent wage increase and a reduction in the hours of labour to 44 per week.[85] Employers rejected the women's demands, stating that the work of women in the binderies lacked 'permanency,' and thus was of less value than the labour of men 'who enter as apprentices, have every intention of making the trade their life-work, and in time, if capable, they become expert binders.'[86] Toronto Bindery Women's Union No. 34 was short-lived. In 1908, the union merged with IBB Local 28, on a directive issued by IBB President Glockling that 'where small locals exist of men and women, separated, ... there be but one local.'[87]

By the early 1900s, however, male bookbinders were perhaps more concerned about their own position in the trade. While the skills of the hand bookbinder were still required to produce quality 'up-market' books, the burgeoning market in cheap books and periodicals, combined with mechanization and fragmentation in the production process, weakened the position of journeymen in the workplace. In the production of cheap books, where casing, stamping, and embossing were carried out by machine by the 1890s, employers increasingly turned to cheaper women piece-rate workers and boy apprentices. In February 1905, IBB President Robert Glockling, asked, 'Why is a girl employed in place of a man?' 'Because she is cheaper,' he declared. 'With our women organized,' Glockling stated prophetically, 'we will be able to educate them in the economic situation, and thus avert much of the future difficulties that will inevitably arise if we keep them apart.' He further stated:

History tends generally to imply the idea of the inferiority of women in the industrial and political field. It remained, however, for the Labor organizations to declare against this doctrine. The Order of the Knights of Labor in the early eighties declared for 'Equal pay for equal work.' And why not? Assuming that wages represent the media of exchange for life's necessities, why should not Women share equally in wage distribution? Does it require any less for life's necessities of woman than man's?[88]

The rhetoric of equal rights as articulated by the Knights of Labor in the 1880s, and by the IBB in the early 1900s, always operated in tension with the prevailing notions of domesticity and woman's sphere. On the one hand, equal pay implied an acceptance of women as equal partners in the 'public sphere' of productive life.[89] On the other hand, the Knights of Labor and the IBB looked forward to the day when women might return to the 'private sphere' of domesticity. The journeymen bookbinders, moreover, used the rhetoric of domesticity to justify their own purposes and goals, specifically, retaining control over the finishing jobs in the bindery by excluding women and boy-apprentice machine operators.

Art Workmen: The British Heritage and the Craftsman Ideal

The 'craftsman ideal,' associated primarily with the writings and practice of the English art critic John Ruskin and his disciple William Morris, was a reaction against industrialization and changes in social relations beginning in the late eighteenth century in Britain, whereby a separation had emerged between artist and artisan, and between artist and craftsman. As Raymond Williams explained, 'An *art* had formerly been any human skill; but *Art*, now, signified a particular group of skills, the "imaginative" or "creative" arts. *Artist* had meant a skilled person, as had *artisan*; but *artist* now referred to these selected skills alone. Further, and most significantly, *Art* came to stand for a special kind of truth, "imaginative truth," and *artist* for a special kind of person.'[90] Social transformations associated with the industrial revolution had divided crafts into the fine arts and the industries. Art became a part of 'culture,' redefined in the late nineteenth century as a privileged domain of refinement and aesthetic sensibility. Art also separated itself into 'high' and 'popular' art, the latter of which was manufactured for urban consumers. The emergent graphic-arts industry contributed to the division between 'high' and 'popular' culture. Artists were employed as illustrators, engravers, and lithographers, but their status was perceived as one of inferiority, as the defenders of fine art placed art in opposition to labour.[91] In contrast to the fragmentation of social life endemic in the burgeoning industrial society, the 'craftsman ideal' offered an alternative culture with powerful symbols aimed at reuniting art and labour. Many of the leaders of the arts and crafts movement that emerged in Britain and in North America in the late nineteenth century were socialists, or had ties to the labour movement. This was not surprising, since both groups appeared to be working toward transforming a social system that degraded workers.

Born in London in 1819, John Ruskin, the only son of a Scottish sherry merchant, provided 'a Christian rendering of the Romantics' vision of nature.' The purpose of art according to Ruskin was to reveal 'Beauty,' which he equated with 'Truth.' His idea of beauty rested on his belief in a universal, divinely appointed order. Ugliness in nature, and in art, was a negation of what Ruskin termed 'Vital Beauty,' which he defined as 'the appearance of felicitous fulfilment of function in living things, more especially of the joyful and right exertion of the perfect life in man.'[92] By equating ideas of beauty with morality, Ruskin was able to eliminate the distinction that had emerged during the nineteenth century between art as an abstract immoral perception and the activities of everyday life. These ideas were summed up by Ruskin in an aphorism: 'So far from Art's being immoral, in the ultimate power of it, nothing but Art is moral; Life without Industry is sin, and Industry without Art, brutality.'[93]

During the 1840s, Ruskin began to question the Protestant evangelicalism he had acquired from his mother, although he retained a fundamental faith in Christianity. His focus shifted from the role of landscape, which had preoccupied him in the early volumes of *Modern Painters*, to a concern with human nature and social reform. 'The Nature of Gothic,' the central chapter of *The Stones of Venice*, published in 1842, is an indictment of the enslavement of workers by machine production. 'You must either make a tool of the creature, or a man of him,' Ruskin wrote. 'You cannot make both.' He continued, 'Men were not intended to work with the accuracy of tools, to be precise and perfect in all their actions.'[94]

For Ruskin and his followers, the Gothic symbolized the freedom and liberty of every workman. In 'The Nature of Gothic,' Ruskin translated the characteristics of Gothic architecture into masculine moral virtues, namely, savageness, love of change, love of nature, disturbed imagination, obstinacy, and generosity. The roughness and imperfections of Gothic architecture symbolized the working of a free, human soul. Perfection, such as that found in the products of machine production, was, by contrast, a sign of slavery. According to Ruskin, there should be no division between art and society, and between intellectual work and manual work. 'Now it is only by labour that thought can be made healthy, and only by thought that labor can be made happy, and the two cannot be separated with impunity,' Ruskin argued.[95] The solution proposed by Ruskin was the reintegration of art with the common life of society, so that all men are good 'handicraftsmen.' The process of creating a design, and then implementing the design, conferred manliness on the craftsman.

William Morris retained Ruskin's moral aesthetics, but he secularized them by judging society on its social relationships rather than by any notion of godliness. Morris worked to spread the socialist cause. He predicted that, under real socialism, people would prefer handicraft as a means of self-expression. Unlike Ruskin, Morris applauded the use of any machinery that freed men from drudgery. His rationale for founding Kelmscott Press in 1891 was drawn directly from Ruskin's chapter 'The Nature of Gothic' in *The Stones of Venice*, particularly Ruskin's association of the Gothic with a certain set of moral values.

Morris's theories about book design were rooted in the practices of fifteenth-century printers. T.J. Cobden-Sanderson, a barrister who was acquainted with Morris, and who apparently took up bookbinding at the suggestion of Morris's wife, Jane, viewed art as the engine of social change rather than its result. Cobden-Sanderson revived the medieval method of sewing books on raised bands, and did much to revive the tradition of craft bookbinding, which had declined with the widespread use of cheaper cloth bindings in the latter nineteenth century.[96]

Bookbinding was one of the crafts taken up by middle-class women who embraced the arts and crafts movement. In the autumn of 1900, Ernest J. Hathaway, secretary of Warwick Bros. and Rutter, a large Toronto book printer and publisher, delivered a lecture on art in bookmaking to the Women's Art Association. In this talk, and in his articles for the *Canadian Printer and Publisher*, Hathaway referred to the work of William Morris at the Kelmscott Press. Hathaway wrote: 'A well-printed and well-bound book may be in itself as true a work of art as the piece of literature which it contain.' In contrast to the well-established gender division of labour in the industrial sector, where women had long been excluded from the artistic finishing component of the binding process, middle-class women reformers were among the arts and crafts enthusiasts who took up hand bookbinding.[97]

Toronto radicals and social reformers who came of age in the 1890s also found inspiration in Ruskin's moral aesthetics for their project of building 'the cooperative commonwealth.' This project had its institutional grounding in the Nationalist Association and the Theosophical Society. Among local theosophists were such radicals as T. Phillips Thompson, Women's Suffrage Association leaders Dr Emily Howard Stowe and her daughter Dr Augusta Stowe-Gullen, Ethel Day MacPherson, F.E. Titus, and Felix Belcher. James Simpson, who in the early 1890s was an apprentice compositor at the *News* and a Methodist youth leader, initiated the formation of the Ruskin Literary and Debating Society.[98]

Toronto engraver Frederick Brigden combined the Protestantism of his Methodist upbringing with the craftsman ideal. Brigden acquired a knowledge of the craftsman's ideal as an apprentice in Linton's London workshop and as a student at the Workingmen's College, where Ruskin conducted classes in drawing and Thomas Hughes, author of *Tom Brown's School Days*, lectured on self-improvement. Many years later, Brigden described Ruskin as 'more of a sort of Art Missionary, introducing a religious sentiment into art culture, than as a teacher of practical work.' Looking back, Brigden indicated that Ruskin's methods did not train to the mastery of drawing required of the commercial engraver. Brigden, however, in the manner of Ruskin, referred to himself as an 'art workman' throughout his career.[99]

As his younger son Frederick, who displayed considerable artistic talent as a member of the Toronto Art Students' League, approached manhood, the elder Brigden told his son that his ambition for him had always been to see him established as a 'skilful art workman.' In the letter, he confided to his son that he had always feared the effect his affiliation with the Art Students' League would have on the development of his character, and was concerned that he might develop a 'sentimental selfishness.' 'The pleasure of following art on one's own devices is of a lower kind than the high uplifting goodness of consciously doing utmost with such talents as we have for the helping of all among us,' the elder Brigden wrote.[100] Frederick H. Brigden incorporated the craftsman ideal taught by his father into his works as an artist, although the division between 'high' art and commercial art was already firmly established in Canada by the twentieth century. He was denied associate membership in the Royal Canadian Academy until 1934, and full membership was delayed until 1939.[101]

Throughout his life, Frederick Brigden Sr thought of himself as an art workman and a Christian, although like Ruskin he came to believe in a broad Christianity founded more on the teachings of Christ than on any organized church.[102] The life of a nineteenth-century Christian craftsman contained a set of assumptions about gender that extended beyond the workplace.[103] Brigden's sense of manly work also encompassed public service and his duties as a husband and father. Sympathetic to the difficulties of the deaf in a hearing world, he organized a Mission to the Deaf along strictly nondemoninational lines, and conducted regular meetings in the family's Rose Avenue home. At the beginning of 1873 Brigden revealed in his New Year's resolutions that he must concern himself with providing for his growing family. In addition to material provisions, Brigden wrote, 'I should seek and be the light and happiness of the house, a free husband and a true father.' He would strive to be a Christ in his own home, 'an annointed of God for the leading and salvation of these dear ones.'[104]

The Apprentice Question and Masculinity

In December 1896, the *Canadian Printer and Publisher* published the indentures signed by Charles Johnson, bindery foreman at Warwick Bros. and Rutter, when he was apprenticed to London stationer George Richards Simmons sometime around the middle of the nineteenth century. Johnson agreed that he

shall not waste the goods of his said master nor lend them unlawfully to any. He shall not commit fornication nor contract matrimony within the said term. He shall not play at cards, dice tables, or any other unlawful games whereby his said master may have any loss ... He shall not haunt taverns or playhouses nor absent himself from his said master's service, day or night unlawfully. But in all things as a faithful apprentice he shall behave himself towards his master, and all his, during the said term.[105]

Until the 1870s apprenticeship was more than a system by which boys acquired the technical skills of the craft, whether it be bookbinding, composition, engraving, or presswork. 'Completion of an apprenticeship,' as Ava Baron has argued in the case of nineteenth-century compositors, 'simultaneously symbolized passage into manhood and into skilled "competent" worker status.'[106] Through apprenticeship boys achieved manly respectability by learning the discipline and self-control needed to practise a craft. As a young apprentice to William Linton, Frederick Brigden engaged in a program of self-improvement that he carefully recorded in his dairy. On 22 March 1858 Brigden wrote: 'My engraving is anything but good and it will take me long even to acquire the first simple exercises but I remember my motto, Industry, Patience, Perseverance, and I fear not I shall get success for my crest.'[107] Steadfastness in pursuing his craft, and in his program of reading and study at the Workingmen's College, were part of the cultivation of manliness of character for Brigden. Upon completion of the term of apprenticeship, usually between five and seven years in duration, a boy entered manhood. In becoming proficient in a craft, he obtained a way of earning a 'family wage' and gained a position of 'honorable independence.'

By the end of the nineteenth century, apprenticeship in large Toronto printing-trades establishments was practically obsolete. Employers preferred the labour of cheaper boy apprentices who could be discharged at their convenience. 'Two-thirds' apprentices from the country wanted the right to leave an office if they found a better position elsewhere. Journeymen resisted the threat these abuses of apprenticeship presented to their privileged position as craftsmen and family providers.

Shortly after its formation in 1832, the York Typographical Society incorporated into its constitution a measure intended to control the number of apprentices allowed to enter the trade: 'That the practice of having a number of apprentices in the different establishments must prove an injury to the journeymen, it is deemed necessary by this society that no member shall consent to work in any office where more than two are employed, except in the event of its being the last year of the elder apprentices time, when a third may be taken on.'[108] In 1867 an attempt was made by the local typographical union to regulate apprenticeship by allowing fifth-year apprentices into the union as 'junior' members.[109] Later, in April 1871, a rule was adopted stipulating that boys must serve five years at the printing trade from the age of sixteen to twenty-one years.[110] The union also monitored the ratio of journeymen to apprentices beginning in the late 1870s to ensure that a ratio of five to one was enforced.

Printers brought their grievances concerning violations of the various apprentice regulations before Local 91. On two occasions, first in November 1876 and again in February 1881, the compositors at the *Mail* chapel charged their employer with putting boys to work on advertisements while the journeymen composed 'straight matter,' thus denying them the more lucrative 'phat.'[111] Journeymen also complained on several occasions about the system of bringing 'two-thirders' into the city from the country before they had completed an apprenticeship.[112] The technical knowledge of the craft that country apprentices received was often inadequate. One country printer revealed that apprentices were generally taught to set straight matter only, and were given no education in job printing.[113] As a result, 'two-thirders' fell far short of the ideal 'all round' practical printer.

The printers' craft, which required intellectual, artistic, and manual capabilities, was viewed by the journeymen as comprising the essential ingredients of manhood. Stewart L. Dunlop, a journeyman printer and member of Local 91, although not working as a printer at the time, testified before the Royal Commission on the Relations of Labor and Capital in 1887 that some of the boys entering the trade were not 'competent' to begin because 'they have not been attending school to any extent.' 'A boy cannot understand anything mechanically to the extent that a boy can who is educated,' commented Dunlop. Boys lacking in education were viewed as 'idle.'[114] A boy who failed to present himself as intelligent and industrious would never develop manliness. Eventually his lack of manly 'character' would culminate in moral ruin.

In April 1892 the business committee of Local 91 reported that one of the greatest evils affecting the trade is the 'boy question.' In its report the committee raised the question, 'Who are to replace these thoroughly practical men fast dying out owing to the present system of get without regard for quality on the part of the employer.'[115] The members of Local 91 adopted a recommendation made by the committee that an apprentice be required to prove that he had served five years.

The demise of the practice of placing an apprentice, or 'devil' as he was called in the tradition of the craft, under the personal tutelage of an experienced journeyman remained a concern for the ITU throughout the remainder of the 1890s. In an article published in the *Typographical Journal*, the issue of apprentice neglect and the failure to inculcate 'manliness' was discussed.

The employer, formerly recognizing a limit to apprenticeship, made an effort through the foreman to give the apprentice the proper tuition against the time of his arrival at the journeyman stage. Now the apprentice keeps on forever – more or less – in that uncertain condition, neither boy nor man, yet in many cases long past the age at which maturity is supposed to come. Apparently the employer cares not a continental whether the boy ever becomes proficient at his calling or not.[116]

Employers were not, however, entirely to blame for the deterioration of the apprenticeship system: the *Typographical Journal* reprimanded journeymen for neglecting apprentices until they had become conditional members of a local union.

During the 1890s printers attributed the poor quality of apprentice training not only to the tendency among employers to try to reduce production costs by shifting more of the typesetting to comparatively cheaper boy labour, but also to the widespread introduction of machine typesetting and fragmentation of the labour process, whereby the 'all round' printer was increasingly displaced by the 'specialist' who was proficient in one particular area of the craft. Local 91's objection to the use of apprentice and women workers on the machines precipitated the strikes of the early 1890s. Regulations governing the use of typesetting machines by apprentices were introduced by Local 91. The wage scale for machine operators put into effect on February 1900 stipulated that apprentices were permitted to practise on the typesetting machines, but only during the last three months of their five-year apprenticeship.[117] The intent of the rule was to ensure not only that journeymen unionists retained control over the operation of the machines, but also that the boys acquired 'competence' in all the other areas of the compositor's craft before learning machine composition.

During the latter decades of the nineteenth century, Toronto's male printing-trades workers defined and redefined meanings of sexual difference in relation to craft and skill. Rather than there being a 'crisis' in masculinity, as some historians have posited, masculinity was transformed and reconstructed. New and different reasons were articulated by male trade unionists to exclude women from the printing trades. This left intact their position of male domination, both in the workplace and in the trade union. The rhetoric of equal rights was used by skilled male printing-trades workers to maintain their position of power in the workplace against attempts by employers to use comparatively cheaper women and boy-apprentice workers.

A discourse of domesticity, with an emphasis on the male breadwinner, forged a connection between work and family. Manliness was still represented as the ability to provide for a family, but by the latter part of the nineteenth century it had been redefined to incorporate wage work. Sexual difference was constructed by journeymen and employers alike to suggest that women's work was temporary, and that they would leave the printing trades upon marriage. Women were denied access to the 'mysteries of the craft' and were never formally apprenticed into the printing trades. The fraternity of brothers organized around the printers' chapel further ensured that women rarely entered the printing trades on the same terms as men and that skill in the trades was defined as masculine. The completion of an apprenticeship symbolized the transition to manhood for a boy, competency in a craft, and the ability to earn a 'family wage.' Both class and gender interests informed both male print-trades workers' discussion of the family wage and women's involvement in the printing trades. Gender was a fundamental component of their articulation of class and class consciousness.

Representations of masculinity shaped the ways in which journeymen and labour reformers dealt with industrial-capitalist transformations. The craftsman ideal imported from Britain, with its origins in the works of Ruskin and Morris, reasserted the power of the skilled working man, and reunited 'art' with 'labour,' contrary to the fragmentation of social life brought about by industrial capitalism. For social reformers and socialists the Gothic represented the moral ideals of the manly craftsman. This discourse was integral to the realization of 'the cooperative commonwealth.'

6

Beyond the Home Circle:
Separate Spheres, Labour Reform,
and Working-Class Women

'The best system of culture and instruction which have yet been devised for men,' declared the *Ontario Workman* on 7 August 1873, 'have been framed in view, not of any specially masculine needs or claims, but of human wants, of the rights and yearnings of the human spirit, of the capacities and forces of the human intelligence; and whatever turns out to be right and wise from this point of view is equally so for woman and for man.' The author of the column went on to state that for both sexes 'there is a complex life to be lived – a life partly of care and duty, partly of leisure and of enjoyment; a life which is in one phase worldly and outward, and in another social and purely domestic and private.' The difference was that the 'proportions of time spent in their different spheres may differ in the case of men and women.'[1]

The metaphor of 'separate spheres' found in the *Ontario Workman* is but one illustration of the use of 'separate spheres' in the late-nineteenth-century English-Canadian labour press to characterize dynamic gender-based power relationships. For some employers, the rhetoric of separate spheres justified the exploitation of women workers as a cheap source of unskilled labour. Woman's sphere of domesticity was used by male trade unionists to reinforce gender segregation in the wage labour force for purposes of protecting men's position of privilege in the workplace and in the family. For married women separate spheres gave them a small measure of power in the home, although this definitely did not translate into social equality between the sexes. Beginning in the 1880s, the rhetoric of separate spheres and domesticity was also used to draw women into the labour movement.

The rhetoric of separate spheres was the foundation of Victorian sexual ideology. In Britain, beginning in the eighteenth century, conduct books mapped out a representation of a domestic and feminine ideal that helped to depoliticize class relations at mid-century by attaching psychological motives to what had previously been class differences, and evaluating these according to a set of moral norms that exalted working-class women over their aristocratic counterparts. As the ensuing discussion of the conduct literature in the late-nineteenth-century Toronto labour press reveals, the rhetorical separation of the spheres bestowed some limited power on working-class women.[2]

The binary model of opposition between the sexes that permeated mid-Victorian culture conferred upon women in the domestic sphere the power of moral influence and surveillance over men. This gave women authority in several domains including the use of leisure, the care of the body, courtship practice, family relations, and the operations of desire and sexual pleasure. During the latter part of the nineteenth century this model of opposition between the sexes was inscribed in different ways into a variety of institutional practices and conventions, including the gender division of labour in the workplace, trade-union organization, and the institutional practices of middle-class women reformers.[3]

A shifting consciousness around gender occurred in Toronto during the 1880s. Wage work among single women was identified as a social problem. The Knights of Labor selectively appropriated strands of domestic ideology for working-class political purposes. While incorporation into the Knights of Labor as the 'peers of men' marked a significant advance for working-class women, this commitment to equal rights and women's involvement in the public sphere always operated in tension with prevailing notions of domesticity and women's sphere. The Knights looked forward to a future in which women would 'return' to their 'natural' sphere of the home.[4]

'The Home Circle': The *Ontario Workman* and the Language of Domesticity during the Early 1870s

The *Ontario Workman* was initiated during the nine-hours movement of 1872 as the organ of the Toronto Trades Assembly. It was published weekly from 18 April 1872 until 9 April 1873. In his inaugural mission statement, editor James S. Williams invited his working-class readers to 'turn aside from the turmoil and strife of the world, and find peaceful enjoyment.'[5] In addition to promoting the cause of a shorter workday, the *Ontario Workman* encouraged the self-elevation of the working class as vital to the project of nation-building and furthering working-class interests in their relations with employers. Literary historian Frank Watt dismissed much of the content of the literary pages of the *Ontario Workman* as 'didactic and hortatory doggerel in favour of the workingman's cause.'[6] The short stories, poetry, temperance tales, and advice columns in the *Ontario Workman*, however, were intended to entertain and educate the working man and his family. In recurring sections of the *Ontario*

Workman, under the headings 'The Home Circle' and 'Grains of Gold,' advice was dispensed through which the ideal of domesticity, and of the 'womanly' woman and the 'manly' man, permeated Toronto working-class culture during the early 1870s. Unfortunately, the source of the conduct and instructional literature was not always provided. Since items reproduced by stereotyped 'boiler-plate' were typically acknowledged by author or source, it seems likely that 'The Home Circle' columns were edited locally. Conduct literature, most of which was produced by women during the nineteenth century, mapped out a field of knowledge that would produce a specifically female form of subjectivity.[7] No explicit racial or ethnic identification was made in this literature. Comparisons to aristocratic and middle-class women, and associations with older traditions of Protestant dissent in some of the columns, suggest that the ideology of womanhood articulated in the columns was that of white, Anglo-Saxon, Protestant women. 'The Home Circle,' moreover, was not intended for an exclusively female audience. Bachelor readers received advice about how to select the ideal wife, and both single men and married men were encouraged to cultivate manly self-improvement in the home.

Whereas masculine subjects were understood in terms of their economic and political qualities in the public sphere, women's roles were defined as 'natural' because of their sex. In this social/masculine and natural/feminine dualism moral value was attached to gender-specific qualities possessed by women. According to 'The Home Circle,' the essence of 'womanliness' was found in the strength of a woman's heart, which sustained her husband through the vagaries of his public life. Women were tender, self-sacrificing, loving, gentle, sympathetic, courageous, and a companion to their husbands. This constituted a female form of desire different from that based on kinship and property, which had dominated marital relations before the nineteenth century. The formation of manly character required the love and reverence of a virtuous woman. 'The Home Circle' informed male readers that they needed women:

A man is sometimes overtaken with misfortunes; he meets with failure and defeat; trials and temptations beset him; and he needs one to stand by and sympathize. He has some stern battles to fight with poverty; with enemies and with sin, and he needs a woman that, while he has something to fight for, will help him to fight; that will put her lips to his ear and whisper words of council, and her hand to his heart and impart new inspirations.[8]

Woman's self-sacrifice for her husband's love was a recurring theme in discussions of marital relations. A good wife, 'The Home Circle' advised readers, 'will do anything, bear anything, suffer anything, for the sake of a husband who truly and tenderly loves her.'[9]

The domestic ideal with woman as man's moral hope and spiritual guide conferred power upon women, and gave them authority over a specific domain of knowledge – that of emotion. Another dimension of woman's power in the domestic sphere was responsibility for the management of the home and household consumption. As the manager of household resources, she had 'to study how long she must make the bag or barrel of flour last,' feed and clothe the children, and generally provide for all the wants of the family. Wives were expected not only to get by on the wages of their husbands, but to economize and build a 'nest egg.' Another column suggested that it would not compromise working men's dignity or manhood to consult their wives as to whether or not 'they should accept a reduction of wages and continue to work during the winter season, or refuse, and pass the winter in idleness.'[10] A specific form of economic relationship between the sexes was in place by the late nineteenth century, whereby men 'earn' and women 'spend.'

In columns published in 'The Home Circle,' the duties of motherhood were singled out as a married woman's paramount and all-absorbing obligation. Women were entrusted with the responsibility of training children 'to thought and virtue, to piety, and benevolence,' and of preparing them to become men and women in their turn. Motherhood bestowed upon women the obligation of moulding the character of children. During a period of mounting anxiety over the future of the nation, and of Canada's relationship with Britain, the mothering roles of women were identified as vital to the prosperity of the nation.[11]

Some of the literature published in the *Ontario Workman* was rooted in the tradition of radical Protestant dissent, which represented the family as composed of opposing and complementary genders, and situated women in a position of moral superiority.[12] As the moral guardians of future generations women were responsible for the creation of a Christian community. With the politicization of the domestic female during the nineteenth century, however, women's power of domestic surveillance extended beyond the home.

The values of the domestic woman were inscribed in the readers of the *Ontario Workman* through the instructional literature in 'The Home Circle' and in poetry, such as 'The Hand that Rocks the World.'

Blessings on the Hand of Woman!
   Angels guard its strength and grace,
In the palace, cottage, hovel –
   Oh, no matter where the place!
Would that never storms assailed it,
   Rainbows ever gently curled

For the hand that rocks the cradle
   Is the hand that rocks the world.

Infancy's the tender fountain
   Power thence with Beauty flows,
Woman's first the streamlet's guidance,
   From its soul with body grows –
Grows on for the good or evil,
   Sunlight streamed or tempest hurled,
For the hand that rocks the cradle
   Is the hand that rocks the world.

Woman, how divine your mission
   Here upon this natal sod,
Yours to keep the young heart open
   To hold the breath of God!
All true triumphs of the ages
   Are from mother love impearled,
For the hand that rocks the cradle
   Is the hand that rocks the world.

Blessings on the hand of woman!
   Father, sons, and daughters cry,
And the sacred song is mingled
   With the ownership in the sky –
Mingles where no tempest darkens,
   Rainbows evermore are curled,
For the hand that rocks the cradle
   Is the hand that rocks the world.[13]

These 'sacred' duties of motherhood were a married woman's paramount and all-absorbing obligation. Her role as a mother was defined as a 'mission,' more important than the work of missionaries in distant lands. In another column entitled 'Self-Supporting Wives,' the author stated that so important and all-consuming was woman's work in the home that it was undesirable for young married women to undertake to contribute to the family income.[14]

Providing emotional support and instilling moral virtue were the obligations of a good wife and mother. The importance of woman's nurturing role in the family was reinforced by the designation of the home as 'Mother's House.' Images of the family gathered around 'the home circle,' where comfort and happiness were found in the company of the family sitting in the evening around the fireside, were presented in several of the columns published in the *Ontario Workman*.[15] The fireside symbolized not only the site where home sentiment and familial love were instilled, but also the place where moral virtue was inculcated by a loving mother carrying out the 'natural' obligations of motherhood. The authority figure implied in the text is the mother.

Instead of speaking of their mothers with derision as the 'old woman,' sons and daughters were instructed to admire their mother more in her old age. Warrior allegories were used to delineate the veneration due an elderly woman after a lifetime of self-sacrifice caring for and raising her children to virtue. Having fought the 'good fight,' and come off the conqueror, an old woman 'stands more honorable and deserving than he who has slain his thousands or stood triumphant upon the proudest fields of victory.'[16] In this instance, the allegory served to further exalt the domestic sphere of woman in comparison to the public sphere of man.

Men were advised 'to try the habit of domesticity,' and 'they would find their labors far more remunerative in every respect than any prizes they may work for, or any investments they might make.'[17] In an editorial, J.S. Williams suggested that if employers wanted a compliant labour force, they must first ensure that the homes of working men are happy and comfortable. The domestic ideal was central to the cause of labour reform. 'One of the first duties of all parties interested in promoting the success of labor,' Williams wrote, 'is to make its homes happy.'[18]

Among contemporary feminists there has been considerable debate as to the ways in which women contributed to the construction and application of the domestic ideal, or, conversely, the extent to which we have participated in our own oppression. Rather than take a particular side, Mary Poovey has argued that both men and women were subject to the constraints imposed by the binary organization of difference.[19] While women were able to construct communities within the terms of the domestic ideal, as Carroll Smith-Rosenberg and Mary Ryan have illustrated, there were also important limitations to this ideology.[20] Women were expected to endure patiently all of the frustrations, fears, and moodiness manifested by husbands, including abusive relationships, for the sake of maintaining some semblance of the domestic ideal. This expectation was revealed in a poignant verse entitled 'For Lillie's Sake,' which was published in the 'The Home Circle.'

When papa drinks he's cross to you,
   I know, my kindest mother,
And sometimes cross, and cruel, too,

To me and little brother.
But, mamma take him back once more,
   'Twill make me feel so glad,
For he is often good and kind,
   He is not always sad.

I know that he has left us oft,
   In sickness and in need,
Nor thought about our misery,
   Your tears he gave no heed;
But should I never see him more
   My heart will surely break,
Please, mamma, take him back again,
   Just once for Lillie's sake.

My days had been as roses fair
   Ere I became his wife,
Till then I never knew a care,
   No shadow crossed my life.
But, Oh! how oft' he caused my heart
   To bleed beneath its pain,
But still, for little Lillie's sake,
   I took him back again.

The golden sun has sunken low.
   Behind the old oak's shade;
'Tis summer twilights silvery glow
   In oakland's quiet glade;
And sitting here beside him now,
   With soul to joy awake,
I don't regret I took him back,
   For little Lillie's sake.[21]

Household cleaning tips, home remedies, and recipes in 'The Home Circle' suggest other 'hidden' topics and implied opposites. For the working man, tranquil hours at home were viewed as a reward for long hours spent in the workplace. 'Yonder comes the laborer; he has borne the burden and the heat of the day; the descending sun has released him of his toil and he is hastening home to enjoy his repose.' In this depiction of blissful domestic life, the labourer's children run down the lane to greet him and 'the companion of his humble life is ready to furnish him with his plain repast.' The labourer's weariness quickly vanishes and his hardships are forgotten.[22] What the author of the column neglected to mention was that the leisure of men at home, and their freedom to pursue the work of the public sphere, was gained through an inequitable division of domestic work in the home that made men the beneficiaries of women's labour. The rhetoric of woman's sphere of domesticity substantiates a key point in the domestic-labour debate of the late 1970s and early 1980s, specifically, that women's household labour has been, and remains, vital to the perpetuation of industrial capitalism. 'A comfortable home makes the workingman all the more ready to work,' the 'Home Circle' advised women.[23]

Mothers were told to begin instructing their daughters in the feminine role of housekeeping at a young age. Helpful tips for teaching girls housekeeping appeared regularly in the *Ontario Workman*. In a column entitled 'The Training of Daughters,' mothers were advised to teach their daughters to bake cookies at the age of eight years, and that this task be presented to daughters as a great privilege. A year or two later, a young girl should be permitted to iron old collars and bosoms, with the promise that if she does this well she will be 'rewarded' with the privilege of ironing one of the nice shirts. 'As a reward for neatly hemming a handkerchief of her own she may be promoted to the hemming of pillowslips for the best bed, and this be in sensible gradation, and without any hardship, she may become a good seamstress and a good cook.'[24] By the age of fourteen a girl ought to be able to fit a pattern and cut and make her own dresses under the supervision of her mother. Education in housekeeping was intended to ensure that girls were 'fit to be married.' This view was based on the belief that a knowledge of household economy, skill in cooking, and neatness in the house would have a great deal to do with making the life of a husband pleasant and comfortable.[25]

The specific form of womanliness defined in the conduct literature held working-class women in high esteem over middle-class women. Women were understood to be different as members of classes. The differences between the classes were illuminated in columns intended to assist bachelor readers in the search for a 'suitable' wife. 'The true girl,' or the desirable woman, according to one advice column, was neither fashionable or rich. The column continues,

But, oh! What a heart she has when you find her! So large, and pure, and womanly! When you see it you wonder if those show things outside were really women ... She'll not ask you for a carriage or a first-class house. She'll wear simple dresses, and turn them when necessary, with no vulgar *magnificat* ... She'll entertain true friends on a dollar, and astonish you with the new thought how very little happiness depends on money. She'll make you love home (if you don't you are a brute), and teach you how to pity, while you scorn, a poor fashionable society that thinks itself rich, and vainly tries to think itself happy.[26]

The womanliness of the ideal working-class wife differed from perceptions of the femininity of middle-class women found in the columns. The women of the upper classes were described as 'dolls' and 'puppets,' 'reverenced today; discarded to-morrow; admired but not esteemed; ruling by passion, not affection.'[27] In contrast, mechanics' wives were portrayed as actively involved in their husbands' concerns. In an overly romanticized interpretation of nineteenth-century tenement life, one author wrote that nothing was more delightful than 'to enter the neat little tenement of the young couple, who within, perhaps, two or three years, without any resources but their own knowledge or industry, have joined heart and engaged together the responsibilities and duties, interests, trials and pleasures of life.' In the small tenement house the 'industrious wife is cheerfully employing her own hands in domestic duties,' as she prepares to welcome home her husband from his toil 'to enjoy the sweets of his little paradise.'[28]

A discourse linking love of finery and woman's character was developed in the advice columns. The artificial modesty of upper-class women who were slaves to fashion was contrasted with the 'rosy-cheeked and bright-eyed daughters' of working-class men. Working-class girls loosen their corset strings in order to breathe fresh air. They dress simply and with economy. Unlike women of the upper classes, working-class women refuse 'to pay court to silk, panniers, frills and chignon.' In 'A Woman's Defense of Dress,' the author denounced the 'wearisome shackles of fashion,' thus pointing to the agency of working-class women in challenging male privilege. A contradiction in the discourse, however, was the attraction that fashionably attired young women held for unmarried working-class men. Fashionable attire was also viewed by women of all classes as a way to attract *beaux*. Drawing on her own experience, the woman further writes: 'I have myself been to parties, and economically clad, and I was despised and rejected by men; again I have been more expensively attired, and I had more beaux than I knew what to do with.' She also recommended that bachelors court and marry working girls as they 'are accustomed to habits of economy.'[29]

The ideal of domesticity and womanhood in the conduct literature published in the *Ontario Workman* between 1872 and 1874 revealed that for women domesticity was organized around the duties of motherhood, which were defined as 'natural' to women because of their sex. The columns published in the *Ontario Workman* never suggest, however, that women were expected to spend all of their time in the domestic sphere. The domestic ideal was extended to spheres outside of the home, where a woman was also a 'friend and benefactor' in the neighbourhood and a 'devout worshipper and exemplary Christian' in the church. The amount of time spent in each sphere differed between women and men, however, with women spending the bulk of their time in the sphere that is purely 'domestic and private' and men spending more time in the sphere that is 'worldly and outward.'[30]

The 'Home Circle' columns and other literature in the *Ontario Workman* suggest that the preferred place for women and girls was in the home, where they fulfilled the duties socially defined as integral to 'true womanhood.' For historians attempting to identify the meanings of femininity for working-class women, what was left unmentioned in 'The Home Circle' is also of significance. No reference was made in the columns to women's wage work, nor was there any mention of appeals for equal pay for women performing the same work as men.

'We won't stitch up a shoetop': The Women Shoe Operatives' Strike of 1882

The first attempt to organize women workers in Toronto occurred in the boot and shoe industry in the early 1870s. This might possibly be attributed to the more centralized organization of boot and shoe production in contrast to the clothing industry, which relied extensively on outwork. The Order of the Knights of St Crispin (KOSC) was introduced in Toronto in the spring of 1869, after employers attempted to place boys and girls at work that journeymen shoemakers alone had previously done. In the late fall of 1870, the KOSC attempted to organize women operatives into a branch of the Daughters of St Crispin.[31]

The following year, in April 1871, the shoemakers at Damer, King & Co. went out on strike. The immediate crisis for the Crispins centred around the hiring of cheap unskilled labourers, namely, an old sailor, a barber, and three boys supporting their widowed mother, to carry out work that had previously been performed by their best hands, who had since removed to Cooper's shoe factory at higher wages. A Knight of St Crispin remarked that Damer, King & Co. 'seem to manifest a strong sympathy for the sons of widows, and why not the *daughters* of widows.' The other firms in the city reportedly paid women operatives from 50 cents to $1.25 per week more than did Damer, King & Co. A combination of several issues precipitated the conflict. The Crispins were dissatisfied with the quality of shoes produced. The defective uppers produced by the unskilled operatives took longer to work, which translated into reduced earnings for journeymen employed at piece rates. Other key issues in the conflict centred around the indignities heaped upon the Crispins by a company eager to bust the union and management's refusal to recognize the female-operatives union and pay a 'fair wage' to women operatives.[32]

The initial attempt to organize women workers was frustrated by an all-out assault on the KOSC by the shoe manufacturers. The comments made by an anonymous Knight of St Crispin, however, suggest that arguments about gender exclusivity among skilled male workers must be nuanced, since there were instances where men and women could work together. Like the New England shoe workers studied by Mary Blewett, Toronto women who were providing for the economic needs of a family in the absence of a male breadwinner received support from the male Knights.[33]

Despite the outcome of the struggle of 1871, the KOSC had a continuous existence in the city until they joined the Knights of Labor as Pioneer Assembly 2211 in September 1882.[34] After 1877 another organization of shoemakers was established. In that year factory operatives organized the Wholesale Boot and Shoemakers' Union. Thereafter, the KOSC included only those journeymen in the custom trade.

The Wholesale Boot and Shoemakers' Union was involved in the first major strike of women workers in Toronto. In March 1882, the union sent a circular to J.D. King & Co., Childs, Charlesworth & Co., and H.B. Hamilton containing a uniform scale of increased wage rates for women operatives. On 3 April 1882, the women operatives at the three establishments suspended work when the employers refused to grant their request for union recognition and a uniform scale of increased prices. A few days later the women operatives at Damer's, and many of the women at Cooper's, a non-union shop, joined the striking women operatives. The average weekly earnings of the best hands for the busiest twenty-six weeks in the year were: King's $6, Hamilton's $4.50, Damer's $6, Cooper's $8.50, and Charlesworth's $5. Some women earned as little as $2 per week. The women were demanding a wage increase of between 15 and 25 per cent.[35]

Some indication of the living conditions faced by independent women shoe operatives living alone in the city was revealed in a letter to the *News*, signed 'One of the Striking Girls.' 'For the last six months,' the woman wrote, 'I do not think I would average $3.50 a week; indeed, scarcely more than would pay my board.' This particular woman had seven years' experience in the trade. She indicated that a woman could not live 'respectably' on less than $7.50 a week, which was the increase the striking women were demanding. Many of her sister operatives, the woman operative revealed, were forced 'to follow a life of shame' by turning to street-walking to supplement their meagre wages.[36]

At the beginning of the strike the pro-labour *News* praised the women for the 'ladylike way' in which they had conducted themselves, bearing 'the reverses which have come upon them quietly and patiently.' 'Those who are in the habit of talking slightingly of working girls,' the reporter continued, 'should attend their meeting to be convinced that they are not only highly respectable, but remarkably intelligent.'[37] The meanings of femininity articulated in the separate-spheres discourse around woman's patience and inner strength of character were attached to the women's struggle with their employers and institutionalized in women's trade unionism. Thus, the conception of what modes of being were appropriate to wage work and collective action had been diversified to included a feminine ideal as well as a masculine one. The newspaper report further suggests that among women operatives economic concerns were paramount. 'They spoke of percentages, the conditions of female labour, the laws of supply and demand, and other matters pertaining to trade with a familiarity which showed that they had mastered the details of their business,' the *News* reporter commented.[38]

A mass meeting of the women shoe operatives' union was held on 7 April. Addresses were delivered by prominent labour reformers, including Daniel J. O'Donoghue, former labour member of the provincial legislature, John Armstrong of the Typographical Union, and Eugene Donovan, also prominent in the Typographical Union and about to embark on his brief career as editor of the *Trades Union Advocate / Wage-Worker*. All three speakers impressed upon the women the importance and advantages of trade unionism. At the meeting arrangements were made for two women from each shop to meet with the employers the following Monday. The deputation of women operatives subsequently met with the employers in the office of J.D. King. According to the *Globe*, several hours were spent discussing the problem, 'but no definite steps towards a final settlement were taken.'[39]

The next afternoon, on 11 April, the male shoemakers gathered in the meeting hall on the corner of Shuter and Victoria Streets and discussed the dispute between the female employees and the five manufacturers. During the course of the meeting, one of the male unionists declared: 'The defeat of the girl's union would also mean the defeat of the men's own union.' Also, the *Globe* remarked, 'in consequence of the female operatives being on strike there is not enough work to keep half the men employed.'[40] Motivated, therefore, both by a need to protect their own interests and a concern for the conditions of the female workers in the trade, the male shoemakers passed a motion to stop work until a settlement with the women's union was reached. Vice-President Beecher of the Toronto Trades and Labor Council (TTLC) offered the council's support and praised the stand taken by the women in the following terms: 'They behaved like men.'[41] Not only was there a measure of acceptance for the women as wage workers, but in stating that the women 'behaved like men,' Beecher was praising the women for conducting themselves in an honourable manner – with dignity and respect for individual rights. Among nineteenth-century male labour reformers these were the characteristics of a 'good' trade unionist. The gender identity of the striking women operatives was experienced in such a way that even as members of a separate women's union the women operatives were sometimes perceived as masculine.

John Giblin, an employee at Cooper's establishment, was appointed spokesman by the women's union to open negotiations with the manufacturers. Coincident with the meeting of the male shoemakers, Giblin met with employer John Cooper in another room.[42] The outcome of the various meetings held that afternoon was that the employers finally agreed to an arbitration. While Giblin functioned as an intermediary in the dispute for the female unionists, the women operatives made their own decisions and conducted their own meetings apart from the men's union. Miss Foster acted as spokesperson for the women's union and frequently chaired their meetings.[43] The women operatives had succeeded in carving out a physical space for themselves in the labour movement. They also controlled their own agenda and exercised disciplinary power over their female members.

The strike was conducted by the women with determination and militancy. Daily strike meetings fostered solidarity. Picket committees stood outside the entrances to the shoe factories and attempted to persuade non-union strikebreakers to join the union by appealing to their interests as women workers. Some of the women were self-supporting, or sole family providers, and hence had economic needs not unlike those of male household heads with families. Further inroads were made in the organization of the women operatives when, on 12 April, forty-three women from Cooper's (non-union) shop joined the union.[44] The following verse composed by one of the women operatives illustrates the resolve with which they conducted the strike:

We won't sew on a button
   Not make a button-hole;
We won't stitch up a shoetop,
   All ready for the sole,
Until the price is raised a peg.
   On all the shops' pay-roll.[45]

Throughout the lengthy strike the women received support and encouragement from the male unionists. The Wholesale Boot and Shoe Workers' Union persisted in their 'sympathy strike,' although with a concern for their own interests in the trade. They provided advice in negotiating with employers. The various trade unions in the city also provided much-needed financial assistance.[46]

At a meeting of the women operatives on 18 April the women extended the 'olive branch' to the employers. They voted to resume work on the condition that the employers give them a written pledge that a uniform bill of wages would be prepared within three weeks, with an advance of 10 per cent. Also, all of the striking women were to be reinstated in their old positions. The women firmly resolved not to abandon their union.[47]

The following day the combined men's and women's unions met in the basement of Temperance Hall. Giblin announced that the employers wanted them to resume work in the interim while a new scale of wages was prepared. The employers estimated that it would take three or four weeks to complete the list. The unionists decided not to return to work until a written pledge had been signed by all five manufacturers. A committee of women operatives met with employers Damer and Charlesworth on 20 April. The employers would settle only if the women abandoned their union and resumed work on 24 April. A uniform bill of wages was to come later. The women refused the offer following the advice of the men's union to 'stand firm.'[48]

Two days later, on 22 April, the committee of women operatives and the employers met again. The employers remained intransigent in their refusal to recognize the Female Operatives' Union, but proposed that if the women resumed work a uniform scale would be drawn up at some unspecified time in the future. The employers refused to promise a wage increase, but would guarantee that wage rates would not be lowered. Although they refused to abandon their union, the women agreed to return to work on the terms offered. The motion to resume work was supported by only two-thirds of the women operatives. Many of the women were unhappy with the settlement.[49] In terminating their strike the women operatives clearly conceded a great deal to the employers.

Some of the employers, furthermore, did not comply with the terms of the settlement. On 4 May, the *Trades Union Advocate* disclosed that after the blockade was raised, the operatives of one establishment found a man working in one of their places. A protest was made by the women. The employer informed the women that 'they might not be afraid of this "man,"' that the male machine operative 'would not make love to them.'[50] The employer defined the morality of the working girls along sexual lines. *Trades Union Advocate* editor Eugene Donovan interpreted the employer's statement differently. Donovan asked: 'Was this language which an employer, claiming a little of manhood should use to his female operatives?' He interpreted the employer's remark as an affront to the femininity of the women operatives. At another establishment, also unnamed in Donovan's editorial, the forewoman blocked the doorway, and with 'Amazonian courage discharged seventeen of her lady operatives.'[51] In this instance, the use of the warrior metaphor suggests that the brand of femininity displayed by the forewoman, specifically, that of a strong 'masculine' woman, was inappropriate. This language was viewed as an asperion on the forewoman's gender identity, and was intended as a disciplinary tactic.

Two weeks later, the *Advocate* revealed that two members of the Female Operatives' Union employed in King and Brown's factory were discharged by the forewoman, Miss Frogham, for collecting union dues from their shopmates.[52] Additional references to tensions between women operatives and forewomen appeared in the *Advocate*: 'When any of the young women in Cooper's Shoe Factory complain of infringements upon their just rights they are consoled by the "governess" with the lady-like remark, "Oh, my but you're bold!"'[53] In this instance, the grievances of the women operatives were couched in inferences from the forewoman that assertiveness was not gender-appropriate behaviour. The tension between the women operatives and the forewoman further reveals that rather than supporting gender solidarity among women workers, the forewoman was siding with management at the expense of her sister workers.

When the employers, who had subsequently organized themselves into an association, failed to produce the promised uniform scale of wages after several weeks, rumours of another strike among the women operatives surfaced. W.B. Hamilton threatened to import operatives from Montreal if the women went out on strike again. The *Trades Union Advocate* denounced the 'boss shoemakers and their promises,' calling into question the manhood of the employers, who refused to grant from their 'smallness of soul' an increase in wages to meet the increasing cost of living.[54] When the employers still had not delivered the bill of wages by October 1882, a deputation from the Female Operatives' Union, accompanied by John Armstrong, now president of the Trades and Labour Council, met with W.G. Charlesworth. Trying to mollify the group, Charlesworth announced that he would do all that was in his power to have the bill completed as soon as possible.[55]

On 6 December, seventy-five women employed by J.D. King & Co. stopped work when a Russian Jewish immigrant woman was employed on the buttonhole machines at cheaper rates than those received by the other operatives. King reluctantly met with the women, and they immediately resumed work.[56] The eagerly awaited bill of wages was not presented to the union until February 1884. Almost two years had passed since the first strike. A special meeting of the Female Operatives' Union was held on 20 February. 'The meeting was largely attended,' the *News* reported, 'and many expressed strong disapprobation at the uncalled for reduction, considering the prices the proprietors were receiving.' Wage reductions estimated at between 20 and 30 per cent were imposed by the employers. At Charlesworth's establishment, for instance, the wages of 'turners' were reduced from $1.70 per case to $0.70. 'Trimming machines had been brought into vogue, and a reduction had taken place in that branch also,' observed the *News*. At the meeting a resolution was passed denouncing Messrs. King and Charlesworth for enforcing a reduction at this season of the year.[57]

In the aftermath of the strike, the Female Shoe Operatives' Union joined the Toronto Trades and Labor Council in September 1882.[58] The women operatives were represented by Misses Swain, Grogan, and Wilson. Attendance by the delegates from the Female Shoe Operatives' Union at the meetings of the TTLC was sporadic, however. The final reference to the union in the minutes of the TTLC was for the meeting held on 21 March 1884, where the 'Women Shoe Fitters' were recorded as 'unrepresented.'[59]

Coincident with the women shoe operatives' strike, the issue of equal pay for both sexes was raised by the Toronto Trades and Labor Council shortly after its formation in August 1881 as replacement for the defunct Toronto Trades Assembly.[60] In May 1882 Eugene Donovan launched the *Trades Union Advocate*, which was renamed *The Wage-Worker* in March 1883.[61] Donovan's newspaper was not only a voice for the reorganized city central, but an early proponent of the Knights of Labor in Toronto. One of the planks of the *Advocate*'s labour platform was 'to secure for both sexes equal pay for equal work.'[62] 'As a worker,' Donovan editorialized, 'woman is man's equal in almost every respect.' Donovan qualified his comments though by suggesting that there were many callings that women could not enter into owing to their 'peculiar organism,' which periodically 'disables' them. 'Man does not have these physical difficulties to contend with,' Donovan wrote, 'yet man finds cheaper female labour gradually driving him out of the labour market.' According to Donovan, if equal pay were given for equal work, employers would certainly hire the worker that brought the greatest return for wages paid. Because of woman's 'physical limitations,' of course, men would be hired over women.[63] Donovan's appeal for equal pay for both sexes using biological justifications was intended primarily to protect the position of male workers in the labour market. He used separate-spheres rhetoric to bolster his argument. 'The physical construction of women proves that they were intended for other purposes than manual or clerical labour, and that purpose was to become a wife and mother,' Donovan commented. 'When she occupies any other she is out of her element.'[64]

In the editorial, Donovan emphasized that men only were responsible for having to compete with cheap female labour, and that they themselves brought about this 'evil.' If male workers demanded equal pay, they would drive out cheap female labour and consequently receive higher wages. For Donovan, this translated into the return of women to the home, and would secure for the working man 'a cheerful home circle when his day's toil was over.'[65] His conceptualization of equality, therefore, was not the same for both male and female workers. Donovan never successfully reconciled equality for women workers with the dominant ideology of women's sphere of domesticity.

The following week, a woman worker named Nellie wrote in a letter-to-the-editor of the *Trades Union Advocate* that she was delighted to read the article on 'Equal Pay,' and felt that if the wages of every women worker in the city were raised they would all be thankful. She remarked, however, that male union members did not always look to the interests of women workers. Nellie wrote: 'If the men ... would only speak for us a little once and while they would soon find out that all the girls would join Unions, and would not work for any less than they receive.' She added that the women were afraid to speak, 'because if we get into trouble the men will not help or advise us.'[66] Nellie interpreted Donovan's editorial from her experience as an independent working woman. She ignored the logic based on the differences between the sexes that Donovan believed would operate if equal pay were implemented. In the same issue of the *Advocate*, Donovan reported that several male wage-workers had congratulated him on the position he had taken on equal pay for the sexes, adding that the men had commented that 'they never looked at the matter in such a light before.'[67]

A few weeks later, in a lengthy letter published in the *Advocate*, W.H. Stevens criticized Donovan's equal-pay strategy as a remedy for cheap female labour competing with male labour. 'Female shoemakers and female tailors are fast taking the places men once occupied,' declared Stevens. What was needed, in Stevens's opinion, was 'a revolution in the home sphere' before 'white slavery,' in this case the abuse of women workers, could be eliminated. He wrote,

If parents and brothers, and young men generally, would by their actions encourage young girls to occupy the positions as helpmates and wives in the household they would not only be doing a service in preventing a surplus of labour in the market and thereby injuring themselves, but they would be fulfilling a great mission, that woman was intended for – the marrying state – and for which men and women present into the work, as the summit of blissful happiness.

Stevens's representation of femininity for working-class women emphasized women's identities as mothers and wives. He believed that the 'finer quality' of women's sphere ought to be encouraged in preference to the 'grosser amazonian feeling,' which wage work brought out in women.[68] Stevens's use of gender as a category to analyse women's wage work, and the content of that category, remained stable, and was consistent with dominant Victorian gender ideology.

Donovan's editorial, and the responses to it by workers of both sexes, points to internal contradictions in how Victorian definitions of femininity were displayed. The issue of equal pay for both sexes would surface again during the course of the decade. It was at the forefront of the 'equal rights' platform of the Knights of Labor.

'The Rights of Women Merit Some Attention': The Knights of Labor, Domesticity, and Equal Rights for Women

During a period of labour-movement resurgence in Ontario in the 1880s, Toronto became a focal point for Knights of Labor activity in the province. Departing from the exclusivity of craft-based unionism, the Knights attempted to organize all workers, including unskilled workers, women workers, and workers from all ethnic backgrounds.[69] Women's involvement in the Knights of Labor in Ontario did not begin with the formation of local assemblies. Women were first exposed to the Knights through socials, dances, and soirées conducted under the auspices of the assemblies to which their fathers, brothers, and boyfriends belonged.[70]

The failed women shoe operatives' strike of the spring of 1882 provided an impetus for the introduction of the Knights of Labor in Toronto. In August of that same year, the city's telegraph workers organized Morse Local Assembly 2163 and joined District Assembly 45, the National Trade Assembly for their craft. Consistent with the Knights' objective of organizing workers of both sexes, women telegraph operators joined Morse LA.[71]

The following summer Morse Assembly was involved in a strike of DA 45, the Brotherhood of Telegraphers of the United States and Canada, against the telegraph companies. On 16 July 1883, the Brotherhood of Telegraphers presented their demands, which included a 15 per cent wage increase, a reduction in hours, and equal pay for both sexes.[72] Upon receiving the telegraphers' demands, Thomas Eckert, acting president of the Western Union Telegraph Co., commented: 'The demand for both sexes shall [sic] be paid the same for like service looks to the driving of women labour from the ranks, as were the company to concede it, it would be to its interests to prefer men operators, who can be availed of for a greater variety of service than women operators.'[73] Eckert's remarks substantiate the statements made by some Toronto labour reformers, notably Eugene Donovan, about the detrimental effects the implementation of equal pay would have for women workers. Despite widespread support from the local labour movement, including the TTLC, this first real test of the Knights' principle of equal pay ended in defeat for the women telegraph operators.[74] By October 1888, the telegraphers had left the Knights of Labor and Morse LA ceased to exist.

In Canada the organization of separate women's assemblies of the Knights of Labor was initiated by Hamilton shoe operative Katie McVicar. In a series of letters to *The Palladium of Labor* in the fall of 1883, written under the pseudonym 'Canadian Girl,' McVicar exposed the plight of sewing girls and women employed as dry-goods clerks and domestic servants, and concluded that 'organization is our only hope.'[75] Another working girl told McVicar that organization would never occur if they used the traditional male techniques, and were forced 'to advertise mass meetings, mount platforms, and make speeches.' McVicar focused her attention on the problem of organizing women workers. Complaining that women lacked the necessary information to organize, McVicar called on the fathers and brothers of working women in the Knights of Labor to assist them.[76] Three weeks later assistance came from a 'A Knight of Labor.' In a letter-to-the-editor of the *Palladium*, the male 'Knight' provided the women with the information needed to organize a women's assembly of the Knights of Labor, and offered to assist them.[77] In January 1884, women shoe operatives and textile workers in Hamilton joined with male workers to form Local Assembly 3040. In April of the same year, McVicar spearheaded the organization of the first all-women's assembly in Canada, Excelsior Assembly No. 3179, composed of operatives in cotton and shoe factories.[78]

Belleville's Marie Joussaye, who would later relocate to Toronto and assist in the organization of the short-lived Workingwomen's Protective Association in 1893, joined the Knights of Labor at some point in the early years of organizing in Belleville in the mid-1880s. Joussaye, who was employed as a domestic, was studious, and read a great deal. She encouraged women to join the Knights of Labor, and like many other nineteenth-century labour reformers, she wrote poetry intended to 'Spread the Light.'[79] In a poem entitled 'Only the Working Class,' published in the *Journal of United Labor*, the official international organ of the Knights of Labor, Joussaye indicated that a woman's femininity would not be damaged by joining the Knights of Labor, since they were struggling for moral 'right.' In this case moral 'right' was equated with women's right to equality with men in the workplace. She wrote,

Do I belong to the Knights of Labor?
Well, yes, my friend, I do,
And if you'll be advised by me
You'll join our order too.
I am sure, my friend, that you will own
Our cause is right and just,
To keep the honest workingman
From being trampled in the dust.

It is not any woman's part,
We often hear folks say,
And it will mar our womanhood
To mingle in the fray.
I fear I will never understand,
Or realize it quite.
How a woman's fame can suffer
In struggling for the right.

They are only the lower classes,
Is the phrase we often meet,
And Ladies sneer at the working girls
As they pass them on the street.
They stare at us in proud disdain,
And their lips in scorn will curl,
As they pass us by we hear them say,
She is only a working girl.

Only a working girl! Thank God!
With willing hands and heart,
Able to earn my daily bread,
And in life's battle take my part.
You could offer me no title
That I'd be more proud to own,
And I stand as high in the sight of God
As the queen upon her throne.[80]

Joussaye articulated a discourse of 'respectability' for working women and helped to carve out a space for women workers in the Knights of Labor. The 'true woman' was called upon to support the cause of labour reform.

In May 1885, Samuel McNab, a local organizer for the Knights and a machinist employed at Massey's agricultural-implements factory, assisted in the organization of Hope LA 7629; the first all-women assembly in Toronto. Hope Assembly was composed of women workers from a variety of occupations, the majority of whom were tailoresses.[81] Later, in March 1887 the city's tailoresses organized an assembly, which was formally chartered in 1889 as Silver Fleece LA 409. Women also served on the executive of Toronto District Assembly 125 from its inception in 1886. For a brief period in 1889, DA 125 had a Director of Women's Work.[82]

In addition to the two women's LAs, women workers were probably present in at least three other Toronto assemblies. Morse LA 2163 of telegraphers, it will be recalled, was organized in August 1882, and Unity LA 3491 of trunk-makers was chartered in November 1884. Both assemblies were chartered before the organization of the two independent women's LAs. Hand-in-Hand LA 5743 of bookbinders, organized in March 1886, almost certainly included women who were employed in the city's binderies as folders and stitchers.[83]

As the 'peers of men,' women came under the same laws and regulations that governed men in the Knights of Labor. Domestic rhetoric was used to bring women into the movement. 'Upon motherhood we base our brotherhood, and in our family circle we pledge ourselves to defend the fair name and reputation of an innocent sister even with our lives.' Implicit in this statement, and stated explicitly by Alexander Whyte Wright in the *Canadian Labor Reformer*, was the notion that the 'potent influence of motherhood, should be enlisted in the cause.'[84] In the Knight's representation of womanhood, a woman was perceived as 'man's best advisor,' and was imparted with the gender-specific quality of sound judgment and strength of heart that was directed towards the man she loves.[85]

Entrenched in the Knights' declaration of principles and aims adopted in 1878, previous to the acceptance of women into the Order, was the stated objective of securing for both sexes equal pay for equal work.[86] For historians, questions arise concerning who benefited from this equal-pay ideology and why. 'The Knights of Labor,' *The Palladium of Labor* asserted, 'are doing more for women than any Women's Rights League ever attempted.'[87] The Order gave women equal rights in membership. The *Palladium* further stated: 'They demand equal pay for equal work, whether performed by man or woman, and by seeking to restrict the employment of women and children in factories they open the door to give employment to more men, and enable them to support wives and families in comfort, instead of dooming both men and women to continuous physical labor at wages barely sufficient to sustain life.'[88] The statements from the *Palladium* suggest that, while the Knights supported equal rights for women, they ultimately looked forward to the day when women would return to their 'natural' sphere in the home.

From the perspective of male workers, the extensive employment of women at lower wages was detrimental to their interests both as workers and as family breadwinners.[89] 'The male factory operative, salesman, clerk or telegrapher,' the *Palladium* argued, 'cannot obtain decent living wages so long as women are capable and willing to work in the same capacities for a great deal less.'[90] Working men perceived themselves as superior to their female counterparts, and believed that employers would refuse to pay higher wages to lesser-skilled women workers as a concession to workers' demands for parity. Thus, equal pay for equal work would protect the position of male workers in the workplace and further ensure a 'living wage,' or a breadwinner wage sufficient to support a male worker, his wife, and any children by preventing an influx of underpaid women workers.[91]

By the late 1880s and early 1890s, women reformers viewed women workers as a presence in the labour market that warranted attention. In 'Women as Competitors in the Labor Market,' Ethel Day MacPherson, editor of the women's column in *The Labor Advocate*, offered a solution to the 'woman question.' She wrote, 'Instead of attempting to fight the women workers, most of the unions recognize their right to work where they can, and endeavor to help them, at the same time protecting their own interests by demanding equal pay for equal work without regard to sex.'[92] 'So great has been the extension of "women's sphere" in recent years,' she continued, 'that it is now impossible to consider any labor question without taking her into account.' The metaphor of separate spheres was applied to women's involvement in the wage labour force as competitors with men. Although she recognized women as a presence in the labour force to be taken seriously as equals to men, MacPherson also accepted the argument made by male trade unionists constructed around the need to defend the status of working men in the workplace. According to MacPherson, working women were 'committing almost a crime in driving their natural protectors and providers out of their occupations by accepting wages on which a man cannot live.'[93] In her use of crime-against-nature language, MacPherson was attempting to reconcile an older political notion of equal rights with a cultural construction of sexual difference for purposes of defining a new gender category, namely that of the respectable woman factory worker.[94]

The equal-pay strategy and the organization of women workers was also perceived by both sexes as protecting the interests of women workers in the workplace. The columnists recognized that poverty, illness, or the death of a male household head forced wives and daughters into the workforce. Middle-class ideals of domesticity had little relevance in the lives of working-class women. 'All the smooth advice, the platitudes, the nice sounding phrases about "woman's sphere" and her "kingdom of home,"' reported the *Palladium*, 'relate only to the few well-cared-for, well-to-do wives and mothers, as though they represented woman-kind in general.'[95] Wage labour was perceived as enhancing the femininity of the daughters of the working class. The 'Women's Department' of the *Palladium* described the 'poorest girls' in the world as those who have never been taught to work, and who are 'petted' by rich parents. Labour reformers argued that every daughter, including the daughters of the upper classes, should be taught to earn a living, as the uncertainty of conditions in an industrial-capitalist society often resulted in the rapid disappearance of fortunes.[96]

The Knights of Labor advocated the organization of women and equal pay for equal work for the additional purpose of protecting women and girls from exploitation by employers, particularly in the city's garment trades.[97] They appealed to masculine chivalry in demanding equal pay for women workers. 'While true Knights love and honor women,' Phillips Thompson wrote using his pen-name 'Enjolras,' 'it is not only in gallant sentiment they demand equal wages for equal work, but because the better payment of women will advance her position in the world.'[98]

The need to organize women workers for purposes of securing higher wages for women was linked to the sexual morality of working girls. The Knights contributed to the 'sex debates' of the late 1880s and early 1890s, and supported seduction legislation. In an editorial in the *Canadian Labor Reformer*, A.W. Wright stated that the employment of girls in the sewing trades at wages of $2 per week was lamentable. Furthermore, independent working women could not live respectably on such low wages. Poverty forced young unmarried women living outside the family into prostitution in order to survive. The result, according to Wright, was a 'lowering of womanhood,' and the tempting of women from 'lives of virtue.'[99]

The association between poverty and vice among working girls followed on the heels of the 'Maiden Tribute' revelations in Britain, and the successful campaign in Hamilton for the commutation of the death sentence of Maria McCabe, an unmarried Hamilton domestic who killed her newborn child when the father deserted them.[100] Through his column in the *Palladium*, Phillips Thompson drew the Knights' attention to the class and gender connotations of the disclosure by the *Pall Mall Gazette* of the widespread existence of juvenile prostitution in London.

Nothing that has occurred for many years is likely to give such an impetus to the impending social revolution by which alone Labor can win its rights, as the terrible disclosures of the Pall Mall Gazette of the manner in which the privileged classes of England use their wealth, position and influence for the systematic debauchery of the female children of the poor ... Horrible, hideous, unspeakable as these revelations of the moral rottenness of the English upper classes are, they are not surprising. They merely disclose a state of things which is the natural accompaniment of the unjust and oppressive social and political system under which Labor is first robbed and then degraded.[101]

During the mid-1880s, the Canadian Knights lobbied for the incorporation of protection for women workers in the seduction legislation. The Order's concerns, however, were not realized in Charlton's bill passed in 1886. In April 1890, a series of criminal-law amendments were adopted, including an employer seduction law. The legislation, however, was narrower than the Knights would have liked. It stipulated that the 'seduced' woman must be under twenty-one years of age, of previously chaste character, and employed in a factory, mill, or workshop, and the 'seducer' had to be an employer, foreman, or workman with supervisory powers.[102]

In addressing the issue of 'moral hazards' for working women and the question of equal pay, the Knights of Labor functioned with the intent of improving conditions for women workers. Another dimension of the equal-rights discourse of the Knights, namely the question of suffrage, must be considered before any conclusions concerning the feminist purposes of the Order can be made. The Knights of Labor endorsed the enfranchisement of women at both the regional and the international level. In 1886, at a special meeting of the General Assembly held in Cleveland, the Knights supported women's suffrage. This was consistent with the objective of the Order to work for the 'complete emancipation and enfranchisement of all those who labor.'[103] This was at a time when total manhood suffrage did not exist in Ontario, and included the period between 1884 and 1889 when the Toronto Women's Suffrage Association ceased to function regularly.[104]

In the serial fiction 'Our Social Club,' probably written by Phillips Thompson, the members of the club debated recent efforts to secure women's suffrage in provincial and municipal elections. Club member Alfred Freeman, who was a carpenter by trade, an avid reader, and an ardent labour reformer, began the discussion by enthusiastically supporting women's suffrage on 'the broad general principle of democratic equality.' Another member of the club, Frank Harcourt, a book canvasser born into a middle-class English family whose parents had lost their fortune, opposed women's suffrage. Harcourt argued that women are incapable of rational thinking because they are controlled by their emotions and impulses. Freeman, by contrast, focuses on the power of the ballot as an educational device for women, and suggests that working-class women in particular need the vote. He states that '[t]he wealthy ladies who have property do not require it nearly as much as the sewing-girls, factory workers, domestic servants and others who are often wronged and abused because they have no political influence.'[105] The argument that working-class women required the vote for their own protection placed a distinct working-class slant on the debates surrounding women's suffrage. In Thompson's narrative, the working-class male character was presented as far in advance of the middle-class male characters with his support of equal rights for women.

In his 'Enjolras' column of 20 March 1886, Thompson addressed the issue of women's suffrage, criticizing the idea that women should be denied the vote on the basis of notions of woman's sphere:

The old idea of husband's proprietory right to the wife still survives in law, and to a certain extent in public sentiment. It is the basis of the opposition to woman suffrage and to the movement for woman's enfranchisement generally. It re-appears in such platitudes as that 'woman's sphere is home' – 'women have no business in politics' and the like ... That 'woman's sphere is home' is of course true in a sense, just as it would be to say, 'Man's sphere is labor.' But the falsehood lies in the implied assertion that woman is to have no interests or duties outside of her home.[106]

Thompson's use of the language of separate spheres anticipated what historians have labelled 'maternal feminism.'[107] In this instance, woman's sphere in the home was used to justify the enfranchisement of women. 'On all questions of temperance, education and social reform generally,' Thompson asserted, 'the addition to the electorate of a large body of voters who make the welfare of the house their chief consideration, will have a tendency to supply the stimulus to effective and progressive legislation that is now wanting.'[108]

The Knights of Labor, thus, represented a significant departure from nineteenth-century craft unionism with their attempts to forge a 'movement culture' that encompassed all workers. The Knights adopted an impressive array of reforms intended to improve the condition of working-class women, including equal rights in membership, equal pay for equal work, and suffrage. These reforms represented a measure of progress for working-class women. While the Knights sought to improve the conditions of women in the workplace, they looked forward to a time when women would 'return' to their 'natural' sphere in the home. The preferred place for married women was in the home carrying out the sacred duties of motherhood, which depended on a breadwinner wage for the male household head. Thus, the Order's 'feminist' reforms were not without limitations and contradictions.

'Separate spheres,' Linda Kerber writes, 'was a trope that hid its instrumentality even from those who employed it; in that sense it was deeply ambiguous.'[109] By unpacking the metaphor of separate spheres, however, historians can see how that sphere was constructed both by and for women. Separate spheres, as the analysis of the conduct literature in the *Ontario Workman* has revealed, conferred a measure of power, albeit a meagre one, upon working-class women. During the nineteenth century, a distinctively female form of desire was articulated that gave women power over the psychological realm of emotion and valued working-class women over women of the upper classes. Industrial-capitalist transformations put into place an economic relationship whereby women became responsible for household consumption. The authority to spend gave women another added measure of power in the domestic sphere. On the other hand, women's power was limited. Men were free to pursue the work of the social and public sphere because of the inequitable division of labour in the home, which made them the beneficiaries of women's domestic labour.

Separate spheres was a rhetorical construction that responded to changing social and economic conditions, including the widespread entry of women into the wage labour force beginning in the 1880s. The Knights of Labor re-coded the values of women's sphere and the ideology of womanhood for the purposes of labour reform. The rhetoric of domesticity was used to draw women into the labour movement. With the organization of women's assemblies in the Knights of Labor, women created their own 'separate sphere' in the nineteenth-century labour movement in the literal sense of physical space. Women workers could set their own agenda, control their own funds, and exercise disciplinary power over members.

The Knights of Labor, in extending women's sphere beyond the home, presented an impressive program of social reform. The equal-rights discourse constructed by the Knights around equality in membership, equal pay for both sexes, and women's suffrage represented real progress for nineteenth-century working-class women. Yet, in continuing to support domesticity at least for married women, they never articulated an ideology based on true equality. The equal-pay strategy had another dimension. In some instances it reinforced the gender division of labour in the workplace, thereby ensuring that women remained in low-paying, unskilled, or semi-skilled jobs. Thus, as members of the working class, and as workers, women were defined and shaped by gender, and gender-based exclusions were built into Toronto labour reformers' ideas of class.

'Bring the Girls into the Fold': Work, Family, and the Politics of Labour Reform in the Toronto Garment Trades

In the summer of 1897, William Lyon Mackenzie King was hired by Bert Woods, of the Toronto *Mail and Empire*, to write a series of special articles on immigrant living conditions and sweated labour in Toronto. A visit to the home of a needlewoman was described by King in his article on sweating in the local garment industry published 9 October:

A woman with a large family, some of whom were sick, was the next person visited. She was about to move to a new residence, and the clothes at which she had been working were lying with a heap of rubbish on the dirty floor. She could hardly speak with a consumptive cough, which is fast taking her life away. She had worked at the garment trade for many years, but had been unable to save enough to permit of her children getting a proper schooling. A little girl, sixteen years of age, who was thin and sickly in appearance, stood by her side and related how she had worked for eight years past for a large wholesale house most of the time at $2 a week. She now intended to help her mother at the machine. She had a little sister, nine years of age, who also sewed at a machine. Another sister got $2 a week in a large shop for making button-holes in coats, the button-hole contractor had to clear a profit after subcontracting the work. They had made up knickerbockers at five cents a pair. They were now making men's pants at from 12½ cents a pair, and were supplying the thread themselves.[1]

As King's narrative disclosed, production in the Toronto garment industry by the late 1890s was reliant on a system of outwork, particularly homework by women and children, and subcontracting to middlemen who, in turn, hired workers at low rates. The term 'sweating' was generally applied to those trades or sections of trades characterized by low wages, long hours, and an unsanitary work environment. Recent studies of the nineteenth-century garment industry have rejected interpretations that outside work and sweating represented the persistence of an antiquated pre-industrial mode of production.[2] The widespread use of sweating in the garment trades was the result of industrial growth rather than stagnation. The latter decades of the nineteenth century were further characterized as a transitional period in the clothing industry, one that witnessed the growth of the ready-made sector of the industry.[3]

The importance of women's work in the home to the growth of the garment industry during the nineteenth century has also been recognized in this historical writing. The evolution and growth of the garment industry during the nineteenth century was founded on a gender division of labour in the household. As Christine Stansell writes, 'The development of the outwork system demonstrates with particular clarity how a gender system tied to the household economy helped to divide, or segment, the work force into a sexual hierarchy that bestowed privileges upon men.'[4] The outside system, in effect, strengthened women's ties to household and family.

Representations of family and sexual difference entered into discussions about economics, the production process, and the organization of workers in the Toronto garment trades. These contests, furthermore, were about power. Strategies for labour reform in the nineteenth-century garment trades addressed issues of skill and the gender division of labour, and revealed a reciprocal relationship between work and family, and family and work. Familial images and the rhetoric of women's sphere were incorporated into the political appeals of Toronto's men and women garment workers.

The Gender Division of Labour in the Toronto Garment Industry

By 1871 the garment industry was the city's leading manufacturing sector and largest employer. Between 1871 and 1900, Toronto became a national clothing centre where ready-made garments were manufactured and then shipped across the country.[5] Timothy Eaton introduced the mail-order service in 1884 to take advantage of the growing market in the West and burgeoning local consumer demand for ready-made apparel from small tradesmen and office workers and their families. Beginning in the late 1880s, he manufactured men's shirts, women's underwear, and boys' knickerbockers in order to eliminate profits to wholesalers. In 1893 a large four-storey factory was completed at the corner of James and Yonge Street, not far from Eaton's store, and women's coats, dresses, capes, and skirts were added to the list of ready-made goods produced by the company.[6]

The late-nineteenth-century garment industry was divided roughly into four broad sectors: menswear, womenswear, hats and furs, and furnishings. The manufacture of men's and women's clothing was further divided into custom-

and ready-made goods. Unfortunately, the distinction between custom- and ready-made production was never made in the nineteenth-century decennial censuses. In each of the three decennial censuses between 1871 and 1891 (see Table 7.1), the garment industry was overwhelmingly dominated by women workers. In 1891, women and girls constituted three-quarters of all workers in the industry. The census figures, however, underestimate women's involvement in the clothing trades. The definition of a manufacturing establishment for purposes of the nineteenth-century decennial censuses was 'any place where one or several persons are engaged in manufacturing, altering, making up or changing from one shape into another, materials for sale, use or consumption.'[7] Thus, the nineteenth-century censuses omitted the substantial volume of outwork carried out by families.

The proportion of women in the trade remained lowest in the custom tailoring sector where skilled journeymen were concentrated. Traditionally, tailoring was defined as skilled men's work, although wives and daughters had always assisted with stitching in the finishing of men's clothing. The nineteenth-century custom trade in men's suits was divided into three component parts, specifically, the production of trousers, vests, and coats. The tailor's craft was further subdivided according to its three major processes of cutting, pressing, and sewing. In the artisan workshop, a journeyman tailor did the cutting and basting, and then passed the garment to a seamstress who stitched the main seams. A journeymen tailor then fitted and pressed the shoulder seams and attached the collar. Women were employed to fell the linings and stitch the buttonholes.[8]

Beginning in the 1820s and 1830s, custom tailors in Britain and the United States engaged in the production of cheap ready-made clothing during the slack season in the trade. This work was called 'slop work,' as these garments were made quickly with no fitting. The ready-made trade developed first in the men's clothing sector. Competition for outside work led merchant tailors to look for cheaper sources of labour, and women and children entered the trade in vast numbers.

A Toronto journalist reported in October 1868 that, in the manufacture of men's ready-made suits, 'frequently the industrious effects of a whole family are employed to fill the orders of the employers.' The journalist further observed, '[T]he female head of the house, a group of daughters, and perhaps the male members of the family, if no better occupation is available, turn to assist the father in adding to their means of support.'[9] Although the wives and children of tailors continued to assist in the production process, women from the surrounding neighbourhood were also hired to sew trousers and vests. Sometimes a tailor hired two or three women to work in the shop, but more often women worked at home.

TABLE 7.1 Divisions by sector, occupation, and gender in the Toronto garment industry, 1871–1891

| Year | Sector | Number of employees | | | | Total number of employees | Percentage of total city garment industry | Percentage of sector male | Percentage of sector female |
| | | Adult | | Child | | | | | |
		M	F	M	F				
1871	Womenswear	0	205	8	38	251	12.2	0.0	96.8
	Menswear	466	764	22	47	1299	63.3	37.6	62.4
	Furriers & hatters	42	114	9	17	182	8.9	28.0	72.0
	Furnishings	27	255	19	30	331	16.1	13.9	86.1
	Total	535	1338	58	132	2053	100.0	28.4	71.6
1881	Womenswear	7	393	7	76	483	17.8	2.9	97.1
	Menswear	537	927	16	23	1503	55.5	36.8	63.2
	Furriers & hatters	85	197	5	3	290	10.7	31.0	69.0
	Furnishings	44	373	7	10	434	16.0	11.8	88.2
	Total	673	1890	35	112	2710	100.0	26.1	73.9
1891	Womenswear	30	1547	15	85	1677	26.3	2.7	97.3
	Menswear	1034	1575	28	17	2654	41.7	40.0	60.0
	Furriers & hatters	230	412	4	1	647	10.2	36.2	63.8
	Furnishings	231	1126	20	15	1392	21.6	18.0	82.0
	Total	1525	4660	67	118	6370	100.0	25.0	75.0

Sources: Canada, Census of Canada 1871, vol. 3, tables XXVIII, XLVI, LV; Census of Canada 1881, vol. 3, tables XXXIX, XLI, XLVII; Census of Canada 1891, vol. 3, table 1.

The availability of a viable sewing machine by the 1850s revolutionized the manufacture of clothing. Although journeymen tailors resisted the introduction of the sewing machine and its woman operator at Walker and Hutchinson's establishment in 1852, the sewing machine significantly reduced the time necessary to manufacture a frock coat from an estimated sixteen hours and thirty-eight minutes by hand to two hours and thirty-eight minutes by machine. The sewing machine increased the rate of production by as much as 500 per cent depending on the type and quality of garment produced.

Sewing machines were a cheap and accessible labour-saving device. A domestic sewing-machine industry sprang up in Ontario during the 1860s. American sewing-machine manufacturers established agencies in Toronto, and Singer sewing machines were manufactured locally.[10] Most of the sewing machines used in small workshops, and by women homeworkers, were purchased on the hire system. Weekly or monthly instalments were made over a period of several months until the machine was paid for. Some women homeworkers, however, particularly those who were also heads of households, experienced difficulties in making the payments. In January 1888 sewing-machine agents George Hall and J.G. Abbott were brought before Magistrate Denison after charges of assault were laid by Grace Bryant. The woman testified that she had purchased a sewing machine more than a year earlier and signed an agreement to pay for it at the rate of $3 per month. Over the course of the year she had paid only $9, and was thus behind in her payments. When the agents came to her house to remove the machine she resisted. Bryant stated that she depended on it to support herself and her children. The agents assaulted the woman, bruising her cheek and blackening her eye.[11]

Another mechanical innovation introduced into the garment trades in the 1850s was the band knife, which made it possible to cut more than one garment at a time. By the 1870s, 'long knives' capable of cutting up to eighteen thicknesses of cloth were widely available. Since cutting required precision to guarantee a proper fit, it was carried out 'in-house' and remained under the purview of skilled journeymen tailors. A decade later, steam presses were introduced to replace hand irons, and devices for buttonhole-making and pocket-stitching appeared.[12]

Outwork proliferated as the local market for ready-made clothing grew during the latter decades of the nineteenth century. Many of the city's journeymen tailors became contractors and subcontractors for wholesale merchants, and for tailors who were also retailers. In Toronto, contractors limited themselves to making up one type of garment, usually either coats, vests, ladies mantles, or overcoats.[13] The system of subcontracting in the Toronto garment industry took one of three forms: (1) the cut cloth was given by a contractor to a subcontractor, who in turn employed workers in his shop, which was unconnected with the place of residence of the subcontractor, (2) the cut cloth was given by a contractor to a subcontractor who employed hands to work in his or her residence, or (3) the cloth was given directly by a wholesaler or a contractor to women homeworkers to make up their homes, where as a rule family labour was engaged to complete the work.

Louis Gurofsky, a local Jewish garment worker and labour-movement leader, testified before the 1896 Wright Commission on sweated labour that competition for contracts pitted contractor against contractor and resulted in price-cutting. He further revealed that often two contractors stood between the contractor and the actual workers who carried out the manufacturing.[14] Many of these subcontractors fared as poorly as their workers. In his 1897 newspaper article on sweating in Toronto, Mackenzie King described his visit to the home of an Italian immigrant subcontractor and his wife, who had been forced to give up the work because they had run into debt:

While they were working for a leading wholesale house they had hired four men at $5 each a week, two boys at $1 each, and one young girl at $4. Frequently they had worked themselves from four in the morning till eleven at night, and then were unable to keep out of debt. They had made Norfolk jackets, which required to be lined, pressed, etc., at from 26 to 40 cents each. After paying for gas, rent on machines, house rent, etc., they could not make ends meet.[15]

Additional changes in the production process occurred with the expansion of the ready-made sector. Garments were made in assortments, A.W. Wright reported, 'and it being no longer necessary to make each special garment to fit a particular wearer, they are cut out by machinery and then each part of the work of making up and finishing is done by men, women and children skilled in doing that particular part.' Pattern-making, sample-making, and cutting were carried out in the factory. The actual sewing, which could be divided into specialized tasks such as sewing sleeves, stitching pockets, sewing bottonholes, and sewing on buttons, was executed by women outworkers. Finishing and pressing were completed 'in-house.' 'In this way what may be called the "team work" system has arisen,' Wright remarked, and has 'practically done away with the necessity for employing completely skilled tradesmen.'[16]

A woman outworker might also work as a subcontractor. She obtained the cut cloth from the contractor or wholesaler and then hired one or two women to assist with the work in her home. A 'Knight of Labor' revealed that married women desperate for work 'persistently take out the work for less than the regular contractors' prices, and ultimately force the general rates down.'[17] Generally, women homeworkers obtained the cloth from a wholesaler, or from a contractor directly, without the intervention of a middleman. They were required to send for and deliver the bundles. By the mid-1890s large numbers of women were seen struggling up Bay Street with great bundles of clothing, some of them barely able to walk. Often baby carriages were used to carry the bundles. The outwork system strengthened women's ties to the household and the family. For married women with children, homework provided a way to contribute to the family economy while allowing them to remain at home. Outside work 'mediated the requirements of the two great employers of women's labor – families and manufacturers.'[18]

Women homeworkers lived in close proximity to wholesalers. Most lived in 'the Ward,' which was the area west of Yonge Street and above Queen Street, or the area encompassed by St John's Ward in the electoral boundaries of the 1880s. The city's labouring poor and destitute immigrants gathered here, particularly Irish immigrants escaping the potato famines during the mid-nineteenth century. Later, beginning in the 1890s Eastern European Jews took up residence in this area.[19]

Jewish garment workers would become prominent in the Toronto labour movement during the early decades of the twentieth century.[20] In 1881, however, there were only 534 Jews in Toronto, representing less than 1 per cent of the total population of the city. These early Jewish immigrants were primarily of British origin, and were merchants rather than artisans. By 1891, the Jewish population in the city had more than doubled to 1425, and increased two-fold once again over the decade to 3044 in 1901. Still, the proportion of the total city population who reported their religion as Jewish was slightly less than 2 per cent in 1901. The presence of Jewish workers in the garment trades, however, exceeded their proportion of the total city population. In 1901, Jews constituted an estimated 15 per cent of the garment workers living in St John's Ward.[21]

The Eastern European Jews who arrived in the city during the last two decades of the nineteenth century were for the most part destitute. Finding few employment opportunities when they arrived, many Jewish immigrants became peddlars, labourers, or factory operatives. Journeymen tailors with access to a small amount of capital established small businesses in the area.[22] In his discussion of 'Foreigners Who Live in Toronto' for the *Mail and Empire*, Mackenzie King reported that many Jewish immigrant men were subcontractors in the manufacture of ready-made clothing. He further stated that a large number of Eastern European Jewish men came to Toronto without their families, and sent for them later after they had saved some money. Some Jewish women did homework at piece rates for local clothing contractors, or found work in the local garment factories. In the article, King referred to American cities and the problem of 'foreigners,' meaning those of non-Anglo-Saxon racial backgrounds, who took up residence in the poorer sections of cities, thereby aiding in the creation of 'dangerous slum districts.' He advised that the tendency among the Eastern European Jewish population of Toronto to form small colonies and 'keep up the old life to which they were accustomed' must be checked. 'Only by spreading these foreign elements are they likely to become adapted to the new surroundings and properly assimilated with the general community,' King concluded.[23]

Early signs of ethnic tensions between Jewish subcontractors and non-Jewish women outworkers, which escalated during the early twentieth century, were already evident in Toronto by the late 1890s. One woman outworker who supported herself on her wages of seventy-five cents a week told King that '[t]he hours were long, from eight in the morning until six every night, incessant work, no one to talk to, for the Polish Jew who was employing her did not know much of English, and she had scarcely enough to eat.'[24]

Piece rates were more prevalent among female outworkers than among male outworkers. Gurofsky informed the Wright Commission that women outworkers in Toronto earned as little as seventy-five cents per week, although the 'usual wage' was between $3 and $4.50 a week, with $3 being considered a 'fair wage.' Wholesalers were in no way responsible for the payment of wages to employees of contractors.[25] Single women contributing to weak family economies were also tied to the household. A 'Knight of Labor' asked a local contractor how he expected the single women in his employ to live on from $1.50 to $3 per week. 'Well I'll tell you how it is,' the contractor replied, 'their brothers or father, I suppose, have to help to keep them.'[26]

The growth of the ready-made trade was accompanied by a subdivision of the labour process that resulted in more unskilled, low-paying jobs for men. 'For men who are operators,' Gurofsky stated before the Wright Commission, 'the best men get $11 a week, and the wages run down to $5 and $4.' He then described the reduction in wages that accompanied the subdivision of the labour process among pressers in the factories: 'At one time pressers used to get $2 per day. Now, instead of having one man to press the whole garment they have four. One for the seams one for the collar and so on. They pay these men from $3 to $5 per week where formerly one man would do the whole thing and make $12 per week. He had been paid as low as $9 per week and as high as $14.'[27]

According to the decennial census compilations, the overwhelming majority of women workers in the garment trades were employed in dressmaking and millinery. In this sector, women constituted fully 95 per cent of the labour force. The local trade in women's custom clothing was carried out largely by women dressmakers assisted by a few seamstresses. Twenty-five dressmaking and millinery establishments were enumerated in 1871: ten employed fewer than five workers, three between five and nine workers, five between ten and twenty workers, six between twenty-one and forty-nine workers, one between fifty and ninety-nine workers, and one over one hundred workers.[28] The classification 'dressmaker' was usually applied to a sewing woman who in effect performed many of the same tasks as tailors, specifically, measuring, drafting patterns, and cutting and pressing. Toronto dressmakers sometimes used the name 'mantua makers,' following the English classification derived from the popular eighteenth-century style of dress with back pleats stitched down to the waist. 'Seamstresses' or 'needlewomen' were typically unskilled women who performed the time-consuming task of sewing seams.[29]

Wealthy women had all of their clothing custom made. By the latter decades of the nineteenth century, middle-class women too had dresses and hats custom-made for special occasions. Dressmaking was particularly prone to seasonal variations and changes in fashion. Dressmakers had to keep abreast of all the latest fashions. This translated into greater control over the production process for dressmakers. Nineteenth-century dressmakers were consulted not only on questions of fashion, but also on questions of etiquette. Dressmakers were expected to be knowledgeable about the appropriate clothing for the various stages of mourning, and the proper attire for weddings and society functions. Definitions of middle-class femininity, which incorporated a concern for 'fashion,' thus affected the organization of the labour market. The more exclusive dressmakers came from middle-class, and even upper-class, backgrounds. They were often described as 'gentlewomen in reduced circumstances.'[30]

Of the twenty-five dressmaking and millinery establishments enumerated in 1871, eleven had women proprietors.[31] For a woman with limited capital assets, dressmaking was a means by which she might become a small proprietor, although ownership was usually combined with her own labour in the shop. Since the ability to sew well had long been important to the definition of womanhood and woman's sphere, operating a dressmaking establishment allowed a woman to earn a living while simultaneously retaining her respectability. J.H. Burnett, an unmarried Englishwoman, established a millinery, dress, and mantle shop at 95 Yonge Street in 1881. By 1886, she employed thirty seamstresses, and she had established a reputation as an 'artiste of taste and elegance' in dress- and mantle-making. Burnett's customers were reportedly drawn from 'the most fashionable class' of Torontonians. Another dressmaker patronized by the local elite during the 1880s, Mrs A.W. Miller, also an Englishwoman, started a dressmaking business in her home in 1876. The volume of business brought about a need for larger quarters, and by the mid-1880s she was established in her own shop at 100 Yonge Street.[32]

Miss Helen Gurnett, the proprietor of a small dressmaking establishment, testified before the Labour Commission in 1887 that her 'best hands' earned between $5 and $7 per week. Seasonal fluctuations characterized the local clothing trades. Commissioner John Armstrong asked Miss Gurnett whether the wages earned by women in the millinery trade were enough to support them during six months of unemployment. She replied: 'I do not think an average milliner would. Their wages are only small, they do not get large wages, that is for a season hand. They are generally not very good hands. In most shops there are only two good milliners, and they retain their situations the year round. The others are season hands, who are there three or four months, and who are then out of employment, and if they have not homes to go to they are in a rather bad position.'[33] Long periods of seasonal unemployment and low wages combined to reinforce the dependency of women garment workers on the family. The meagre wages earned by women garment workers were not sufficient to support single women boarding in the city during the 1880s. The total cost of living in 1889 for a woman over sixteen years of age without any dependants was $214.28.[34]

Gurnett further revealed that girls in her shop were apprenticed for six months. During this period they were not remunerated. The practice in several of the city's dressmaking establishments of taking in large numbers of apprentices and improvers during the peak seasons, and later dismissing them was criticized by Gurnett.[35] Another Toronto dressmaker, Miss M.J. Watson, spoke disparagingly about the absence of a system of apprenticeship in the establishment in which she had been employed for fifteen years. Commissioner Samuel Heakes asked Watson how long an apprentice should serve at dressmaking before she is considered competent. 'I don't think they could be first-class without serving three years,' Watson stated, 'but, as it is, they come without any knowledge at all, and they are supposed capable right from the first.'[36]

In the ready-made clothing trade an apprenticeship system did not exist. 'Learners' were employed, but the employer was under no obligation to teach them the trade. A.W. Wright explained,

These learners, usually girls, are kept at some trivial and easily mastered work, such as pulling out basting threads, sewing on buttons, or running up seams on a sewing machine, and then, when the term for which they agreed to work without wages expires, they are discharged, without having had an opportunity to learn any trade by which they can earn a livelihood, their places being filled by other 'learners' who are in turn defrauded out of several months of work and time.[37]

In addition to seasonal fluctuations in the trade, low wages, and the exploitation of family labour, unsanitary conditions and the spread of disease were associated with the living and working conditions of Toronto garment-trades workers. In November 1886, an outbreak of smallpox spread by a tailoress was reported by the Medical Health Officer. The tailoress had contracted the disease in a mild form, and several members of the family with whom she was living at the time became infected. Meanwhile, she continued to work at a local tailoring shop while carrying the virus. As a result, her employer and several coworkers contracted the disease. The disease quickly spread to several different parts of the city.[38]

Outbreaks of diphtheria in Toronto during the 1880s and 1890s were attributed to the living conditions of the city's garment workers, particularly where the family living quarters was used as a workshop. A local subcontractor told Mackenzie King that on one occasion he was forced to quit work when it was discovered that some of his children were sick with diphtheria. The subcontractor also indicated that he 'would not have stopped if the authorities had not found him out.'[39]

Family, Work, and the Organization of Garment Workers

In June 1882, editor Eugene Donovan announced in the *Trades Union Advocate* that the organization of a union of tailoresses in the city was being contemplated, but that no action had been taken in the matter. The young women 'eking out a miserable existence in the corset factories' were also reportedly interested in forming 'some association whereby they might advance their interests.' Donovan concluded his editorial with an offer to assist the women in their 'laudable' efforts.[40]

Over the next several weeks the *Trades Union Advocate* continued to criticize the treatment of the city's women needleworkers by employers, and urged that they be organized into a union. One scathing critique of shirt manufacturer J.M. Treble revealed that his shirt hands 'work the treadle of a sewing machine 54 or 60 hours for less than would pay for one mid-day lunch for Vanderbilt – $2.50 per week.' 'Chinese labour is bad enough,' Donovan wrote, 'but when Mr. Treble pays Chinese wages to young women for making perfect fitting shirts, the purchasers of his goods should know it.' The comparison to Chinese labour, which Toronto labour reformers fought to exclude during the latter part of the nineteenth century, was intended to foster militance among unionists. It was an injustice that the daughters of working men were remunerated at rates comparable, or below, those received by Chinese labourers. The grievance of labour reformers based on race was thus used to contest another, different grievance based on gender. The injustice done to the sewing girls was intensified with a reference to Treble's prominent role in the community as a middle-class Christian gentleman. Treble's generous financial donations to the Church, while he simultaneously permitted his women workers to labour until their constitutions were broken by hard work, was brought to the attention of the *Advocate*'s working-class readers. 'When Mr. Treble can afford to give $300 to a church he should be charitably disposed to his employees, and allow his shirt hands to lay by for broken constitutions, at least one cent per week after paying their board,' Donovan remarked.[41]

The plight of women workers in the city's garment factories was disclosed in a series of letters-to-the-editor, many of them from women factory workers or family members, that appeared in the daily *News*. 'A Factory Girl' wrote that she did not mind paying for needles and thread out of her meagre wages as much as she resented the forewoman who bestowed privileges on a handful of favourites. The forewoman in the corset factory where she was employed would 'sometimes give all the large sizes to one girl that she dislikes, and then, let her work as hard as she can, she can't make a quarter of her wages, while the girl that gets the small sizes has a soft thing.'[42]

More disclosures of abuses suffered by women factory workers soon followed. A few days later another letter signed 'Indignant' revealed that the fourteen-year-old sister of the correspondent had been whipped by a forewoman. 'Indignant' wrote that her sister was 'told to remain during noon recess, and had to partly undress, when the forewoman gave her twelve cuts with a leather strap.' According to the correspondent, the practice of 'punishing' girls was quite common in the city's factories. 'Indignant' then asked the editor of the *News* to expose the cruel treatment of factory girls. 'The girls are afraid to say much about this themselves, for fear their names get to the bosses.'[43]

Another correspondent, who signed her letter 'A Sufferer,' wrote: 'One day I spoiled a piece of work and when dinner hour came, the forewoman told me to remain. She said she would punish me for carelessness, or if I objected to that, she would dismiss me. I did not want the latter so I said she might punish me.' The correspondent then described the 'punishment' she received. The forewoman took a one-inch leather strap and fastened it around the girl's wrist. She then passed a piece of stout cord between the leather straps, and hung the cord through a pulley several inches above the ground. The girl was suspended above the ground by her wrists for more than half an hour. The correspondent indicated that '[s]carcely a day passes but a girl, sometimes two or three, are punished in this way.'[44]

The letters prompted a response from a forewoman employed in one of the city's corset factories. The forewoman revealed that she did indeed whip the girls under her supervision, but only when they 'deserve' it. She compared her position in the factory to that of a mother who 'has to punish her child, whom she is constantly looking after.' Arguments based on woman's sphere of motherhood were used by the forewoman to justify the beating of sewing girls, a significant percentage of whom were very young. 'The majority of girls who work in factories are not refined young ladies,' she wrote. 'They are a rough lot, and the fear of bodily pain is the best way to get the work out of them.'[45] The discourse about the mothering role of women in the home entered into discussions of the workplace. The forewoman viewed punishment as a 'mothering' obligation of mature women intended to ensure that the sewing girls in her charge developed into respectable women.

Subsequently, the *Trades Union Advocate* issued a rebuttal to the forewoman's letter. The text of the commentary called into question the womanliness of the forewoman. 'She cannot rate with that portion of her sex who are "a little more than angels,"' editor Eugene Donovan declared, 'when she wields with Amazonian audacity a stout leather strap upon the shoulders of delicate young girls.' Rather than being an example of ideal motherhood, this particular forewoman was represented using the warrior metaphor of the 'Amazon' – a type of masculinized femininity. In opposition to the forewoman, Donovan asserted that all young women who work for an 'honest living' are 'refined young ladies.' Working women, Donovan continued, 'profess dignity and independence of character sufficient to refuse to work under a forewoman who would even cast a reflex upon them.'[46]

The letter from the forewoman generated another round of letters-to-the-editor from working girls, both from their parents and from employers. A proprietor of a local dressmaking establishment agreed with the forewoman that punishment for girls was the only effective means of making the girls 'prompt and attentive.' 'A Father of a Family' and a mother who signed her letter 'Mrs H.' also favoured the punishment of factory girls. Mrs H., like the forewoman, viewed the punishment of boys and girls as an obligation of motherhood. 'I see that if my boys and girls are to grow up good men and women their misconduct must be corrected,' she wrote, 'and I know no more effective and wholesome means than the judicious application of the rod.' Mrs. H indicated that she whipped her children rarely, and never in anger, but the severity of the punishment when it was administered functioned as a 'deterrent power.' In a similar vein, 'A Father of a Family' wrote: 'I have three daughters. The youngest is at home, and if she commits a fault, she is punished. The second is at school, where her offences are punished, and I don't see any reason why the third, who is in a factory, should be exempt from punishment, if she is neglectful or disobedient. Girls are not such ethereal creatures that a good, sharp, chastisement will do them any harm.'[47] These particular parents viewed the use of disciplinary power in the workplace, and in the home, as a deterrent that would ultimately benefit children by making them respectable adults. Generational differences were evident in the letters, however. The factory girls tended not to share the view of those in positions of authority. In response to the letter from 'A Father of a Family,' a single woman, 'Miss H.,' wrote that 'he can require but two more legs to make him a brute.' In Miss H.'s opinion this particular father was 'unmanly.' Another correspondent appealed to the 'public morality' to protect girls both in the factory and at home, and recommended that legislation be introduced to protect minors.[48]

A few weeks later, in March 1883, a scandal occurred in local newspaper-publishing circles. The *News* accused the rival *Telegram* of slander after the latter newspaper published a sensationalized account of the conditions of women and girls employed at A. Friendly & Company's shirt factory at 15 Front Street.[49] While the proprietors of the *Telegram* eventually confessed that they had lied about conditions in the shirt factory, the pro-labour *News*, surprisingly, emerged on the side of the employers. A journalist from the *News* visited Friendly's factory and reported: 'Every one of them expressed herself thoroughly satisfied with her lot, and, what is more conclusive than words, looked satisfied.'[50]

The column generated several letters to the two newspapers from women employed in the city's garment factories. A correspondent named Katie wrote that the *Telegram* had proved itself a friend of every working girl in Toronto. She described her living conditions as follows:

Me and another girl make $3 a week each. We have got a room on Adelaide street for which we pay $1.50 a week and we board ourselves. In the morning we have bread and butter and cheese, and sometimes a bit of red herring or head-cheese or Bologna sausage to make it tasty as we have no stove to cook anything. We take our lunch with us and that is only bread and butter, and we eat it with a glass of water. At night we make tea at our landlady's stove and we pay 40 cents a week for the priviledge [*sic*] and buy our own tea.

Katie further indicated that their clothes were of such a poor quality that they were 'ashamed' to go out walking at night.[51]

Another 'One of the Girls' accused the *News* of taking great care to tell the public 'only the brightest side.' She inquired, 'What else could girls do, with the head of the establishment standing by, but appear to be contented, when they know that although their pay is small it keeps them from starvation?' A different view was presented in a letter published in the *News*. A woman who signed her letter 'An Employee' remarked: 'I am by no means one of the smartest operators, but can earn from $4 to $4.50 a week, can pay my board and keep myself respectably clothed.'[52] Although the conditions under which the sewing girls toiled clearly were deplorable, independent working women who did manage to get by emphasized, with considerable pride, that they also maintained their feminine respectability. This was contrary to middle-class representations of working girls as sexually immoral.

The women employed in the Toronto garment factories during the late nineteenth century were never simply passive victims of employers' abuses. In November 1879 the women employed at Telfer's corset factory walked off the job in procession to protest wage reductions. On 26 November, two meetings were organized that were attended by the flossers, boners, stitchers, and laundry girls employed in the factory. A spokeswoman, whose name was given only as Miss O.D. in the *Telegram*, addressed the meeting. She explained that 'this is the third time our wages have been cut down for no good reason that I can discover.' When she appealed to the strikers to stand 'manfully,' a voice in the audience admonished, 'Womanly you mean.' Miss O.D. continued: 'We will assert our rights and if necessary seek other employment before we will give in. Am I not right? ... Our flossers and our boners have been reduced a cent on the dozen, and our stitchers are docked fifteen cents, and I would ask if this is justice: is it fair?' She concluded with an appeal to her sisters 'to stand firm,' for in 'unity is strength.'[53] This group of politically active corset stitchers demanded women's right to work and a living wage. Their rights as women workers were discussed in gender terms, and gender entered into the woman corset stitchers' discussions about economics.

Later, in the midst of the disclosures of the abusive treatment of women operatives, sixty sewing-machine operators at Telfer and Harold's corset factory went on strike on 30 January 1883, after the employers announced a reduction in piece rates of 10 cents per dozen. 'When the list was presented to them,' the *News* reported, 'they tore it to pieces and left the factory in a body.' The strike ended favourably for the women, and on 1 February they resumed work at the previous scale.[54]

In the fall of 1884, fifty women operatives at Telfer's corset factory went out on strike when they were given a 'new class' of work, which translated into a reduction in wages from between $1 and $1.20 on piecework to $0.60. According to the *News*, this was the third time the women employed in the factory had gone out on strike within six weeks.[55] On each occasion the women were successful.

Throughout the early 1880s, both the Toronto Trades and Labor Council (TTLC) and the Knights of Labor encouraged the organization of tailoresses and women workers in the garment factories. On 1 December 1882 the organization committee of the TTLC reported that preliminary steps had been taken to organize the tailoresses. In its report the committee alluded to the plight of independent working women who did not earn enough to support themselves. Central to the TTLC's endorsement of the organization of women garment workers was the image of the morally adrift working girl. The committee argued that the effort to raise the standards of morality among those low-paid workers was to a large extent useless unless they were assisted to earn sufficient to keep themselves as respectable members of society.[56] Nothing apparently came out of this initiative by the TTLC to organize the tailoresses.

With the emergence of the Knights of Labor in Ontario during the early 1880s, the drive to organize women workers, particularly women garment workers, began in earnest. In May 1885, Samuel McNab, a local organizer for the Knights and a machinist employed at Massey's agricultural-implements factory assisted in the organization of Hope LA 7629, the first all-women assembly in the city. Hope Assembly consisted of women workers from a variety of occupations, but the majority of the members were tailoresses.[57]

Unlike the first Canadian women's assembly of the Knights of Labor organized in Hamilton in January 1884, which relied on male leadership, Hope Assembly was administered entirely by its women members. They organized 'socials' to heighten the visibility of the assembly in the community. A fruit social was organized by Hope LA in October 1886. On New Year's Eve a concert and ball was held in St Andrew's Hall. The self-determination of the women of Hope LA was illustrated again the following year, when steps were taken to start a cooperative shirt and ladies' underwear factory.[58]

The plight of women in the needle trades remained an important concern for male labour reformers even after the organization of Hope LA. An appeal was made in the *Canadian Labor Reformer*, the organ for the Knights in Toronto, to bring more tailoresses 'into the fold.' 'The girls' work is equally as good as that of the men,' editor A.W. Wright declared, 'but they receive little more than half men's pay, and all because the girls have no organization, while the men have.'[59] Journeymen tailors' interest in the plight of women workers was double-edged. While they were concerned with eradicating the sweated labour of women in the industry, journeymen tailors were preoccupied with protecting their position of gender privilege in the trade with the growth of the ready-made trade and the expansion of the system of outwork.

In March 1887, approximately seventy tailoresses gathered in Richmond Hall to discuss some form of organization, either under the Knights of Labor or, alternatively, as a separate trade union. A committee of men from the tailors' LA 8527, composed of Master Workman W.H. Geary, Alfred Jury, and Donald Grierson, explained the rules and constitution of the Order to the women, and the benefits of organization. Mrs Keefer from the Woman's Christian Temperance Union was present to lend the support of that organization. The committee from LA 8527 referred to a statement made by the employers that women's work was superior to that of men. Consequently, the committee told the gathering, they should set at least 'equal value' upon women's work. In this instance, the equal-pay-for-equal-work argument was used to mollify any concerns the tailoresses might have about being replaced by men. 'When the male coatmakers had applied for an increase in pay,' the *Globe* reported, 'they were told their places could be filled by ladies who were better finishers of dress coats, so those present need not fear being thrown out of work by the competition of men's labor.'[60]

Another meeting of the tailoresses was held on 28 March. The meeting was chaired by Mrs Thomlinson of Hope Assembly. Donald Grierson of Golden Fleece Assembly addressed the meeting. He described the benefits that organization would have for the tailoresses, including an increase in wages. The tailoresses voted unanimously to join the Knights of Labor, and approximately one hundred women signed then and there. Silver Fleece LA 409 was not formally chartered, however, until 1889.[61]

On 20 April the tailoresses gathered in Temperance Hall. They voted unanimously to demand a 20 per cent wage increase. The *Canadian Labor Reformer* praised the tailoresses for the 'businesslike' way in which they dealt with the question of wages. Significantly, similar comments were never made in newspaper accounts of men's union activites. The *Labor Reformer* further stated that the women would receive the support of Golden Fleece Assembly, as 'their obligation and the principles of the Order make it obligatory on all Knights to do so.'[62]

In June 1888, the women corset stitchers at the Telfer Manufacturing Company deliberately chose the busy season in the trade to demand an increase in wages. 'The girls are paid 78 cents a dozen and few can make that number in less than a day and a half, so that they get from $4 to $4.50 per week,' the *Globe* reported.[63] The women were asking for an increase of 12 cents per dozen. Telfer rejected the demand, and thirty-five women walked off the job. The forewoman, Miss Burns, was discharged by Telfer, who accused her of encouraging the women to strike. The corset stitchers, however, denied any involvement by the forewoman. Another issue behind the job action centred around working conditions. The windows in the factory had been screwed down, despite the unbearable summer heat, to prevent the women from spending their work-time flirting with the workmen in the *Empire* newspaper office across the street. The women demanded that the windows be opened.[64]

The strike lasted ten days and ended in a victory for the women. They secured an increase in piece rates of 10 per cent. In the aftermath of the strike the corset stitchers at Telfer's organized into an assembly of the Knights of Labor. This assembly, however, was short-lived.[65]

Two years later, on 25 July 1890, the corset makers at Telfer's went out on strike again. The issue in this conflict was Telfer's refusal to pay the women for extra work at cording the strips, three of which were required for each corset. Previously, Telfer had employed a woman to do only this work. She was paid a piece rate of six cents a strip, and could complete two cords per hour. When Telfer reduced her wages she quit.[66]

The *News* used the renewed conflict at Telfer's factory to reiterate its concern for the sexual morality of single working women. Vice was constructed discursively as a social problem prevalent among working-class women exclusively. On 26 July the masthead on the front page of the *News* blazoned 'White Slaves, The Trouble in Telfer's Corset Factory.' 'The oppression of working girls struggling for a bare livelihood has almost become a conflict between life and death,' the *News* disparaged. 'It is not surprising that under such pressure so many girls are driven into lives of immorality.' The stitchers at Telfer's reportedly made between $2 and $4 a week. A woman who had worked at the factory for two years stated that she made about $3 a week, but had to work very hard to make that amount. 'If I had not been living at home, I don't know what might have become of me,' she remarked.[67]

Andrew Telfer was an elder in St James Square Presbyterian Church and a pillar of the community. A former bookkeeper and manager at Telfer's establishment described him as a tyrannical employer who was unkind to his employees and cut their wages at every opportunity. He further stated that 'some of the girls were afraid to work too hard on piece work, as they expected that their wages would be reduced if they made too good a showing during the week.'[68]

The strike ended in another victory for the women. On the evening of 27 July, Telfer sent a messenger around to the various residences of the women inviting them to return to work as usual the following morning. When the women returned to work the next morning, they were informed that they would either be paid for the extra work in cording corsets or, alternatively, another woman would be paid to do the work of cording strips. The women agreed that preferably one or two women would be employed at cording strips in order to eliminate costly delays. If, however, the work was performed by the employees generally, they would be paid 18 cents per dozen extra.[69]

A male worker commented on the corset girls' strike in a letter-to-the editor of the *News*. 'What is the Trades Council doing?' he asked. 'Surely they are not going to allow these poor girls to be bested because they are not organized.'[70] In response, TTLC president Robert Glockling stated that in the aftermath of a strike at the Telfer corset factory two years earlier the labour council had persuaded the women to organize to prevent a recurrence of difficulties with their employers. He wrote:

We succeeded in organizing them, placed a goodly sum of money at their disposal, attended their meetings, encouraged and instructed them in the principles of organization – in fact did all that could be done for them. As a result, however, of preconceived ideas and a false sense of dignity, they deemed it somewhat degrading to belong to a labor organization, and it gradually fell away. There were a few who, to their credit be it said, strove to keep their organization intact, but finally it had to succumb for lack of the support of their fellow-workers in the factory.

Glockling's comment that the women found it 'degrading' to belong to a labour organization suggests that some women perceived trade unionism as an affront to their femininity. Clearly there were ambiguities and contradications among the women garment workers in defining femininity within the institutional context of trade-union participation. Glockling concluded by reiterating the previous offer made by the TTLC to assist in the organization of the women garment workers.[71]

Another attempt was made to organize the city's women garment workers under the United Garment Workers of America (UGWA). Formed in 1891, the UGWA concentrated on the men's ready-made clothing branch of the garment industry, and later branched out to other sectors of the ready-made trade. Two locals of the UGWA were chartered in Toronto in 1895: Local 99 and Local 81, composed of cloak and mantle makers. Louis Gurofsky assisted in the organization of Local 81.[72] The attempts by the UGWA to organize women workers proved unstable. At a meeting held in Richmond Hall in late March 1899, Miss Doody from Detroit, acting on behalf of the executive of the UGWA, assisted in the organization of a women's local. This union was short-lived, and another attempt at organization was made the following year. The UGWA, however, gave only limited support to the women workers under its jurisdiction. Its approach centred around the union label campaign, which was used as leverage in an attempt to convince employers to conform to union standards.[73]

The inroads made in the organization of women garment workers during the late 1880s under the Knights of Labor were temporary. Historians have attributed the difficulties in organizing women workers to a weak attachment to the labour market. Domestic obligations, the prevalence of homework in the garment industry, a view among women that wage work was only temporary before marriage, appeals to femininity and sexual morality, exclusion by male unionists, and the failure of male unionists to consider the needs of women were without a doubt detrimental to women garment workers' trade-union initiatives.[74] During the 1880s and 1890s, women workers did, however, enjoy some measure of success in their struggles with employers in the garment factories. In several instances they resisted employers' attempts to implement reductions in piece rates.

Journeymen tailors were at the forefront of protests against changes in the labour process brought about by the growth of the ready-made section during the latter decades of the nineteenth century, and by the concomitant expansion of women's outwork. On 14 March 1887, the journeymen tailors notified the merchant tailors that they would not begin any new work until the merchants adhered to the new log of prices that had been mutually agreed upon the previous week. The Merchant Tailors' Association accepted a proposed increase of 8 to 10 per cent on fine custom-made goods. They refused, however, to increase the rates paid for ready-made garments, which the journeymen had classified as 'rough work.' The following day Master Workman W.H. Geary and Secretary George Kelz of Golden Fleece LA met with J.W. Cheeseworth and H.A. Taylor of the Merchant Tailors' Association. The employers agreed to the time scale after some changes were made in the classification of goods. A week later approximately forty tailors went on strike when several members of the Merchant Tailors' Association announced that they would not pay the negotiated scale. The outcome of the strike was a victory for Golden Fleece LA 8527.[75]

With the decline of the Knights of Labor in Ontario, the custom tailors turned to the Journeymen Tailors' Union of America (JTU), which was formed earlier in 1883. In March 1890, at the invitation of Golden Fleece Assembly, General Secretary John B. Lennon from New York visited Toronto with the intent of organizing the custom tailors into a local of the JTU.[76] Local 132 was formally chartered a few weeks later.

In 1887 the JTU, through its organ *The Tailor*, issued a plea for the organization of all custom tailors: 'Our trade is specially in need of organization. Our work is largely done at our homes, our wives and children having to help. Is not a tailor as good as a machinist or blacksmith? Why should we not have workshops and tools provided as well as other mechanics? Simply because we have not except in a few instances had sufficient manhood to assert together our right and practically maintain the brotherhood of man.'[77] Not only was the relationship between masculinity and the collective interests of the unionists clearly stated, but the JTU associated the masculinity of the skilled journeyman tailor with shop work.

As for the tailors studied by Joan Scott in mid-nineteenth-century France, '[w]ork located at the shop was, by definition, skilled; work performed at home was unskilled, whether the homeworker was female or male.' Male garment workers employed in the home 'were demeaned by an implicit association with femininity' and identification with women's sphere of domesticity. The debate over the organization of the labour process, and the location of work, linked home and family. The self-exploitation associated with homework, which relied extensively on the labour of the wives and children of journeymen tailors, was seen as undermining the moral fabric of the home. 'The moral standard of any class of mechanics, and their families also, who work in their homes, is almost sure to be lowered,' *The Tailor* observed.[78]

One solution proposed by the JTU to the problem of non-union tailors working at home was the provision of 'back shops.' These were small workrooms furnished by employers at the back of merchant tailoring establishments. In some communities the local union set up back shops and charged for seat room to cover maintenance costs. According to *The Tailor*, the advantages of back shops were as follows: 'Your homes are made more pleasant by having the workshop removed from it; the hours of labor become more regular and less; work can be done to much better advantage, and for the time consumed, much more rapidly.' St Thomas tailor S.F. Simmons reported that the organization of back shops in that community had allowed them to drive out non-English-speaking 'foreigners' who went to work in a house at rates below that paid to union tailors.[79]

In June 1891, Local 132's correspondent to *The Tailor*, George Pennington, wrote that the union back shop had been abandoned in the city, but several other back shops had been since started 'with a view to have good places to work in.' Among Toronto's journeymen tailors, paying a fee for a seat in a shop remained an area of contention. 'Why pay seat room when the bill of prices remains the same, when you cannot get the extra on and above your start?' Pennington asked. Throughout the 1890s the provision of free back shops furnished by employers remained a key demand for union tailors.[80]

In his 1897 newspaper article on sweating in the Toronto garment trades, King described his visit to a union back shop in glowing terms. The shop employed only union men and every garment manufactured went out with the union label on it, 'which is a guarantee that it has been made in a shop subject to inspection, where proper sanitary conditions have been complied with, and where the hours of labour and rate of wages are such as are considered fair and right.' King concluded that the extension of union back shops was one way that the problem of sweated labour in the home might be overcome.[81]

At every annual meeting of the Trades and Labor Congress of Canada (TLCC) held following its formation in 1883 a resolution was passed calling for the abolition of sweating in the garment industry.[82] At its annual convention in September 1895, the TLCC, upon receiving a petition from the Toronto garment workers, agreed to ask the federal government to appoint a commission to investigate the sweating system as practised in Toronto, Hamilton, and Montreal.

On 29 October 1895, Alexander Whyte Wright was appointed by the Conservative government to inquire 'whether, and if so, to what extent the sweating system is practiced in the various industrial centres of the Dominion.' Wright was given only ninety days to complete his investigation. He submitted his final report on 6 March 1896. Given the time limitations of his commission, Wright decided against attempting to make visits to all the sites of production relevant to the scope of his inquiry, or to ascertain except in a 'general way' the rates of wages paid.[83] Public meetings were held in Toronto at Richmond Hall on the evenings of 8 and 9 January 1896. This occurred in the midst of a strike by the city's journeymen tailors. Among those who took an active part in the discussions were Messrs D.J. O'Donoghue, Todd, and Tweed of the Trades and Labor Council; Messrs. Love, Mackey, Davis, and Pennylegion, local contractors; Alfred Jury and Louis Gurofsky of the Garment Workers' Union; Messrs. Strachan and Sims of the custom tailors' union; and Miss Carlyle, Mr Brown, and Mr Barber, the factory inspectors resident in the city.[84] Women factory workers and homeworkers were not present at either of the two meetings.

Contrary to the position taken by the JTU, Wright stated in his final report that custom tailors, particularly married men, preferred to work at home rather than in back shops. 'Where the trade is organized the unions generally limit the number of hours per day for work in shops, and, by taking their work home, some who wish to work longer than the union rules permit, can do so without the knowledge of the union,' Wright indicated. 'The advantage of having the assistance of their families is further inducement.' Elsewhere in his report Wright cited the expansion of the ready-made trade, and the concomitant subdivision of the labour process, as the reason for the widespread use of homework. According to Wright, homework was 'but another development of the "team system," as under it the family becomes a "team."'[85]

In his recommendations, which were largely derived from similar investigations completed in New York, and from the 1888–90 House of Lords Select Committee on Sweating in Britain, Wright called for an extension of the Factories Acts to include all factories and workshops, and 'all dwellings in which more than the husband and wife are employed.'[86] Significantly, homework by women and children was excluded. Rather than advocating the abolition of homework, Wright suggested that in order to prevent the introduction of the tenement-house shop system in Canada, manufacturers and contractors should be required to provide factory inspectors with lists of persons to whom they give work to be completed outside their own factories or warehouses.

Wright further recommended that more factory inspectors be appointed, and that the Factories Acts concerning the inspection of factories and workshops be made uniform across the country. A licensing system similar to those used in Massachusetts and New York, which prohibited the manufacture of garments in living apartments except by family members, was also suggested. Licences would be granted to shops with not less than 250 cubic feet of air space for each person employed in the day, and not less than 400 cubic feet for each person employed at night, except in rooms lighted by electricity, when the allowance of air space might be less than 400 cubic feet at night.[87]

The federal government chose not to act on the report of the Wright Commission. When the issue was raised in the House of Commons on 1 April 1897, Charles Tupper cited jurisdictional problems as one reason why the recommendations could not be implemented. No distinction was made in the report between legislative remedies that were within the purview of the federal government and legislation that would have to be enacted by the provincial governments. Tupper further stated that 'owing to the pressure of other business' it was doubtful whether the government could give the legislative measures recommended by the commissioner due consideration during the session.[88]

Women employed in the custom trade in men's clothing also posed a threat to the status of journeymen tailors in the production process. Although many journeymen opposed the work of women in the custom trade, the JTU regularly called for the admission of tailoresses into local unions during the 1880s and 1890s. The underlying intent of the male unionists was, however, double-edged. On the one hand, the male unionists argued that women should be brought into the union for their own protection. The journeymen defined the interests of tailoresses in the trade in both sexual and economic terms. If prohibited from earning an 'honest living,' they argued, the women would be forced to turn to 'dishonorable means' (meaning prostitution) to earn a living. On the other hand, the organization of women workers also served the interests of men in the trade. 'What is needed is that for the same work they should have the same pay; by having them in the union this can be secured; but if they are not in the union employers will use them to cut down men's wages.'[89] According to the established gender division of labour in the garment trades, however, women performed those tasks socially defined as unskilled for which they were remunerated at comparatively lower piece rates. Although concerned with the plight of women in the trade, the 'equal pay for equal work' rhetoric of the JTU actually reinforced women's oppression in the workplace and in the home.

Like the journeymen tailors, social reformer and Toronto mayor William Howland also referred to women garment workers in sexual rather than economic terms in his testimony before the Labour Commission. Howland described the needlewomen as a 'helpless class.' He further indicated that wage cutting occurred in the contracting out of work to women homeworkers. These conditions, Howland told the commission, ultimately drew many women into prostitution. 'A good woman will die first,' Howland stated, 'but there are a great many unfortunate girls, who are young and careless and like pleasure and who have not had a good training, who are under the influence of temptation, with possible starvation, in spite of the best work they can do.' In Howland's view, the 'rooted laziness' of working-class women, rather than low wages, was the crux of the problem. For these women, Howland indicated, prostitution was a moral failing, and thus 'unavoidable' because of 'the temptation' it offered for an 'easy living.'[90]

Tailoresses were a minority presence in Local 132 during the early 1890s. Following his visit to Toronto in November 1895, JTU general secretary John B. Lennon reported: 'The cause of trade unionism is considered of first importance, and the tailors of Toronto are in consequence, men and women in the broadest and best sense.' As members of Local 132, the tailoresses carried out the domestic tasks defined as women's work. For example, following the meeting of the local trades council held on 15 November in conjunction with Lennon's visit, the women members served a 'first-class' lunch.[91]

In December, between 130 and 150 tailors and tailoresses belonging to Local 132 were locked out by the King Street West merchant tailors.[92] Employer R.J. Score stated that the issue in the lockout was an attempt on the part of the union 'to dictate to us what we shall do and what we shall not do in regard to the employment of non-union tailors, tailoresses, and dressmakers.'[93] The merchant tailors declared their firms closed to the union.

President Couch of JTU Local 132 responded that the 175 members of the union were not affected by a strike at this time anyway, as they were in the midst of the slow season in the trade. The journeymen tailors complained that the sweating system associated primarily with the work of women was weakening their position in the trade. Employers paid the union scale of $1.25 to $2.50 for making trousers, but the women who actually did the work received only 50 or 60 cents per pair. Couch explained, '[A] man who gets a lot of this work from the merchants tailors has a shop in which he employs a large number of girls, who work under a veritable sweating system, earning less than half of the price their employer gets for the work.'[94]

Surprisingly, Secretary William Merritt of JTU Local 132 continued to work at No. 31 King Street West. It was a custom of the union, Merritt disclosed, to finish the work already started previous to engaging in any job action. During the early stages of the lockout several women were initiated into JTU Local 132, many of them from shops where the workers were locked out.[95]

By January 1896 the lockout was at a standstill. On 3 February, the General Executive Board of the JTU issued an official circular asking for financial assistance from the membership to support the Toronto tailors. General Secretary Lennon reported that he had visited Toronto, and 'found the lockout to be one that the Union could in no way avoid without disbanding.'[96]

A Board of Conciliation was appointed by the province to settle the dispute.

But when the board met on 25 March there were no representatives from the Master Tailors' Association present. The ruling delivered on 9 April was in favour of the union: 'There being no dispute between the parties as to the rate of wages, we see no reason why the difficulty should not be adjusted, if the employers were desirous of it, and we are compelled to report that, in our judgment, the responsibility rests with the employers.'[97] Although the JTU referred to the resolution of the struggle as a 'drawn battle,' it was not, in effect, favourable for all of the city's tailors and tailoresses. When the men and women who had been locked out sought work at their former places of employment, a substantial percentage found that their places had been filled in the interim. The lockout also had a crippling effect on the union.

In April 1897, JTU general organizer E.S. Christopherson visited Toronto for the purpose of reorganizing Local 132. At a meeting of the tailors' union held in Richmond Hall, Christopherson made special reference to the accomplishments of the female membership. During his stay in the city he also met with a group of King Street merchants. An agreement was reached that no worker would be fired for belonging to the union.[98]

In the summer of 1897, during the course of his investigation of sweated labour and immigrant living conditions in Toronto, Mackenzie King discovered that many of the women homeworkers he interviewed were making letter carriers' uniforms.[99] On 19 September, King and his father visited Postmaster General Mulock, a family friend and colleague of King's father on the University of Toronto Senate.[100] Two days later, King was appointed by the government to study the methods used to carry out government clothing contracts.

Louis Gurofsky was King's main source for his investigations into the sweating system in Toronto. In addition to providing King with information, Gurofsky served as King's entré into the workshops and homes of the city's garment workers. He accompanied King on many of these visits. Gurofsky also provided King with letters of introduction to trade unionists in Montreal and Hamilton.[101]

Disturbed by King's revelations in his articles for the *Mail and Empire*, Mulock introduced new regulations for carrying out Post Office contracts only a few days after King was commissioned. In consultation with King, Mulock drafted an amended contract form which ensured that all work on Post Office contracts for clothing and mail bags would be carried out on the contractor's premises unless special permission was obtained from the government. It was further stipulated that henceforth the wage rates paid in the execution of the contracts must be those generally accepted as prevailing in the trade for 'competent' workmen in the district where the work was to be carried out. If these conditions were not observed the contract would be cancelled, and the contractor could also be fined.[102]

King submitted his report to the Postmaster General on 5 January 1898. The scope of his investigation extended beyond the city of Toronto, and included Montreal and Hamilton. Together the three cities had accounted for the bulk of federal-government clothing contracts over the previous decade. King's report was based almost entirely on his interviews with subcontractors and wage-earners, particularly his exchanges with Gurofsky. In his report King indicated that for 'obvious' reasons the identity of the 'informants' was not publicly exposed. Fear of instant dismissal from employment was cited as the reason for anonymity. A 'private' list of the names and addresses of those consulted by King was apparently submitted with the report for purposes of establishing its 'authenticity.'[103]

Significantly, King did not feel at liberty to interview any government con-tractors.[104] Perhaps he did not want to jeopardize his prospects for a political career by disclosing the operations of government contractors. He found that virtually all of the clothing manufactured for the federal government under the contract system had been made on premises other than those of the government contractors. Culpability for sweating was placed on the shoulders of the subcontractors, thus shifting much of the responsibility away from the govern-ment contractors.

King reported that most of the work on government clothing was actually carried out by women and girls. 'Where these have been employed in shops their wages have been, on the whole, exceedingly low,' King remarked, 'and where the work was performed in homes the prices paid were often such as to necessitate long hours of labour for a very meagre return.' In the case of women employed by subcontractors, 'the general rule has been to require a maximum amount of work for a minimum amount of pay.'[105]

According to King, the homework of women led to the 'injury of the home.' Where women were compelled to work from early morning until late at night in order to earn a living, he argued, children were neglected and the duties of the home were 'sacrificed to the imperative demands of the needle or the machine.' The abuse of women workers in the home was tied to women's mothering role in the home and the project of nation-building. 'To what degree children were thereby neglected, and the duties of the home sacrificed to the imperative demands of the needle and to the machine, are questions,' King wrote, 'the answers to which might prove to be of great and far-reaching importance. The home is still the nursery of the nation.'[106]

King offered no specific recommendations for further government action in his report. Some reform measures had already been implemented by Mulock previously in September 1897, shortly after King was commissioned. These measures were subsequently duplicated by the Militia Department. More than two years later, Mulock introduced the 'Fair Wages Resolution' in the House of Commons, which was formally passed on 17 July.[107] Contractors were required to submit a 'Fair Wages Schedule,' consisting of a list of the different classes of workers to be employed in the work along with the wage rates that were considered the minimum rate for that class. In May 1898, Toronto labour reformer Daniel J. O'Donoghue was appointed Fair Wages Officer. O'Donoghue was responsible for establishing schedules of wages for various areas of the country, investigating complaints of non-compliance, and answering enquiries concerning the fair-wages regulation.[108] A fair-wage resolution was also passed by the Ontario government on 4 April 1900.

Analogous to the previous resolutions, the legislation was intended to guarantee that workers on government contracts were remunerated at rates currently accepted in the district where the work was carried out – meaning the union wage. In an election year, the legislation was clearly aimed at winning labour-movement support. The demand for fair wages and an end to sweating was, however, a limited one. The notion of 'fairness' implied acceptance of an employment hierarchy based on gender. The 'fair wage' reaffirmed male dominance both in the craft and in the home. While male unionists benefited from the legislation, and would no longer have to worry about competition from non-union workers, the legislation was of little benefit to women garment workers, most of whom were unorganized. The gender division of labour and women's oppression in the garment trades were thus reinforced by the fair-wage legislation.

The images of family and woman's sphere incorporated into the workplace and trade-union rhetoric of garment workers and labour reformers was deeply ambiguous, and drew on a variety of representations. Gender, nevertheless, was crucial to the political appeals of Toronto garment-trades workers and the formation of work identities during the latter decades of the nineteenth century.

Custom tailors viewed the long hours, low wages, and exploitation of women and children in the garment trades as a direct result of the ready-made trade and the corruption of women's sphere. According to the JTU, the struggle was over the location of work. For journeymen tailors the solution lay in the continued separation of the spheres. Masculinity was associated with the work carried out by skilled journeymen in the shop. Work performed at home, regardless of whether the worker was male or female, was socially defined as unskilled.

Women in the garment trades were rarely described as 'skilled' workers, although dressmakers performed many of the same jobs as male tailors. Girls were taken into the garment trades as 'learners' or 'improvers.' By the late 1880s the apprenticeship system had virtually ceased to exist in the ready-made trade.

The plight of women garment-trades workers emerged as an issue among Toronto labour reformers in the early 1880s in the aftermath of disclosures in the daily press about the abusive treatment of girls employed in the factories. The rhetoric of woman's sphere of domesticity entered into discussions of the workplace and factory discipline. Forewomen imported ideas of motherhood and mothering from the home sphere into the workplace. This form of factory discipline also met with the approval of the parents of sewing girls who were concerned that their daughters be raised as examples of respectable femininity.

The independent working women who organized separate women's unions in Toronto focused on their rights as women workers and demanded justice and equal pay with male workers. While the women focused on economic concerns, middle-class reformers and some male trade unionists discussed the plight of the women garment workers in sexual terms only.

8

Conclusion

In April 1887 a poem by James Fax of Toronto entitled 'Only a Laboring Man' appeared in the *Canadian Labor Reformer*. The chorus of the poem attests to the importance of masculinity in the subjective identity of working men during the later nineteenth-century.

> I'm only a laborer, only a laborer, only a laboring man
> His dress may disguise him and you may despise him,
> If only his clothing you scan,
> But a man I am sure may be noble and pure,
> Though he's only a laboring man.[1]

Gender, as I have argued, permeated the experience and consciousness of Toronto's working-class men and women during the latter nineteenth century, and was constituted and reconstituted as labour reformers contested multiple notions of masculinity and femininity.

This book has explained the meanings of masculinity and femininity defined by late Victorian Toronto labour reformers, and by working-class men and women, as material productive activities in relation to broader social and cultural transformations, including industrial capitalism, immigration, colonialism, imperialism, and nation-building. I have argued that the meanings of gender articulated by labour reformers were integral to how power was exercised. The analysis of the meanings of masculinity for male labour reformers further contributes to the historical study of men as gendered subjects.[2]

The coded set of representations by which labour reformers articulated their own definition of working-class masculinity was not completely autonomous from that of the dominant middle-class culture. Instead, they had their own 'mechanic accents' that served working-class political purposes. Employers sought to maximize their investment in labour, and implemented measures aimed at disciplining the working class. During the early 1870s the nascent Toronto labour movement through its central institution, the Toronto Trades and Labor Council, and its organ, the *Ontario Workman*, constructed a counter-discourse that emphasized worker independence and the collective goals of trade unionism. Masculinity for labour reformers embraced the honour and class pride of working men as producers, citizens, husbands, and fathers. In addition to the institutions of the labour movement, and the various social-reform clubs and associations, fiction and poetry composed by labour's 'intellectuals' helped to both shape the message of labour reform and spread that message to a wider working-class audience.

The rhetoric of domesticity was used by labour reformers during the later nineteenth century to defend the manliness of workmen against attacks from employers. The working man as father and husband was integral to the masculine gender identity constructed by Toronto labour reformers during this period. The male worker as primary family breadwinner was at the forefront of labour reformers' conceptualizations of manhood. Yet, recent research has shown that the male-breadwinner wage was never an accurate depiction of the way the working class has supported and reproduced itself.[3] Male printing-trades workers and journeymen tailors, nevertheless, used male-breadwinner rhetoric to protect their position of gender privilege in the labour market against incursions from lesser-paid, unskilled workers, particularly women and immigrants.

Education was central to the project of 'spreading the light' of labour reform. 'Brainworkers,' notably Phillips Thompson, instructed workers in the collective goals of trade unionism, and emphasized the importance of self-elevation to the project of labour reform. Thompson was more than an activist who disseminated the message of labour reform with the intent of initiating change from within the working class. From his vantage point as a labour reformer at the centre of Knights of Labor activity in Canada during the 1880s, Thompson articulated a vision of radical political economy counter to that of the dominant middle class. He exalted the 'brotherhood of man' over 'mammon worship.' Class, gender, and race were interwoven into Thompson's narratives on political economy.

The comic art of moderate reformer and Protestant moralist J.W. Bengough relied on powerful symbols and visual images that organized the work of social reform. Through his cartoons in *Grip*, Bengough conveyed his disdain for monopoly, partisan politics, and the National Policy. Following Henry George, Bengough presented the single tax and free trade as the solution to 'the labor question.' Although both Bengough and Thompson were critical of the established churches, both remained committed to the principles of Christianity.

Consistent with recent feminist scholarship, I have argued that class, gender, and race had an autonomous but interconnected existence in the politics of nine-teenth-century labour reform. Late-nineteenth-century labour-reform discourse was based on pre-existing power relationships that privileged skilled white Anglo-Saxon Protestant working men. While the rhetoric of labour reformers typically promoted the creation of a Canadian nation that incorporated all work-ers regardless of race, unskilled immigrants and Chinese workers were effec-tively excluded as a threat to the status of Anglo-Saxon and British-Canadian workers in the workplace. Thus, at times, skill, gender, and race could frag-ment, as much as they consolidated, the working class.

Both Thompson and Bengough were vehement anti-imperialists, and both spoke in Anglo-Saxon absolutes that excluded outsiders who did not share them. In the midst of widespread anxiety about the future of the nation Thomp-son and Bengough rejected Canada's colonial relationship with Britain. Bengough's representations of 'Miss Canada' illustrate how ideas about gen-der, sexuality, and nation were used to provoke reaction to the political issues of the day, particularly the project of nation-building.

During the 1880s, Toronto labour reformers were preoccupied with the plight of women workers. Representations of femininity for working women in the *Ontario Workman* between 1872 and 1874 associated true womanhood with woman's sphere in the home, where the 'good woman' performed the care-giving obligations associated with motherhood and domesticity. Although the popular metaphor of woman's sphere is deeply ambiguous, I argue, along with other feminist historians, that we must unpack the metaphor and study how it was articulated in specific social and historical circumstances. During the later nineteenth century woman's sphere conferred a limited measure of power upon women over a specific domain of knowledge – that of emotion. Women, fur-thermore, exercised the power of domestic surveillance, which extended beyond the home into the public sphere of work. This meagre measure of power never translated into social equality between the sexes, however. Male printers and tailors used the rhetoric of separate spheres to retain their position of privi-lege in the workplace. Ultimately, male dominance both in the family and in the workplace remained intact.

The Knights of Labor extended the meaning of woman's sphere beyond the home, and presented a program of social reform that represented progress for working-class women. The Knights supported equality in membership, equal pay for both sexes, and women's suffrage. Nevertheless, the equal-rights strat-egy forged by the Knights of Labor was double-edged. Equal pay also func-tioned to reinforce the gender division of labour, and ultimately disadvantaged women workers, who were forced to work at low-paying, unskilled jobs. The

Knights of Labor, furthermore, in continuing to support domesticity, particularly for married women, never articulated a gender ideology based on true equality.

Tensions and clashes in class and gender relations can be illuminated through case studies of labour processes and the sex-labelling of jobs. Within the late-nineteenth-century Toronto printing and garment trades, definitions of skill were associated with the work of journeymen exclusively. These findings are not new, but they do, however, reinforce the writings of socialist-feminist theorists who have argued that skill classifications are socially organized around definitions of men's work as skilled and women's work as unskilled or semi-skilled, and bear little relationship to the amount of actual training or ability required to perform them.[4]

Since the publication of Harry Braverman's *Labor and Monopoly Capital* in 1974, labour historians have debated whether the fragmentation of the labour process with industrial-capitalist growth might be equated with 'deskilling.'[5] The analysis of the printing industry suggests that fragmentation actually involved a certain amount of 'reskilling.' Between roughly 1850 and 1890 press feeding was a job for unskilled women workers and boy apprentices. During the 1890s, the international pressmen's union defined the work of the press feeder as skilled men's work. In addition, the male-dominated typographical union succeeded in defining the job of linotype operator as skilled men's work during the early 1890s. This occurred despite attempts by employers to use unskilled women and boy apprentices as operators.

Toronto women who worked outside the home were limited to lesser-skilled, low-paying, and low-status jobs such as needlework in the clothing industry, and folding, collating, and stitching in bookbinding and stationary manufacture. The paltry wages earned by these women were seldom enough to support a single unmarried woman living alone in the city.

Working women, furthermore, endured abuses at the hands of supervisors and employers. In February 1883, in the midst of the disclosures about the brutal treatment of women workers in the city's garment factories, one of the women in a letter-to-the-editor of the *News* wrote that the law could not help them as it would 'kill' them to appear as witnesses. The woman, whose name was not disclosed, wrote, 'I get my share of whippings. They are bad enough when they come, but we must grin and bear it.'[6] While 'grin and bear it' was what many working women probably did, the experience of women workers was not a victimizing one. Militant women operatives in the shoemaking and garment trades successfully resisted wage cuts and employer incursions, and articulated a variant of femininity that incorporated wage work and trade-union membership.

With the expansion of the ready-made clothing trade, sweating proliferated, and was attributed to the work of women outworkers and homeworkers in the trade. Representations of family and sexual difference entered into discussions about economics, the production process, and the organization of workers in the Toronto garment trades. Debates over the organization of the labour process and the location of work linked family and work.

This study has contributed to the integration of gender and race into the writing of Canadian working-class history. It has also pointed to the importance of drawing on the approaches of both poststructuralism and historical materialism to explore the ways in which language and culture, in addition to material social relations, shaped the Canadian working-class experience.

In the late twentieth century the system of homework in the garment industry continues to rely on the relationship between work and family in a gender system that ties women to the home and perpetuates women's disadvantaged position in the labour market. In September 1996, the Ontario Ministry of Labour estimated that the province's garment industry employed between four thousand and six thousand homeworkers, the bulk of them in Toronto, and most of them women and child workers. Mei Iok, a forty-one-year-old Chinese immigrant woman living in Toronto, makes between $5 and $6 an hour sewing garments that retail for $100. The minimum wage in Ontario is $6.85 per hour. During peak periods in the trade she works twelve hours per day to meet deadlines, and does not receive overtime or vacation pay. In today's global market, however, Toronto's women and child homeworkers compete with garment workers in Third World countries who earn $1 a day.[7] The similarities with, and connection to, conditions for women and immigrant workers in late-nineteenth-century Toronto are obvious. The struggle for change, however, continues.

Notes

Chapter 1: Introduction

1 Phillips Thompson, *The Politics of Labor* (New York and Chicago 1887), 77

2 Ibid.

3 Ibid., 178

4 Michael Bliss has been a vocal opponent of the 'fragmentation' of the old Canadian nationalist historiography. See Michael Bliss, 'Privatizing the Mind: The Sundering of Canadian History, the Sundering of Canada,' *Journal of Canadian Studies* 26:4 (Winter 1991–2), 5–17. For responses by social historians, see Linda Kealey, Ruth Pierson, Joan Sangster, and Veronica Strong-Boag, 'Teaching Canadian History in the 1990s: Whose "National" History Are We Lamenting?' *Journal of Canadian Studies* 27:2 (Summer 1992), 129–31; Gregory S. Kealey, 'Class in English-Canadian Historical Writing: Neither Privatizing, Nor Sundering,' *Journal of Canadian Studies* 27:2 (Summer 1992), 123–9; Ruth Roach Pierson, 'International Trends in Women's History and Feminism: Colonization and Canadian Women's History,' *Journal of Women's History* 4:2 (Fall 1992), 146–8; Franca Iacovetta, 'Manly Militants, Cohesive Communities, and Defiant Domestics: Writing about Immigrants in Canadian Historical Scholarship,' *Labour / Le Travail* 36 (Fall 1995), 220–1

5 The structural organization of Toronto's industrialization has already received considerable scholarly attention, notably in Gregory Kealey's important study of the nineteenth-century Toronto working class. See Gregory S. Kealey, *Toronto Workers Respond to Industrial Capitalism, 1867–1892* (Toronto 1980), 18–34. See also J.M.S. Careless, *Toronto to 1918: An Illustrated History* (Toronto 1984), 109–17; and D.C. Masters, *The Rise of Toronto, 1850–1890* (Toronto 1947).

6 Gregory S. Kealey and Peter Warrian, eds, *Essays in Canadian Working Class History* (Toronto 1976), 7–8

7 In the Canadian context see Kealey, *Toronto Workers*; and Bryan D. Palmer, *A Cul-*

ture in Conflict: Skilled Workers and Industrial Capitalism in Hamilton, Ontario, 1860–1914 (Montreal 1979).

8 Joan Wallach Scott, 'Women in *The Making of the English Working Class,*' in Scott, *Gender and the Politics of History* (New York 1988), 68–90; Carolyn Steedman, 'The Price of Experience: Women and the Making of the English Working Class,' *Radical History Review* 59 (1994), 108–19; Sally Alexander, 'Women, Class and Sexual Differences in the 1830s and 1840s: Some Reflections on the Writing of a Feminist History,' *History Workshop* 17 (Spring 1984), 128; Catherine Hall, *White, Male and Middle-Class: Explorations in Feminism and History* (New York 1992), 9–13; Ava Baron, 'Gender and Labor History: Learning from the Past, Looking to the Future,' in Baron, ed., *Work Engendered: Toward a New History of American Labor* (Ithaca and London 1991), 15–16; Laura L. Frader, 'Dissent over Discourse: Labor History, Gender, and the Linguistic Turn,' *History and Theory* 34:3 (1995), 217; Anna Clark, *The Struggle for the Breeches: Gender and the Making of the British Working Class* (Berkeley and Los Angeles 1995), 2–3; Sonya O. Rose, *Limited Livelihoods: Gender and Class in Nineteenth-Century England* (Berkeley and Los Angeles 1992), 2–4

9 Janice Acton, Penny Goldsmith, and Bonnie Shepard, eds, *Women at Work in Ontario, 1850–1930* (Toronto 1974)

10 In the introduction to *Gender Conflicts*, the editors wrote that 'from the start women's history in Canada revealed a strong preoccupation with articulate, white, middle-class women.' In a polemical essay that debated the merits of women's history versus gender history from a Canadian perspective, Joan Sangster rejected the statement published in *Gender Conflicts* as 'something of a caricature,' and reasserted that class analysis was central to feminism at the time, and to the writing of Canadian women's history in particular. Franca Iacovetta and Mariana Valverde, eds, *Gender Conflicts: New Essays in Women's History* (Toronto 1992), xiii–xiv; Joan Sangster, 'Beyond Dichotomies: Reassessing Gender History and Women's History in Canada,' *left history* 3:1 (Spring/Summer 1995), 114–17

11 Anne Phillips and Barbara Taylor, 'Sex and Skill: Notes Towards a Feminist Economics,' *Feminist Review* 6 (1980), 82–4; Cynthia Cockburn, *Brothers: Male Dominance and Technological Change* (London 1983). My earlier writing on the printing trades posited an intersection of class, gender, and skill in the organization of the labour process. See Christina Burr, '"That Coming Curse – The Incompetent Compositress": Class and Gender Relations in the Toronto Typographical Union during the Late Nineteenth Century,' *Canadian Historical Review* 74:3 (September 1993), 344–66; Burr, 'Defending "The Art Preservative": Class and Gender Relations in the Printing Trades Unions, 1850–1914,' *Labour / Le Travail* 31 (Spring 1993), 47–73

12 Judith M. Bennett, 'Feminism and History,' *Gender and History* 1:3 (Autumn 1989), 251–72; Joan Hoff, 'Gender as a Postmodern Category of Paralysis,' *Women's His-*

tory Review 32 (1994), 149–68; Joy Parr, 'Gender History and Historical Practice,' *Canadian Historical Review* 76:3 (September 1995), 358–9; Sangster, 'Beyond Dichotomies,' 109–21

13 Barbara Taylor, ' "The Men Are as Bad as Their Masters ...": Socialism, Feminism and Sexual Antagonism in the London Tailoring Trade in the 1830s,' in Mary P. Ryan and Judith Walkowitz, eds, *Sex and Class in Women's History* (London 1983), 187–220

14 Scott, 'Women in *The Making*,' 72–3; Clark, *The Struggle for the Breeches*, 1–2; Bettina Bradbury, 'Women's History and Working-Class History,' *Labour / Le Travail*, 19 (Spring 1987), 23–43

15 Baron, 'Gender and Labor History,' 38–9; Mary H. Blewett, *Men, Women and Work: Class, Gender, and Protest in the New England Shoe Industry, 1798–1910* (Chicago 1988); Patricia A. Cooper, *Once a Cigar Maker: Men, Women, and Work Culture in American Cigar Factories, 1900–1919* (Urbana and Chicago 1987)

16 Joan Scott, 'Gender: A Useful Category of Historical Analysis,' in Scott, *Gender and the Politics of History*, 28–50; Laura L. Frader and Sonya O. Rose, 'Gender and the Reconstruction of European Working-Class History,' in Frader and Rose, eds, *Gender and Class in Modern Europe* (Ithaca and London 1996), 1–33

17 Michèle Barrett, 'The Concept of "Difference," ' *Feminist Review* 26 (Summer 1987), 30–3; Evelyn Brooks Higginbotham, 'African-American Women's History and the Metalanguage of Race,' *Signs* 17:2 (1992), 251–74; bell hooks, *Ain't I a Woman? Black Women and Feminism* (Boston 1981); Chandra Mohanty, 'Under Western Eyes: Feminist Scholarship and Colonial Discourses,' *Feminist Review* 30 (Autumn 1988), 60–88; Barbara Christian, 'The Race for Theory,' *Cultural Critique* 6 (Spring 1981), 51–63

18 Gisela Bock, 'Women's History and Gender History: Aspects of an International Debate,' *Gender and History* 1 (1989), 8

19 For recent Canadian historical writings that have incorporated this recognition of diversity and difference see Joy Parr, *The Gender of Breadwinners: Women, Men, and Change in Two Industrial Towns, 1880–1950* (Toronto 1990); Franca Iacovetta, *Such Hardworking People: Italian Immigrants in Postwar Toronto* (Montreal and Kingston 1992); and Ruth Frager, *Sweatshop Strife: Class, Ethnicity, and Gender in the Jewish Labour Movement of Toronto 1900–1939* (Toronto 1992).

20 My thinking here has been influenced by my reading of Himani Bannerji's writings. See Himani Bannerji, 'Introducing Racism: Notes towards an Anti-Racist Feminism,' *Resources for Feminist Research* 16:1 (March 1987), 10–12; 'Writing "India," Doing Ideology: William Jones' Construction of India as an Ideological Category,' *left history* 2:2 (Fall 1994), 5–36; and 'But Who Speaks for Us?: Experience and Agency in Conventional Feminist Paradigms,' in Bannerji, *Thinking Through: Essays on Feminism, Marxism and Anti-Racism* (Toronto 1995), 55–95.

See also the special issues of *Gender & History* and *Feminist Review* on gender, nationalism, and national identities: *Gender and History* 5:2 (Summer 1993) and *Feminist Review* 44 (Summer 1993).

21 The term 'counter-identification' is borrowed from Diane Macdonell's *Theories of Discourse: An Introduction* (Oxford and New York 1986), 112.

22 Gareth Stedman Jones, *Languages of Class: Studies in English Working Class History 1832–1982* (Cambridge 1983), 90–238; Joan Scott, 'On Language, Gender, and Working-Class History,' in Scott, *Gender and the Politics of History*, 53–67. For critiques of Scott and Stedman Jones see Bryan D. Palmer, *Descent into Discourse: The Reification of Language and the Writing of Social History* (Philadelphia 1990); see also the responses to Scott by Palmer and Christine Stansell in *International Labor and Working-Class History* 31 (Spring 1987), 14–29. For an interesting debate about the merits and promises of a post-structuralist historical approach see the book reviews by Joan Scott and Linda Gordon of each other's work in *Signs* 15:4 (Summer 1990), 848–60.

23 Lynne Marks, *Revivals and Roller Rinks: Religion, Leisure, and Identity in Late-Nineteenth-Century Small-Town Ontario* (Toronto 1996); Cecilia Morgan, *Public Men and Virtuous Women: The Gendered Languages of Religion and Politics in Upper Canada, 1791–1850* (Toronto 1996)

24 The phrase 'active-while-acted-upon' agents is taken from Bannerji, 'But Who Speaks for Us?' 82.

25 Teresa de Lauretis, *Feminist Studies / Critical Studies* (Bloomington 1986), 8; Linda Alcoff, 'Feminist Politics and Foucault: The Limits to a Collaboration,' in Dallery and Scott, eds, *Crises in Continental Philosophy* (Albany 1990), 78–80; Linda Alcoff, 'Cultural Feminism versus Post-Structuralism: The Identity Crisis in Feminist Theory,' *Signs* 13:3 (1988), 423; de Lauretis, 'Eccentric Subjects: Feminist Theory and Historical Consciousness,' *Feminist Studies* 16:1 (Spring 1990), 115–50

26 Kealey, *Toronto Workers*, 124–45; Palmer, *A Culture in Conflict*, 125–52; John Battye, 'The Nine Hour Pioneers: The Genesis of the Canadian Labour Movement,' *Labour / Le Travailleur* 4 (1979), 25–56

27 Careless, *Toronto to 1918*, 201

28 *Grip*, 1 Aug. 1874, 23 March 1878, 28 April 1883. The Orange Order, as Kealey has illustrated, had a solid working-class membership. During the nineteenth century the civic establishment was a bastion of Orange-Tory strength. Kealey, *Toronto Workers*, 98–123; Kealey, 'Orangemen and the Corporation: The Politics of Class during the Union of the Canadas,' in Victor L. Russell, ed., *Forging a Consensus: Historical Essays on Toronto* (Toronto 1984), 41–86

29 David Montgomery, *Beyond Equality: Labor and the Radical Republicans 1862–1872* (New York 1967), 215–16

30 Gene Howard Homel, '"Fading Beams of the Nineteenth-Century": Radicalism

and Early Socialism in Canada's 1890s,' *Labour / Le Travailleur* 5 (Spring 1980), 7–32

31 Ramsay Cook, *The Regenerators: Social Criticism in Late Victorian English Canada* (Toronto 1985), 153

32 Cook, *The Regenerators*, 153; Henry James Morgan, ed., *The Canadian Men and Women of the Time* (Toronto 1912), 1097–8

33 Russell Hann, 'Brainworkers and the Knights of Labor: E.E. Sheppard, Phillips Thompson, and the Toronto News, 1883–1887,' in Kealey and Warrian, *Essays in Canadian Working Class History*, 35–57; Cook, *The Regenerators*, 152–73; Kealey, *Toronto Workers*, 279–80

34 Cook, *The Regenerators*, 142–4; Carman Cumming, *Sketches from a Young Country: The Images of Grip Magazine* (Toronto 1997), 21

35 Jean Thomson Scott, *The Conditions of Female Labor in Ontario* (Toronto 1892)

36 Veronica Jane Strong-Boag, *The Parliament of Women: The National Council of Women of Canada 1893–1929* (Ottawa 1976); N.E.S. Griffiths, *The Splendid Vision: Centennial History of the National Council of Women of Canada, 1893–1993* (Ottawa 1993); Carolyn Strange, *Toronto's Girl Problem: The Perils and Pleasures of the City, 1880–1930* (Toronto 1995), 57–62; Diana Pederson, ' "Keeping Our Good Girls Good": The YWCA and the "Girl Problem," 1870–1930,' *Canadian Women's Studies* 7:4 (1986), 813–34; Alice Klein and Wayne Roberts, 'Besieged Innocence: The "Problem" and Problems of Working Women – Toronto, 1896–1914,' in Janice Acton et al., eds, *Women at Work, 1850–1930* (Toronto 1974), 211–57

37 Linda K. Kerber, 'Separate Spheres, Female Worlds, Woman's Place: The Rhetoric of Women's History,' *Journal of American History* 75:1 (June 1988), 9–39; Sonya O. Rose, 'Gender and Labor History: The Nineteenth-Century Legacy,' *International Review of Social History* 38 (1993), Supplement, 145–62

38 Christine Stansell, *City of Women: Sex and Class in New York, 1789–1860* (Urbana and Chicago 1987), 106–15

39 Phillips Thompson, *The Labor Reform Songster* (Philadelphia 1892), 13–14

Chapter 2: 'The Other Side'

1 'The Toronto Trades Assembly, How It Originated,' Toronto Trades Assembly (TTA), Minutes, vol. 6, February 1871, National Archives of Canada, MG 28 I 44

2 Gregory S. Kealey, *Toronto Workers Respond to Industrial Capitalism, 1867–1892* (Toronto 1980), 325; John Battye, 'The Nine Hour Pioneers: The Genesis of the Canadian Labour Movement,' *Labour / Le Travailleur* 4 (1979), 32. Hewitt was also active in the Orange Order, and was a Conservative party supporter.

3 Kealey, *Toronto Workers*, 130

4 *Ontario Workman*, 5 Sept. 1872; Kealey, *Toronto Workers*, 138; Ron Veruh, *Radical Rag: The Pioneer Labour Press in Canada* (Ottawa 1988), 19–23

5 Michael Denning, *Mechanic Accents: Dime Novels and Working-Class Culture in America* (London 1987); Mary Grimes, *The Knights in Fiction: Two Labor Novels of the 1880s* (Urbana and Chicago 1986), 1–23; Martha Vicinus, *The Industrial Muse: A Study of Nineteenth Century British Working-Class Literature* (New York 1974); Anna Clark, 'The Rhetoric of Chartist Domesticity: Gender, Language, and Class in the 1830s and 1840s,' *Journal of British Studies* 31 (January 1992), 62–88; Frank William Watt, 'Radicalism in English-Canadian Literature since Confederation' (Ph.D. dissertation, University of Toronto, 1957)

6 J.M.S. Careless, *Brown of the Globe: Statesman of Confederation 1860–1880, Volume Two* (Toronto and Oxford 1989), 288–300

7 *Globe*, 16 Feb., 27 Feb., 23 March, 20 May 1872

8 *Globe*, 20 May 1872; Louis James, *Fiction for the Working Man, 1830–50* (Harmondsworth 1973), 48–9; Catherine Gallagher, *The Industrial Reformation of English Fiction: Social Discourse and Narrative Form 1832–1867* (Chicago 1985), 88–110

9 George Fowler, *Language in the News: Discourse and Ideology in the Press* (London and New York 1991), 16, 208–12

10 *Globe*, 23 March 1872

11 *Globe*, 16 Feb. 1872

12 See Leonore Davidoff and Catherine Hall, *Family Fortunes: Men and Women of the English Middle Class, 1780–1850* (Chicago 1987), 229–71

13 *Globe*, 16 Feb., 23 March 1872

14 *Globe*, 15 Feb. 1872

15 *Ontario Workman*, 25 April 1872.

16 Ibid.

17 *Ontario Workman*, 18 April 1872

18 *Ontario Workman*, 22 Jan. 1874

19 *Ontario Workman*, 18 April 1872

20 *Ontario Workman*, 6 March 1873, 31 Oct. 1872. This demand for universal manhood suffrage was reiterated in editorials, and in several letters-to-the-editor of the *Ontario Workman*. However, the Macdonald government's long-awaited franchise bill, read for the first time in 1869, and announced in the Speech from the Throne in the spring of 1873, and again in the fall, was dropped in the crisis surrounding the Pacific Scandal.

21 The Election Act of 1868 gave the vote to male British subjects twenty-one years of age and older who owned, rented, or occupied real estate assessed at a minimum of $400 in cities, $300 in towns, and $200 in villages and townships. The bill, passed by the Mowat government in 1874, added to the list of eligible voters any male with an

annual income of at least $400 without regard to real estate and a new category of 'enfranchised Indians.' Attempts to extend the municipal franchise to women in 1875 and 1877 were defeated, although married and single women with property gained the right to vote for school trustees in 1850. Catherine Cleverdon, *The Woman Suffrage Movement in Canada*, 2nd ed. (Toronto 1974), 22; Randall White, *Ontario 1610–1985: A Political and Economic History* (Toronto and London 1985), 143

22 *Ontario Workman*, 30 Jan. 1872

23 Palmer, *A Culture in Conflict*, 99–100; Kealey, *Toronto Workers*, 130

24 *Ontario Workman*, 22 Aug. 1872

25 *Globe*, 15 Feb. 1872; *Ontario Workman*, 15 Aug. 1872, 10 April, 4 Sept. 1873

26 *Ontario Workman*, 23 May 1872. During the early 1870s, McCormick, an Irish Catholic, was a correspondent for Patrick Boyle's *Irish Canadian*. In 1880 he published a pamphlet entitled *Conditions of Labour and Modern Civilization*, much of it consisting of reprints of columns for the *Irish Canadian*. The articles contain an extensive critique of Malthusianism and liberal political economy. John McCormick, *Conditions of Labour and Modern Civilization* (Toronto 1880)

27 *Ontario Workman*, 18 April 1872

28 Michel Foucault has argued that during the late nineteenth century the body became directly involved as a political field. See Foucault, *Discipline and Punish: The Birth of the Prison*, trans. Alan Sheridan (New York 1979; originally 1975), 25–6.

29 See also Vicinus, *The Industrial Muse*, 95.

30 *Ontario Workman*, 4 July 1872

31 *Ontario Workman*, 17 Oct. 1872

32 *Ontario Workman*, 29 Jan. 1874

33 *Globe*, 15 Feb. 1872

34 *Ontario Workman*, 9 May, 26 Sept. 1872

35 *Ontario Workman*, 23 May 1872

36 TTA, Minutes, 2 May 1873; *Ontario Workman*, 26 June 1873

37 *Ontario Workman*, 23 Jan. 1873. Peter Bailey has argued that working-class culture was more additive than substitutive, and that workers engaged in the concurrent pursuit of 'thinking and drinking.' While I agree with Bailey's argument, my intent here is to illustrate how labour reformers used the rhetoric of working-class respectability and sobriety for political purposes. See Peter Bailey, '"Will the Real Bill Banks Please Stand Up?" Towards a Role Analysis of Mid-Victorian Working-Class Respectability,' *Journal of Social History* 12:3 (Spring 1979), 336–53.

38 *Ontario Workman*, 8 Jan. 1874

39 For a similar argument concerning Chartist domesticity, see Clark, 'The Rhetoric of Chartist Domesticity,' 62–88.

40 *Globe*, 23 March 1872; *Ontario Workman*, 9 May 1872

41 *Ontario Workman*, 18 April 1872

42 *Ontario Workman*, 23 May 1872

43 TTA, Minutes, 19 May 1871; *Coopers' Journal* II: 7 (July 1871). The lecture was attended by approximately one thousand mechanics and toilers representing various branches of industry.

44 *Ontario Workman*, 27 June 1872

45 Charles Reade, *Put Yourself in His Place* (New York 1970, reprint from 1896 edition). According to Reade's original agreement with his publisher George Smith, the novel was to be completed in thirteen instalments. Smith was to pay outright £2000, with a right of purchasing the copyright for £2000 more four months before completion. Reade was to have the exclusive right of sending early sheets to American publishers for publication after the completion of the series. On 28 May 1870, Reade presented a dramatic version of novel under the title 'Free Labour.' Malcom Elwin, *Charles Reade* (New York 1931, reissued 1969), 201–2; Elton E. Smith, *Charles Reade* (Boston 1976), 20

46 Elwin, *Charles Reade*, 206

47 *Ontario Workman*, 27 June 1872

48 Martha Vicinus, '"Helpless and Unfriended": Nineteenth-Century Domestic Melodrama,' *New Literary History* 1 (Autumn 1981), 131

49 Vicinus, *The Industrial Muse*, 114; Denning, *Mechanic Accents*, 173–5

50 Peter Brooks, *The Melodramatic Imagination: Balzac, Henry James, Melodrama, and the Mode of Excess* (New Haven and London 1976), 11–14; Vicinus, 'Nineteenth-Century Domestic Melodrama,' 127–43; David Grimsted, 'Melodrama as Echo of the Historically Voiceless,' in Tamara K. Hareven, ed., *Anonymous Americans: Explorations in Nineteenth-Century Social History* (Englewood Cliffs, NJ 1971), 80–98

51 Vicinus, 'Nineteenth-Century Domestic Melodrama,' 129

52 Born in 1840, Martin Foran grew up in rural Pennsylvania, where his father owned a farm and a cooper shop. After a brief stint in the cavalry, Foran taught school briefly and worked as an oilfield hand. In 1868 he moved to Cleveland, where he found work as a journeyman cooper. Foran helped to organize the International Coopers Union and the Industrial Congress while simultaneously attending law school. In 1882, Foran, a Democrat, was elected to Congress. He was re-elected twice before retiring to private law practice in 1899. David Montgomery, *Beyond Equality: Labor and the Radical Republicans 1862–1872* (New York 1967), 214–15

53 Denning, *Mechanic Accents*, 82–3. Denning borrows the term 'accents' from Voloshinov, a Soviet-language theorist associated with the circle of Mikhail Bakhtin. These theorists argue that the ambiguity of ideological signs comes not only from their rhetorical character, but from the different class accents with which they are inflected.

54 *Ontario Workman*, 25 July 1872

55 *Ontario Workman*, 22 Aug. 1872; emphasis in the labour press reprint

56 Vicinus, 'Nineteenth-Century Dometic Melodrama,' 139

57 Carolyn Strange, *Toronto's Girl Problem: The Perils and Pleasures of the City, 1880–1930* (Toronto 1995), 21–52

58 Foucault described this power relationship as the 'deployment of sexuality.' See Michel Foucault, *The History of Sexuality, Vol. I: An Introduction*, trans. Robert Hurley (New York 1978, 1990), 106–8.

59 *Ontario Workman*, 27 June 1872

60 Bryan D. Palmer, *Working-Class Experience: Rethinking the History of Canadian Labour, 1800–1991*, 2nd ed. (Toronto 1992), 112–16; Battye, 'The Nine Hour Pioneers,' 51–6

61 For a discussion of the British context see Anna Clark, 'Manhood, Womanhood, and the Politics of Class in Britain, 1790–1845,' in Laura L. Frader and Sonya O. Rose, eds, *Gender and Class in Modern Europe* (Ithaca and London 1996), 263–79.

Chapter 3: 'Spread the Light'

1 Russell G. Hann, 'An Early Canadian Labour Theorist,' *Bulletin of the Committee on Canadian Labour History* 4 (Autumn 1977), 38

2 T. Phillips Thompson, *The Future Government of Canada* (St Catharines 1864), 13

3 Ibid., 22

4 In the late 1890s, *Saturday Night* ran a special feature entitled the 'Newspaper Club,' where leading journalists commented on important issues of the day and replied to special-interest questions. In response to the question, 'How did you make your first $100?' Thompson stated that he received $25 for his work as a correspondent to the Montreal *Herald* during the Fenian raids, and $8 per week for his work for the Presbyterian clergymen, which lasted for only about a month before the enterprise folded. See *Saturday Night*, 21 Oct. 1899.

5 *The Political Experiences of Jimuel Briggs, D.B.* (Toronto 1873), ii

6 Ramsay Cook, *The Regenerators: Social Criticism in Late Victorian English Canada* (Toronto 1985), 157–8; *The National*, 18 Feb. 1875

7 *The National*, 8 July 1875

8 *The National*, 13 Aug. 1874

9 *The National and Weekly Sun*, 21 Oct., 3 Dec., 31 Dec. 1875. In September 1875 *The National* merged with the Sun Publishing Company and the masthead was changed to *The National and Weekly Sun*, although the paper remained independent in politics.

10 *The National*, 19 July 1879; Cook, *The Regenerators*, 158; Gregory S. Kealey and Bryan D. Palmer, *Dreaming of What Might Be: The Knights of Labor in Ontario, 1880–1900* (Toronto 1987), 303

11 *Globe*, 4 Jan. 1882

12 Bryan D. Palmer, *Working-Class Experience: Rethinking the History of Canadian Labour, 1800–1991* (Toronto 1992), 121

13 Kealey and Palmer, *Dreaming of What Might Be*

14 *News*, 26 Nov. 1883; Russell Hann, 'Brainworkers and the Knights of Labor: E.E. Sheppard, Phillips Thompson, and the Toronto News, 1883–1887,' in Gregory S. Kealey and Peter Warrian, eds, *Essays in Canadian Working-Class History* (Toronto 1976), 35–57

15 Phillips Thompson, *The Labor Reform Songster* (Philadephia 1892), 14–15

16 Mariana Valverde, *The Age of Light, Soap, and Water: Moral Reform in English Canada, 1885–1925* (Toronto 1991), 36

17 *Palladium of Labor*, 5 Jan. 1884, 17 Oct., 26 Dec. 1885

18 *Palladium of Labor*, 26 Dec. 1885

19 Ramsay Cook and Russell Hann also have attributed the authorship of 'Our Social Club' to Thompson. See Cook, *The Regenerators*, 162; Hann, 'Brainworkers and the Knights of Labor,' 40–1.

20 *Palladium of Labor*, 8 Sept., 22 Sept., 29 Sept., 6 Oct., 13 Oct., 20 Oct., 27 Oct., 3 Nov., 10 Nov., 17 Nov., 24 Nov. 1883

21 Victor Hugo, *Les Misérables*, trans. Norman Denny (London 1982), 556–7. An editorial, probably written by Thompson, appeared in the *News* following the death of Victor Hugo in May 1883, in which it was stated that Hugo was 'the ideal Democrat – the believer in the progress and freedom of humanity.' *News*, 23 May 1883

22 Hann, 'An Early Canadian Labour Theorist,' 40–1

23 The series on landlordism in Ireland, 'Troubled Ireland,' ran in the *Globe* between 15 November 1881 and 10 January 1882. Thompson's investigation of the impact of the National Policy on the cotton industry appeared in the *Globe* in nine instalments between 13 May 1882 and 10 June 1882.

24 *Globe*, 21 March, 23 March, 25 March, 28 March, 3 April, 4 April 1885

25 Hann, 'An Early Canadian Labour Theorist,' 40–1; Frank William Watt, 'Radicalism in English-Canadian Literature since Confederation' (Ph.D. dissertation, University of Toronto, 1957)

26 Thompson, *The Politics of Labor*, 9–10, 17. Thompson reiterated his critique about the inadequacies of the language of political economy in his response to a review of *The Politics of Labor* by Goldwin Smith in *The Week*. See Phillips Thompson, 'The Defective Terminology of Political Economy,' *The Week*, 29 Dec. 1887, 67.

27 Ibid., 21–2

28 Cook, *The Regenerators*, 104–22

29 *Palladium of Labor*, 8 Sept. 1883. Thompson was personally acquainted with George. He interviewed him in Ireland in December 1881 while on assignment for the *Globe*. Later, in August 1884, the Knights of Labor brought George to Hamilton for their annual labour demonstration, during which Thompson also addressed the

crowd. It was George who arranged for the publication of *The Politics of Labor*. Phillips Thompson Papers, Correspondence from Henry George, 1884–1887, National Archives of Canada, MG 29 D 71, file #10; Ramsay Cook, 'Henry George and the Poverty of Canadian Progress,' *Canadian Historical Association Historical Papers*, 1977, 143–56; *Palladium of Labor*, 9 Aug. 1884

30 *Globe*, 14 Dec. 1881

31 Gregory S. Kealey, *Toronto Workers Respond to Industrial Capitalism, 1867–1892* (Toronto 1980), 274–5; *Globe*, 16 May 1881

32 *Palladium of Labor*, 8 Aug. 1885

33 *Palladium of Labor*, 11 July 1885. Sheppard supported the military intervention in the Northwest and argued that Riel ought to be hanged for treason. Thompson, obviously, disagreed with Sheppard and used his column in *The Palladium of Labor* to present his counter-argument.

34 John L. Thomas, *Alternative America: Henry George, Edward Bellamy, Henry Demarest Lloyd and the Adversary Tradition* (London 1983), 61–3, 186–7; Cook, *The Regenerators*, 115–21

35 Thompson, *The Politics of Labor*, 28

36 Ibid., 51

37 *Palladium of Labor*, 7 June 1884

38 Kenneth Fones-Wolf, *Trade Union Gospel: Christianity and Labor in Industrial Philadelphia, 1865–1915* (Philadephia 1989), xv, 64; Lynne Marks, 'The Knights of Labor and the Salvation Army: Religion and Working-Class Culture in Ontario, 1882–1890,' *Labour / Le Travail* 28 (Fall 1991), 103–4

39 *Palladium of Labor*, 27 Oct. 1883, 2 Feb. 1884, 7 Nov. 1885

40 Cook, *The Regenerators*, 164; *Palladium of Labor*, 2 Feb. 1884

41 Thompson, *The Politics of Labor*, 178

42 Thomas, *Alternative America*, 61–2

43 *Palladium of Labor*, 6 Oct. 1883. In the summer of 1884, following the discovery of a Chinese opium den on Adelaide Street in a building occupied by a laundry, the *News* attempted to arouse public sentiment against Chinese immigration by using rhetoric that defined Chinese immigrants as morally 'degenerate.' 'It is high time that our people were roused to the magnitude of the danger to the morals and health of the community from the impending opium curse,' the *News* declared. The editor continued, 'The only way to ward it off is to keep out the Chinese. Legal measures of prevention are likely to fail on account of the clannish and secretive character of the race. They keep their concerns to themselves. They have their own codes of social regulations, their own tribunals for the punishment of offences, and their peculiar and mysterious ways which separate them from the Caucasians, and render it possible for even more abominable practices than opium-smoking to be carried on among them without detection.' *News*, 21 Aug. 1884

44 Thompson, *The Politics of Labor*, 73–4; *Palladium of Labor*, 12 July 1884

45 *Palladium of Labor*, 3 Jan. 1885. Much of this column also appeared later in *The Politics of Labor*, 95.

46 *Palladium of Labor*, 3 Nov. 1883

47 *Palladium of Labor*, 19 July 1884; *News*, 11 Jan., 17 July, 27 Dec. 1884

48 *Palladium of Labor*, 26 Jan., 19 July 1884; *News*, 11 Jan., 3 July 1884, 14 Aug. 1885

49 *Palladium of Labor*, 19 July 1884. As Enjolras, Thompson also commented on the revelations made by William Stead in the *Pall Mall Gazette* and his 'Maiden Tribute to Modern Babylon' in Britain. He wrote: 'For generations this over-fed lazy and worthless crew have been rioting in luxury at the expense of the workers. They have robbed them of their lands, they have robbed them of their manhood, of their means of existence, of their rightful share in the government of the country – why should they hestiate at robbing their daughters of their virtue? From beginning to end, the British governmental and social system is based on robbery, oppression, injustice and all manner of infamy.' *Palladium of Labor*, 18 July 1885. See also Karen Dubinsky, *Improper Advances: Rape and Heterosexual Conflict in Ontario, 1880–1919* (Chicago 1993), 66–71.

50 *News*, 16 July 1884. As Russell Hann has indicated, editorial material in the *News* is easily attributed to either Sheppard or Thompson. Sheppard's editorials are characterized by short, broken sentences intended for emotional impact. Thompson's editorials were well argued and written in tight paragraph format. Thompson produced most of the editorial material published in the *News*. Hann, 'Brainworkers and the Knights of Labor,' 200

51 *News*, 18 July 1884

52 Carl Berger, *The Sense of Power: Studies in the Ideas of Canadian Imperialism 1867–1914* (Toronto 1970), 5; P.B. Waite, *Canada 1874–1896: Arduous Destiny* (Toronto 1971), 201

53 Berger, *The Sense of Power*, 117–18. In 1884 the Toronto Trades and Labor Council and the Knights of Labor confronted the Imperial Federationists over the celebration of the city's Semi-Centennial. Previously, in December 1883, the trades assembly expressed its opposition to the celebration, noting that the committee appointed to organize the celebrations held their meetings during working hours, and thus excluded workers from taking part. The local Typographical Union also complained that the bulk of the printing of circulars for the celebrations was completed in rat offices. The organization committee set aside 3 July 1884 as 'Loyalist Day.' In the aftermath of the celebration, William Rowe, editor of *The Palladium of Labor*, declared that those in charge of the demonstration had perverted its spirit with their self-glorification and anti-Canadian speeches that exalted the British connection. Rowe further remarked that nearly all the working men of Toronto believed in democracy, and they 'have no faith in alien government or institutions modelled

upon those of Britain in which the basic idea is that of caste and class prerogative.'
Predictably, the *News* was also critical of the Loyalist Day celebrations and of
'Denison's diatribe' before the crowd assembled for the anniversary, wherein Denison described the advocates of Independence as 'Bohemians' and 'men without any
stake in the country.' See Berger, *The Sense of Power*, 78–84; TTLC, Minutes,
7 Dec. 1883, National Archives of Canada, MG 28 I 44; *Palladium of Labor*, 5 July
1884; *News*, 4 July 1884

54 *Palladium of Labor*, 16 May 1885
55 *Palladium of Labor*, 13 Sept. 1884
56 Ibid.; *News*, 15 Feb. 1884
57 *News*, 28 May 1885
58 *News*, 12 Dec. 1883. A few days later, a letter-to-the-editor signed 'Struggler,' and
probably composed by a woman, appeared in the *News*. The correspondent wrote:
'The ground you take is the only safe one. Women are entitled to the franchise
because they are women, or not at all. For my part I cannot see how there can be any
two sides to the question. No country can afford to deal injustly [*sic*] with any class
of its people. The law is simply and only a compact or agreement by which the
people of a country agree to regulate their conduct towards each other; and to say to
any class that they must be bound by this agreement, while refusing them all a voice
in the making of it, is such an injustice that I can only wonder than men can be found
with so little sense of shame as to advocate it.' *News*, 14 Dec. 1883
59 *Palladium of Labor*, 20 March 1886
60 *Palladium of Labor*, 12 April 1884, 5 Sept. 1885, 8 May 1886
61 *Palladium of Labor*, 5 Sept. 1885. Thompson never provided the actual names of the
'party heelers' he was referring to in his columns. By the 1880s, however, a number
of leading Toronto labour reformers had been rewarded for their services to the Conservative party. For instance, printer and former editor of the *Ontario Workman* J.S.
Williams was a full-time party organizer, and cooper John Hewitt had gone to work
as a clerk at the Toronto Water Works. As a reward for their work for the Grits, D.J.
O'Donoghue received a clerical position in the Mowat government's Bureau of
Industry, and tailor Alfred Jury was appointed to a provincial Royal Commission on
Ontario prisons.
62 *Palladium of Labor*, 1 May 1886
63 *Palladium of Labor*, 8 May 1886
64 *Palladium of Labor*, 24 Nov. 1883. This sentiment was reiterated by Thompson later
in a column he wrote as Enjolras. See *Palladium of Labor*, 7 June 1884.
65 Kealey, *Toronto Workers*, 218–22; *Globe*, 20 May, 27 May 1882
66 *Globe*, 10 June 1882
67 Ibid.
68 For an excellent discussion of middle-class pronouncements on the morality of

working girls see Carolyn Strange, *Toronto's Girl Problem: The Perils and Pleasures of the City, 1880–1930* (Toronto 1995), 21–52.

69 *Mail*, 15 June, 16 June, 17 June, 19 June 1882
70 *Mail*, 14 June, 15 June 1882
71 *Mail*, 16 June 1882
72 *Mail*, 19 June 1882
73 Kealey, *Toronto Workers*, 222–4
74 *News*, 5 Jan., 7 Jan. 1886
75 *Palladium of Labor*, 7 March, *News*, 30 June 1885, 5 Nov. 1886
76 Charles March was also a former president of the TTLC, having occupied that position in 1884 and 1884. He worked with fellow Liberal-party supporters D.J. O'Donoghue and Alfred Jury to orchestrate consistent criticism of the Tory's immigration policy. John Roney, in addition to being an active member of Maple Leaf Assembly of the Knights of Labor and a delegate to District Assembly 125, was a strong temperance advocate. *News*, 4 Dec. 1886; Kealey and Palmer, *Dreaming of What Might Be*, 234; Christina Burr and Gregory S. Kealey, 'Charles March,' and 'Daniel John O'Donoghue,' in *Dictionary of Canadian Biography*, vol. 13 (Toronto 1994), 681–2, 778–81
77 *News*, 7 Dec. 1886
78 *News*, 24 Dec. 1886
79 *Palladium of Labor*, 4 Dec. 1886
80 *News*, 24 Feb. 1887
81 Thompson, *The Politics of Labor*, 85
82 *Palladium of Labor*, 23 Feb. 1884; Thompson, *The Politics of Labor*, 83–4
83 *Palladium of Labor*, 28 March, 11 April, 2 May 1885; Thompson, *The Politics of Labor*, 87–9
84 *Palladium of Labor*, 3 May 1884, 24 April 1886
85 Thompson, *The Politics of Labor*, 82–3, 151; *Palladium of Labor*, 22 Nov. 1884, 3 May 1884, 24 April 1886
86 Thompson, *The Politics of Labor*, 153–9
87 Ibid., 160–1; *The National*, 17 Oct. 1878

Chapter 4: 'An Artist of Righteousness'

1 Ramsay Cook, *The Regenerators: Social Criticism in Late Victorian English Canada* (Toronto 1985), 122–51; Stanley Paul Kutcher, 'John Wilson Bengough: Artist of Righteousness,' MA thesis, McMaster University, 1975; Carman Cumming, *Sketches from a Young Country: The Images of Grip Magazine* (Toronto 1997)
2 *Grip*, 12 May 1883
3 Mariana Valverde, 'The Rhetoric of Reform: Tropes and the Moral Subject,' *Inter-*

national Journal of the Sociology of Law 18 (1990), 61–73; Keith Moxey, *The Practice of Theory: Poststructuralism, Cultural Politics and Art History* (Ithaca and London 1994), 48–50, 57; Griselda Pollock, 'Feminism/Foucault – Surveillance/ Sexuality,' in Norman Bryson, Michael Ann Holly, and Keith Moxey, eds, *Images and Visual Culture: Interpretations* (Hanover, NH 1994), 14–41; Griselda Pollock, '"With My Own Eyes": Fetishism, the Labouring Body and the Colour of Its Sex,' *Art History* 17:3 (September 1992), 343–82. In response to older interpretations that presented a history of art as a record of the creation of aesthetic masterpieces, some art historians have turned to poststructuralist theories in search of a broader understanding of the cultural meaning of a particular work.

4 Cook, *The Regenerators*, 132

5 Biographical information on J.W. Bengough is taken from Cook, *The Regenerators*, 123–6; Kutcher, 'John Wilson Bengough,' in Henry Morgan, *The Canadian Men and Women of the Time* (Toronto 1912), 90–1; Hector Charlesworth, *The Canadian Scene* (Toronto 1927); W.W. Withrow, 'An Artist of Righteousness: J.W. Bengough, Canadian Caricaturist and Humourous Poet,' *Canadian Methodist Magazine and Review* 46 (September 1897), 202–16; Fraser Sutherland, *The Monthly Epic: A History of Canadian Magazines* (Markham, Ont. 1989), 69–79; Thomas Bengough, 'Life and Work of J.W. Bengough, Canada's Cartoonist, By His Brother,' Address to the Bell Club, Toronto, 20 Jan. 1937, J.W. Bengough Collection, Box 3, McMaster University Library; and J.W. Bengough, *Chalk Talks* (Toronto 1922), 3–39.

6 Bengough, *Chalk Talks*, 4

7 Ibid., 9; Morton Keller, *The Art and Politics of Thomas Nast* (New York 1968); Ralph E. Shikes, *The Indignant Eye: The Artist as Social Critic in Prints and Drawings from the Fifteenth Century to Picasso* (Boston 1969), 311–17; Cumming, *Sketches from a Young Country*, 38

8 Bengough, *Chalk Talks*, 11–12

9 Charles Dickens, *Barnaby Rudge* (London, repr. 1973), 99

10 *Grip*, 24 May 1873. Bengough remained a Dickens enthusiast throughout his life. For many years Bengough was vice-president of the Dickens Fellowship. He also wrote several dramatic works that were inspired by Dickens's writings. One of the best-known plays was Bengough's 'The Trial of Bardell vs. Pickwick,' which was staged by the Dickens Fellowship of Toronto in 1922. A memorial 'Bengough' cot was endowed at the Toronto Sick Children's Hospital with the proceeds from the performance. See Hector Charlesworth, 'J.W. Bengough: Pioneer Cartoonist,' *Saturday Night*, 13 Oct. 1923. See Bengough Papers, Box 1, for a copy of the manuscript of the play 'The Trial of Bardell vs. Pickwick.'

11 Thomas Bengough, 'Life and Work of J.W. Bengough'

12 Shikes, *The Indignant Eye*, xxiv

13 *Grip*, 29 March 1879

14 Bengough, *Chalk Talks*, 13

15 *Grip*, 5 Nov. 1873; Pollock,'Feminism/Foucault – Surveillance/Sexuality,' 34;
    Leonore Davidoff and Catherine Hall, *Family Fortunes: Men and Women of the
    English Middle Class, 1780–1850* (Chicago 1987), 445–9

16 *Grip*, 15 Nov. 1873; *Globe*, 26 Nov. 1873

17 *Grip*, 26 July 1873

18 *Flapdoodle: A Political Encyclopedia and Manual for Public Men*, edited by an Ex-
    Minister, illustrated by J.W. Bengough (Toronto 1881), 14, 17, 19

19 *Grip*, 23 April 1892. Also reprinted in J.W. Bengough, *Motley: Verses Grave and
    Gay* (Toronto 1895), 103–4

20 Joy Parr, *The Gender of Breadwinners: Women, Men, and Change in Two Industrial
    Towns, 1880–1950* (Toronto 1990), 140–2

21 *Grip*, 23 April 1892. While the emblematic reading of botanical signs and floral
    imagery was widely used by Victorian artists and writers to communicate various
    moral and spiritual truths, Bengough suggests that Mackenzie's character was above
    such 'vain floriture.' See Beverly Seaton, 'Considering the Lilies: Ruskin's "Pros-
    perpina" and Other Victorian Flower Books,' *Victorian Studies* 28:2 (Winter 1985),
    255–82

22 Peter Bailey, 'Ally Sloper's Half-Holiday: Comic Art in the 1880s,' *History Work-
    shop*, 16, (Autumn 1983), 4–31; Judith R. Walkowitz, *City of Dreadful Delight:
    Narratives of Sexual Danger in Late-Victorian Canada* (Chicago 1992), 43–4

23 Doug Fetherling, *The Blue Notebook: Reports on Canadian Culture* (Oakville 1985),
    121

24 See Carolyn Strange, *Toronto's Girl Problem: The Perils and Pleasures of the City,
    1880–1930* (Toronto 1995), 53–88; and Mariana Valverde, 'The Love of Finery:
    Fashion and the Fallen Woman in Nineteenth-Century Social Discourse,' *Victorian
    Studies* 32:2 (Winter 1989), 169–88.

25 *Grip*, 2 July 1887

26 *Grip*, 12 July 1890

27 George L. Mosse, *Nationalism and Sexuality: Respectability and Abnormal Sexual-
    ity in Modern Europe* (New York 1985), 17; Catherine Hall, 'Gender, Nationalisms
    and National Identities: Bellagio Symposium, July 1992,' *Feminist Review* 44 (Sum-
    mer 1993); C. Hall, *White, Male and Middle-Class: Explorations in Feminism and
    History* (New York 1992), 17–21

28 *Grip*, 2 Feb. 1889

29 *Grip*, 12 July 1890

30 Grace Irwin, *Trail-Blazers of American Art* (New York 1971), 204; Cook, *The
    Regenerators*, 126; Keller, *The Art and Politics of Thomas Nast*, viii–ix

31 J.W. Bengough, *A Caricature History of Canadian Politics, Volume I*, with intro. by
    Rev. Principal Grant (Toronto 1886), 418

32 Gregory S. Kealey, *Toronto Workers Respond to Industrial Capitalism, 1867–1892* (Toronto 1980), 155–6, 162; R.W. Phipps, *Free Trade or Protection* (Toronto 1878)

33 Bengough, *Caricature History, Vol. 1*, 420; Thomas Bengough, 'Life and Work of J.W. Bengough'

34 Bryan D. Palmer, *A Culture in Conflict: Skilled Workers and Industrial Capitalism in Hamilton, Ontario, 1860–1914* (Montreal 1979), 113–16; Kealey, *Toronto Workers*, 160–9; Christina Burr and Gregory Kealey, Biography of A.W. Wright, *Dictionary of Canadian Biography*, vol. 14 (Toronto 1998)

35 Keller, *The Art and Politics of Thomas Nast*, 110; Cook, *The Regenerators*, 126; Palmer, *A Culture in Conflict*, 115

36 *Grip*, 5 April 1879

37 *Grip*, 21 Jan. 1882

38 *Grip*, 12 Sept. 1885

39 *Grip*, 28 July 1888

40 *Grip*, 3 Nov. 1883

41 *Grip*, 27 Oct. 1888

42 *Grip*, 19 Jan. 1889

43 *Grip*, 27 Dec. 1890

44 *Grip*, 5 July 1890

45 Cook, *The Regenerators*, 130–2

46 J.W. Bengough, *The Up-to-Date Primer: A First Book of Lessons for Little Political Economists* (New York 1896), 13

47 John L. Thomas, *Alternative America: Henry George, Edward Bellamy, Henry Demarest Lloyd and the Adversary Tradition* (London 1983), 14–15

48 Catherine Gallagher, *The Industrial Reformation of English Fiction: Social Discourse and Narrative Form 1832–1867* (Chicago 1985), 34; Thomas, *Alternative America*, 5, 13

49 *Grip*, 23 July 1887

50 J.W. Bengough, *The Whole-Hog Book, Being George's Thoro' going Work, 'Protection or Free-Trade?' Rendered into Words of One Syllable, and Illustrated with Pictures, Or, a Dry Subject Made Juicy* (Boston 1908), 95

51 David R. Roediger, *The Wages of Whiteness: Race and the Making of the American Working Class* (London and New York 1991), 95–131

52 Bengough, *The Whole-Hog Book*, 14–15; Bengough, *Chalk Talks*, 110

53 Bengough, *Chalk Talks*, 122

54 Ibid., 119, 123–4

55 Bengough, *The Up-to-Date Primer*, 46–7, 58–9; Bengough, *The Whole-Hog Book*, 87–92

56 My thinking here has been influenced by my reading of Mariana Valverde's work on the social-purity movement in English Canada. Valverde, *The Age of Light,*

Soap, and Water: Moral Reform in English Canada, 1885–1925 (Toronto 1991), 34–41

57 Bengough, *The Up-to-Date Primer*, 74

58 Kealey, *Toronto Workers*, 277, 279

59 Uncle Thomas, 'The Regenerators,' *Canadian Magazine of Politics, Science, Art and Literature* 1:1 (March 1893), 64–7. See also Cook, *The Regenerators*, 3; Gene Howard Homel, '"Fading Beams of the Nineteenth Century": Radicalism and Early Socialism in Canada's 1890s,' *Labour / Le Travailleur* 5 (Spring 1980), 7. 'Uncle Thomas' was probably Toronto journalist Sam Wood, also known as 'Single Tax' to his friends.

60 *Labor Advocate*, 4 Sept. 1891

61 *Labor Advocate*, 18 Sept. 1891

62 *Labor Advocate*, 16 Jan. 1891; Gene Howard Homel, 'Fading Beams of the Nineteenth Century,' 24

63 *Labor Advocate*, 23 Jan. 1891; Cook, *The Regenerators*, 117–18

64 *Grip*, 31 Jan. 1891

65 *Labor Advocate*, 20 Feb. 1891

66 *Grip*, 25 April 1891

67 Carolyn Strange, *Toronto's Girl Problem*, 13–14; Valverde, *The Age of Light, Soap, and Water*, 17

68 Walkowitz, *City of Dreadful Delights*, 16

69 Ibid., 21; Strange, *Toronto's Girl Problem*, 9–10

70 *Grip*, 25 Oct. 1870

71 *Grip*, 25 April 1874

72 Valverde, *The Age of Light Soap and Water*, chap. 5; Angus McLaren, *Our Own Master Race: Eugenics in Canada, 1885–1945* (Toronto 1990), chap. 4; Strange, *Toronto's Girl Problem*, 16

73 J.W. Bengough, 'At Winnipeg Station,' J.W. Bengough Collection, Box 4; Bengough, *Chalk Talks*, 30, 52; *Grip*, 3 Jan. 1880, 10 June 1882, 28 April 1883

74 *Grip*, 1 Dec. 1883

75 Walkowitz suggested that the swell image compensated for a 'troubled' working-class masculinity brought about by industrial-capitalist transformations. Joy Parr, however, has criticized what she calls the 'crisis approach' to the historical study of masculinity, whereby a 'crisis' alert is issued each time masculinity is found to be mutable, when instead 'change' or 'response' might seem adequately to serve as descriptors. Walkowitz, *City of Dreadful Delights*, 44; Joy Parr, 'Gender History and Historical Practice,' *Canadian Historical Review* 76:3 (September 1995), 367–8

76 *Grip*, 25 April 1874; Louis James, 'Cruikshank and Early Victorian Caricature,' *History Workshop* 6 (Autumn 1978), 108; James Parton, *Caricature and Other Comic Art in All Times and Many Lands* (New York 1878), chap. 12; Gerard Curtis, 'Ford

Madox Brown's "Work": An Iconographic Analysis,' *Art Bulletin* 74:4 (December 1992), 626–7

77 Valverde, *The Age of Light, Soap, and Water*, 23

78 *Grip*, 27 March 1880

79 J.W. Bengough, *The Prohibition Aesop: A Book of Fables* (Hamilton, n.d.), J.W. Bengough Collection, Box 4; J.W. Bengough, *The Gin Mill Primer* (Toronto 1898)

80 Bengough, *Chalk Talks*, 65

81 Peter Bailey, 'Parasexuality and Glamour: The Victorian Barmaid as Cultural Prototype,' *Gender and History* 2:2 (Summer 1990), 161–2

82 Bengough Papers, Box 7, Newspaper clippings from the Toronto *Globe*, 1896–7

83 Bengough, *The Gin Mill Primer*, 14–15

84 *Grip*, 16 March 1889

85 *Grip*, 5 Sept. 1874

86 *Grip*, 22 Dec. 1883, 24 May, 8 March 1884, 27 June 1885

87 Desmond Morton, *Mayor Howland: The Citizens' Candidate* (Toronto 1973), 3–6, 57–63; *Grip*, 12 Dec. 1885, 16 Jan. 1886, 12 Nov. 1887

88 *Grip*, 10 Aug. 1889, 26 Dec. 1891

89 For comprehensive discussions of the street-railway question see Kealey, *Toronto Workers*, chap. 14; and Christopher Armstrong and H.V. Nelles, *The Revenge of the Methodist Bicycle Company* (Toronto 1977).

90 *Grip*, 23 May 1891. *Grip*'s satirical petition is as follows:

PETITION TO THE HONORABLE FRANK SMITH, SENATOR ETC.

SIR,– We the undersigned citizens and ratepayers of the city of Toronto, being desirous of securing for ourselves the benefits of efficient civic government,

And Whereas we are far from satisfied with the management of the various Departments, as now and for years past conducted,

And Whereas we have taken note of the fact that you possess, in an eminent degree the qualities of Determination, Firmness and Gall, which qualilities are essential to the proper conducting of the Business of the city,

We therefore humbly beg that you will forthwith take full charge and control not only of the Street Railway but of all and sundry the other Civic Departments, and conduct the same in such manner as may please your own sweet will, rendering the city treasury such portion of the receipts as may to you seem meet.

And your petitioners will ever pray.

91 *Grip*, 4 Jan., 9 Aug., 6 Dec. 1890, 21 March, 6 June, 1 Aug. 1891; *Labor Advocate*, 5 Dec. 1890, 12 June, 24 July 1891

92 *Grip*, 1 Aug. 1891

93 Withrow, 'An Artist of Righteousness,' 202

94 *Grip*, 25 April 1891

Chapter 5: 'The Art Preservative'

1 *Souvenir 1905 Convention ITU*, Toronto, 14–19 Aug. 1905, Archives of Ontario, MS 423; emphasis in the original.
2 Ava Baron, 'An "Other" Side of Gender Antagonism at Work: Men, Boys, and the Remasculinization of Printers' Work, 1830–1920,' in A. Baron, ed., *Work Engendered: Toward a New History of American Labor* (Ithaca and London 1991), 69
3 Joy Parr, 'Gender History and Historical Practice,' *Canadian Historical Review* 76:3 (September 1995), 367–8; Steven Maynard, 'Rough Work and Rugged Men: The Social Construction of Masculinity in Working-Class History,' *Labour / Le Travail* 23 (1989), 159, 161, 166
4 Christina A. Burr, 'Class and Gender in the Toronto Printing Trades, 1870–1914,' (Ph.D. thesis, Memorial University of Newfoundland, 1992); Thomas L. Walkom, 'The Daily Newspaper in Ontario's Developing Capitalist Economy: Toronto and Ottawa, 1871–1911' (Ph.D. thesis, University of Toronto, 1983); Paul Rutherford, *A Victorian Authority* (Toronto 1981), 53–4
5 Geoffrey Crossick, 'The Petite Bourgeoisie in Nineteenth-Century Britain: The Urban and Liberal Case,' in Geoffrey Crossick and Heinz-Gerhard Haupt, eds, *Shopkeepers and Master Artisans in Nineteenth-Century Europe* (London and New York 1984), 62–94; Clive Behagg, 'Masters and Manufacturers: Social Values and the Smaller Unit of Production in Birmingham, 1800–50,' in ibid., 137–54
6 F.H. Brigden, 'Methods and Processes of Illustration,' in Toronto Typothetae, *Art as Applied to Typography* (Toronto 1931), 17
7 Elizabeth Hulse, *A Dictionary of Toronto Printers, Publishers, Booksellers and the Allied Trades, 1798–1900* (Toronto 1982), 21, 113
8 *Canadian Printer and Publisher* 3:10 (October 1894), 10
9 Gregory S. Kealey, *Toronto Workers Respond to Industrial Capitalism, 1867–1892* (Toronto 1980), 303
10 Ontario Census Returns 1871, City of Toronto, District 46, Schedule 6, Census of 1871, National Archives of Canada, RG 31, vol. 801
11 Frederick Brigden Diary, 21 June 1873, Brigden Collection, Baldwin Room, Metro Toronto Reference Library
12 For evidence of seasonality in the late-nineteenth-century Toronto printing industry see *Canadian Printer and Publisher* 3:12 (December 1894), 1; 3:11 (November 1893), 3; 9:8 (August 1900), 14
13 See Angela Davis's *Art and Work* (Montreal and Kingston 1995) for a history of the graphic-arts industry in Canada. Davis relies extensively on the Brigden Collection in her attempt to understand artists as workers, albeit without an analysis of gender. For the business reorganization of Beale Bros. as the Toronto Engraving Company, of which Frederick Brigden became sole proprietor in 1887, see Hulse, *Dictionary of*

Toronto Printers, 16, 30; J. Russell Harper, *Early Painters and Engravers in Canada* (Toronto 1970), 20, 44–5.

14 Geoffrey Crossick and Heinz-Gerhard Haupt, 'Shopkeepers, Master Artisans and the Historian: The Petite Bourgeoisie in Comparative Focus,' in Crossick and Haupt, eds., *Shopkeepers and Master Artisans*, 9

15 Brigden, 'Methods and Processes of Illustration,' 17

16 See John Armstrong's serial history of the Toronto Typographical Union, originally published in the *Toiler*, and contained in a scrapbook in the Robert Kenny Collection, Fisher Rare Book Room, University of Toronto.

17 Kealey, *Toronto Workers*, chap. 6; Wayne Roberts, 'The Last Artisans: Toronto Printers, 1896–1914,' in Gregory S. Kealey and Peter Warrian, eds, *Essays in Canadian Working-Class History* (Toronto 1976), 125–42

18 Siân Reynolds, *Britannica's Typesetters: Women Compositors in Edwardian Edinburgh* (Edinburgh 1989), 15

19 *Printer's Miscellany*, 1:9 (March 1877), 131

20 An 'em' is a unit or measurement used in the printing trades. The letter 'm' in the majority of type fonts has a body as wide as it is high, and the letter 'n' occupies half of this area

21 Minutes of the Toronto Typographical Union [hereafter TTU], 4 March 1882. Archives of Ontario, MS 423

22 *Printer's Miscellany* 2:9 (March 1879), 217; Red Ink, *'Pi': A Compilation of Odds and Ends Relating to Workers in Sanctum and Newsroom Culled from the Scrap-Book of a Compositor* (Hamilton 1890), 162

23 Red Ink, *'Pi'*, 200–1

24 Ibid., 160–1, 172–3

25 Reynolds, *Britannica's Typesetters*, 18–22; Cynthia Cockburn, *Brothers: Male Dominance and Technological Change* (London 1983), 14–19. An interpretation of the origins of the printers' chapel was provided nearly two hundred years earlier by British printer Joseph Moxon in his 1683 *Mechanick Exercises of the Whole Art of Printing*: 'Every *Printing-house* is by Custom of Time out of mind, called a *Chappel*; and the Oldest Freeman is *Father of the Chappel*. I suppose the stile was originally conferred upon it by the courtesie of some great Churchman, or men, (doubtless when Chappels were in more veneration than of late years than they have been here in *England*) who for the Books of Divinity that proceeded from a *Printing-house*, gave it the Reverent Title of *Chappel*.' Moxon further described the rules of deportment expected of members in the chapel. Any violation of this code of conduct was a *Solace*; the penalty for which was a fine. The fine was set by the members of the chapel 'according to the nature and quality of the *Solace*.' Among the behaviours identified as a *Solace* by Moxon were swearing, fighting, abusive language and lying, being drunk in the chapel, leaving a candle burning at night, letting the com-

posing-stick fall, and allowing another to take it up. Every year the master printer was obliged to give the journeymen a feast or *Way-goose* at his own house, and give them money to spend for drink at the local tavern.

26 *Printer's Miscellany* 1:3 (September 1876), 26
27 Cynthia Cockburn, 'Formations of Masculinity,' *Gender and History* 1:2 (Summer 1989), 163
28 George A. Tracy, *History of the Typographical Union* (Indianapolis 1913), 235
29 Ibid., 253–6; William Leach, *True Love and Perfect Union: The Feminist Reform of Sex and Society* (New York 1980), 165–89; Ava Baron, 'Questions of Gender: Deskilling and Demasculinization in the U.S. Printing Industry, 1830–1915,' *Gender and History* 1:2 (Summer 1989), 183–4
30 Tracy, *History of the Typographical Union*, 268
31 *Typographical Journal* 1:3 (15 Sept. 1889)
32 *Report of the Royal Commission on the Relations of Labour and Capital in Canada* [hereafter *RCRLC*], 1889, Ontario Evidence, 109
33 Ibid., 40–1, 109, 135. Composition on the morning dailies required night labour, for which the union had negotiated a higher rate, as the work was deemed more taxing than day labour.
34 Ibid., 48
35 See also Joan Wallach Scott, 'Work Identities for Men and Women: The Politics of Work and Family in the Parisian Garment Trades in 1848,' in J.W. Scott, *Gender and the Politics of History* (New York 1988), 93–112
36 *Printer's Miscellany* 1:7 (January 1877), 104
37 *Printer's Miscellany* 3:10 (April 1879), 308
38 *Typographical Journal* 42:4 (April 1913), 413–15; Mergenthaler Linotype Co., *Speed and How to Attain It* (New York, n.d.), TTU Records, Archives of Ontario, MS 423
39 *Canadian Printer and Publisher* 3:5 (May 1894), 1
40 *Typographical Journal* 1:1 (15 July 1889), 4; George E. Barnett, *Chapters on Machinery and Labor* (Carbondale and Edwardsville, IL 1926), 3–29
41 Tracy, *History of the Typographical Union*, 453–5. The emphasis on an maximum of eight hours for machine operators had further significance, as the ITU was about to enter a lengthy struggle with employers for the eight-hour workday.
42 Gregory S. Kealey, 'Work Control, the Labour Process, and Nineteenth-Century Canadian Printers,' in Craig Heron and Robert Storey, eds, *On the Job: Confronting the Labour Process in Canada* (Kingston and Montreal 1986), 89; *Canadian Printer and Publisher* 1:4 (August 1892), 3; *Typographical Journal* 2:5 (October 1890), 5. Like the Mergenthaler machine, the Rogers typograph dispensed a solid line of type in one operation. The Rogers machine, however, was smaller and cheaper. The typograph was invented by Professor John R. Rogers of Cleveland,

Ohio. A civil engineer by occupation, Rogers had three brothers who were practical printers.

43 A typesetting machine was purchased from the Linotype Company of Montreal in October 1894 for the sum of $3000, with the agreement that the management of the Methodist Book and Publishing House could return the machine at the end of a two-month trial period free from all costs if the machine was deemed unsatisfactory to them. This stipulation apparently stemmed from dissatisfaction with the Rogers typograph in the production of the *Christian Guardian*. The new linotype machine met with the approval of the management of the Book Room and a second machine was purchased from the Montreal company in October 1895. See Copy of the Agreement between the Linotype Company of Montreal and the Methodist Book and Publishing House, 17 Oct. 1894, in the Ryerson Press Collection, United Church Archives; *Canadian Printer and Publisher* 2:8 (August 1893), 15.

44 *Canadian Printer and Publisher* 2:9 (September 1893), 116; 1:5 (September 1892), 8; 2:7 (July 1893), 16; 4:12 (December 1895), 14

45 *Canadian Printer and Publisher* 1:4 (April 1894), 8

46 TTU, Minutes, 6 Feb. 1892

47 TTU, Minutes, 3 Sept. 1882, 22 Oct. 1892; *Canadian Printer and Publisher* 1:7 (November 1892), 14

48 TTU, Minutes, 26 Oct. 1892

49 *Globe*, 2 Nov. 1892

50 Globe, 27 Oct., 29 Oct., 3 Nov. 1892; *Canadian Printer and Publisher* 1:7 (November 1892), 13; *Typographical Journal* 4:10 (November 1892), 3

51 TTU, Minutes, 3 Dec. 1892

52 *Typographical Journal* 4:15 (1 Feb. 1893), 6; TTU, Minutes, 16 Feb. 1893

53 TTU, Minutes, 16 Feb. 1893; *Globe*, 10 March 1893

54 TTU, Minutes, 1 April 1893

55 TTU, Minutes, 8 July 1893

56 TTU, Minutes, 25 April 1895

57 TTU, Minutes, 3 Aug. 1895

58 TTU, Minutes, 5 Oct. 1895

59 *Typographical Journal* 1:1 (15 Aug. 1895), 2

60 *Printer's Miscellany* 5:12 (June 1881), 177

61 *American Pressman* 3:1 (December 1892), 407

62 TTU, Minutes, 8 March 1870; Elizabeth Faulkner Baker, *Printers and Technology* (New York 1957), 69

63 Ontario, *First Report of the Bureau of Labor of the Province of Ontario for the Year Ending December 31st, 1900* (Toronto 1901), 27; Pressmen's Union Local 10, Minutes, 13 Feb. 1885, National Archives of Canada, MG 28 I 93

64 Pressmen's Union Local 10, Minutes, 13 Jan. 1888

65 Baker, *Printers and Technology*, chap. 10; *Report of the Bureau of Labor of the Province of Ontario 1900*, 28
66 Baker, *Printers and Technology*, 175–80
67 *American Pressman* 7:12 (November 1897), 349
68 Ibid.
69 *American Pressman* 15:12 (November 1905), 386
70 Felicity Hunt, 'Opportunities Lost and Gained: Mechanization and Women's Work in the London Bookbinding and Printing Trades,' in Angela V. John, ed., *Unequal Opportunities: Women's Employment in England 1800–1918* (Oxford and New York 1986), 73; Edith Abbott, *Women in Industry: A Study in American Economic History* (New York 1919), 248–9; Elizabeth Faulkner Baker, *Technology and Woman's Work* (New York 1964), 47–8; J. Ramsay MacDonald, ed., *Women in the Printing Trades* (New York and London 1980; originally 1904), 3–14; Mary Van Kleeck, *Women in the Bookbinding Trade* (New York 1913)
71 Ontario, *Annual Report of the Bureau of Industries for the Province of Ontario, 1889* (Toronto 1890)
72 Ontario, *Annual Report of the Bureau of Industries for the Province of Ontario* (Toronto 1891), 45–7
73 Joseph W. Zaehnsdorf, *The Art of Bookbinding* (London 1880), 25–6
74 MacDonald, *Women in the Printing Trades*, 96
75 Hunt, 'Opportunities Lost and Gained,' 84; *Annual Report of the Bureau of Industries, 1889*, 84
76 *Canadian Printer and Publisher* 1:2 (June 1892), 14
77 MacDonald, *Women in the Printing Trades*, ix, 102
78 *Labor Advocate*, 19 Dec. 1890; Ontario, *Eleventh Annual Report of the Bureau of Industries for 1892* (Toronto 1893), 18; Gregory S. Kealey and Bryan D. Palmer, *Dreaming of What Might Be: The Knights of Labor in Ontario, 1880–1900* (Toronto 1987; originally 1982), 102, 322
79 *International Bookbinder* 6:6 (June 1906), 170–1; Constitution and By-laws of the International Brotherhood of Bookbinders, 1892, in *American Labor Unions Constitutions and Proceedings*. At the IBB convention in 1896, Miss Kate V. Smoot of Washington was elected second vice-president. Miss Nannie T. Daniel, also from Washington and employed in the Government Printing Office, was elected second vice-president of the IBB at the 1898 convention.
80 *Report of the Bureau of Labour 1900*, 28
81 *Labor Advocate*, 19 Dec. 1890; *International Bookbinder* 1:4 (May 1900), 4; 14:2 (February 1913), 50; Kealey, *Toronto Workers*, 324; Wayne Roberts, 'Studies in the Toronto Labour Movement, 1896–1914,' Ph.D. dissertation, University of Toronto, 1978, i–ii
82 *Eleventh Annual Report of the Bureau of Industries*, 18; *Report of the Bureau of*

Labour 1900, 28; *International Bookbinder* 19:11 (November 1981), 392; Kealey, *Toronto Workers*, 325. Mrs May Darwin, who was prominent in the labour-reform and socialist movements in the early twentieth century, was the sister of Robert and William Glockling. See Wayne Roberts, *Honest Womanhood: Feminism, Femininity and Class Consciousness among Toronto Working Women 1893 to 1914* (Toronto 1976), 43–5

83 Constitution and By-Laws of the International Brotherhood of Bookbinders, 1899

84 *Typographical Journal* 19:2 (15 July 1901), 81

85 Ibid.; Ontario, *Report of the Bureau of Labour 1902* (Toronto 1903), 58; Roberts, *Honest Womanhood*, 47

86 *Canadian Printer and Publisher* 9:8 (August 1902), 4

87 Proceedings of the Annual Convention of the International Brotherhood of Bookbinders, Cincinnatti, 8 June 1908, in *American Labor Unions Constitutions and Proceedings*

88 *International Bookbinder* 6:2 (February 1905), 43

89 Karen Dubinsky, 'The Modern Chivalry: Women and the Knights of Labor, Ontario, 1880–1891,' MA thesis, Carleton University, 1985; Susan Levine, *Labor's True Woman: Carpet Weavers, Industrialization, and Labor Reform in the Gilded Age* (Philadelphia 1984), 10–11, 129–53

90 Raymond Williams, *Culture and Society 1780–1950* (New York 1983; originally 1958), xv

91 Eileen Boris, *Art and Labor: Ruskin, Morris, and the Craftsman Ideal in America* (Philadephia 1986), xi–xii; Davis, *Art and Work*, 7–8

92 John Ruskin, *Modern Painters*, vol. 2, part 3, sect. 1, chap. 3, para. 16, cited in Williams, *Culture and Society*, 135

93 John Ruskin, *The Works of John Ruskin*, ed. E.T. Cook and A. Wedderburn (London 1903–12), vol. 17:423, 20:93

94 John Ruskin, *The Stones of Venice*, vol. 2 (New York 1900; originally 1853), 162

95 Ibid., 169–70

96 William S. Peterson, *The Ideal Book: Essays and Lectures on the Arts of the Book by William Morris* (Berkeley and Los Angeles 1982), 75–8; Bernard C. Middleton, *A History of English Craft Bookbinding Technique* (New York and London 1963), 271–5; May Morris, *William Morris: Artist, Writer, Socialist*, vol. 1 (New York 1966), 1–105; E.P. Thompson, *William Morris: Romantic to Revolutionary* (London 1955)

97 Ellen Gates Starr was notable among North American women bookbinders. Starr befriended Jane Addams, and she was a co-founder of Hull House in Chicago in 1889. In 1897, Starr learned the craft of bookbinding from Cobden-Sanderson at his Doves Press. Fifteen months later she returned to Hull House and set up a hand bindery. See Boris, *Art and Labor*, 180–1

98 Gene Howard Homel, ' "Fading Beams of the Nineteenth Century": Radicalism and Early Socialism in Canada's 1890s,' *Labour / Le Travailleur* 5 (Spring 1890), 13; Homel, 'James Simpson and the Origins of Canadian Social Democracy' (Ph.D. thesis, University of Toronto, 1978)

99 Frederick Brigden Sr, 'My Acquaintance with Ruskin,' paper delivered to the Saturday Club at one of the regular fortnightly meetings of the Club held at 103 Rose Ave., Toronto, 1915. National Gallery of Canada Library, Ottawa

100 Frederick Brigden to F.H. Brigden, August 1894, Bridgen Collection, Metro Toronto Reference Library. For a history of the Toronto Art Students' League see William Colgate, *The Toronto Art Students' League, 1886–1904* (Toronto 1954).

101 Davis, *Art and Work*, 89; J.E. Middleton, *Canadian Landscape as Pictured by F.H. Brigden* (Toronto 1944), 84

102 'Notes on Father's Character by F.H. Brigden,' Brigden Collection

103 Joy Parr, *The Gender of Breadwinners: Women, Men, and Change in Two Industrial Towns, 1880–1950* (Toronto 1990), 140–1

104 Brigden Diaries, 1873, Brigden Collection

105 *Canadian Printer and Publisher*, December 1896, 8

106 Baron, 'Questions of Gender,' 181

107 Brigden Diaries, 22 Feb. 1858, Brigden Collection

108 Armstrong, History of the TTU (see n. 16 above)

109 TTU, Minutes, 10 Feb. 1867

110 TTU, Minutes, 4 April 1871

111 TTU, Minutes, 4 Nov. 1876, 6 Feb. 1881. The 'phat' was the more easily composed matter such as blank slugs in advertising work. For piece-rate workers this practice translated into higher wages. In the *Empire* chapel part of the business at the regular monthly meeting was the distribution of the 'phat' among compositors. See *Empire* Chapel, Minutes, 25 Jan. 1890, Robert Kenny Collection, University of Toronto Archives.

112 See, for example, TTU, Minutes, Nov. 1870, 4 April, 24 July, 14 Oct. 1871, 8 Jan., 2 April 1881, 6 May 1893, 1 May 1897, 2 Dec. 1899

113 *Canadian Printer and Publisher* 8:8 (August 1899), 12

114 RCRLC, Ontario Evidence, 41–2, 46

115 TTU, Minutes, 2 April 1892

116 *Typographical Journal* 9:2 (15 July 1896), 49

117 TTU, Minutes, 3 Feb. 1900

Chapter 6: Beyond the Home Circle

1 *Ontario Workman*, 7 Aug. 1873

2 My argument contradicts that made by Mary Poovey in the British context. She

argues that the rhetoric of separate spheres and the image of domesticated, feminized morality were integral to the consolidation of bourgeois power, 'because linking morality to a figure (rhetorically) immune to the self-interest and competition integral to economic success preserved virtue without inhibiting productivity.' I argue that gender was integral to the articulation of distinct working-class counterdiscourse to bourgeois hegemony. Mary Poovey, *Uneven Developments: The Ideological Work of Gender in Mid-Victorian England* (Chicago 1988), 10

3 Michel Foucault, *The History of Sexuality, Volume I: An Introduction*, trans. Robert Hurley (New York 1978, 1990), 103–14; Nancy Armstrong, *Desire and Domestic Fiction: A Political History of the Novel* (New York 1987), 3–26; Poovey, *Uneven Developments*, 3–10

4 Susan Levine, *Labor's True Woman: Carpet Weavers, Industrialization, and Labor Reform in the Gilded Age* (Philadelphia 1984), 129–53; Karen Dubinsky, '"The Modern Chivalry": Women and the Knights of Labor in Ontario, 1880–1891,' MA thesis, Carleton University, 1985

5 *Ontario Workman*, 18 April 1872

6 F.W. Watt, 'Literature of Protest,' in Carl F. Klinck, ed., *Literary History of Canada* (Toronto 1973; originally 1965), 464

7 Armstrong, *Desire and Domestic Fiction*, 14–20

8 *Ontario Workman*, 15 Aug. 1872, 21 Aug., 18 Dec. 1873

9 *Ontario Workman*, 1 May 1873

10 *Ontario Workman*, 14 Aug. 1873, 1 Jan. 1874

11 *Ontario Workman*, 19 Dec. 1872, 2 Jan., 16 Jan. 1873

12 Armstrong, *Desire and Domestic Fiction*, 18

13 *Ontario Workman*, 19 Sept. 1872

14 *Ontario Workman*, 16 Jan. 1873

15 *Ontario Workman*, 12 Sept., 21 Nov. 1872, 3 April, 1 May, 3 July 1873

16 *Ontario Workman*, 27 June 1872

17 *Ontario Workman*, 8 May, 23 Oct. 1873

18 *Ontario Workman*, 12 Sept. 1872

19 Poovey, *Uneven Developments*, 21–2

20 Carroll Smith-Rosenberg, 'The Female World of Love and Ritual: Relations between Women in Nineteenth-Century America,' in C. Smith-Rosenberg, *Disorderly Conduct: Visions of Gender in Victorian America* (New York and Oxford 1985), 53–76; Mary P. Ryan, *Cradle of the Middle Class: The Family in Oneida County, New York, 1790–1865* (Cambridge, UK 1981), 196–229

21 *Ontario Workman*, 31 July 1873. See also Linda Gordon, *Heroes of Their Own Lives: The Politics and History of Family Violence, Boston, 1880–1960* (New York 1988), chap. 2

22 *Ontario Workman*, 21 Nov. 1872

23 *Ontario Workman*, 12 Sept. 1872

24 *Ontario Workman*, 1 Jan. 1874

25 *Ontario Workman*, 15 May 1873

26 *Ontario Workman*, 16 Jan. 1873

27 *Ontario Workman*, 2 Jan. 1873

28 Ibid.

29 *Ontario Workman*, 10 Oct., 26 Dec. 1872. See also Mariana Valverde, 'The Love of Finery: Fashion and the Fallen Woman in Nineteenth-Century Social Discourse,' *Victorian Studies* 32:2 (Winter 1989), 169–88; Kathy Peiss, *Cheap Amusements: Working Women and Leisure in Turn-of-the-Century New York* (Philadelphia 1986); and Christine Stansell, *City of Women: Sex and Class in New York, 1789–1860* (Urbana and Chicago 1987), 89–101

30 *Ontario Workman*, 9 Jan., 7 Aug. 1873

31 *Leader*, 10 April 1871; *Globe*, 10 April 1871. For an in-depth discussion of the early organization of shoemakers in Toronto from the perspective of male artisans' struggles for workplace control, see Gregory S. Kealey, *Toronto Workers Respond to Industrial Capitalism* (Toronto 1980), 43–8.

32 *Leader*, 10 April 1871

33 Mary Blewett, *Men, Women, and Work: Class, Gender, and Protest in the New England Shoe Industry, 1780–1910* (Urbana and Chicago 1988), 322

34 Gregory S. Kealey and Bryan D. Palmer, *Dreaming of What Might Be: The Knights of Labor in Ontario, 1880–1900* (Toronto 1987), 97

35 *News*, 5 April 1882; *Trades Union Advocate*, 4 May 1882

36 *News*, 18 April 1882

37 *News*, 5 April 1882

38 Ibid.

39 *Globe*, 8 April, 11 April 1882

40 *Globe*, 13 April 1882; *News*, 11 April 1882

41 *Globe*, 12 April 1882

42 Ibid.; *News*, 11 April 1882

43 Unfortunately no biographical information on Foster has been found. There were no detailed accounts of the meetings of the women's union in any of the city's daily newspapers or in the labour press.

44 *News*, 13 April 1882

45 *Trades Union Advocate*, 4 May 1882

46 The *News* reported on 13 April 1882 that the Female Operatives Union had $300 on hand. The union expected to pay every woman who had been on strike two weeks $3.50, or one-half of their already meagre weekly wages. Clearly, the strike imposed tremendous hardships on the women operatives.

47 *News*, 19 April 1882

48 *News*, 19 April, 21 April 1882
49 *News*, 24 April 1882
50 *Trades Union Advocate*, 4 May 1882
51 Ibid.
52 *Trades Union Advocate*, 25 May 1882
53 *Trades Union Advocate*, 1 June 1882
54 *Trades Union Advocate*, 15 June 1882
55 *Trades Union Advocate*, 23 Oct. 1883
56 *News*, 7 Dec., 8 Dec. 1882
57 *News*, 21 Feb. 1884
58 Toronto Trades and Labor Council [hereafter TTLC], Minutes, 15 Sept. 1882, National Archives of Canada, MG 28 I 44
59 TTLC, Minutes, 21 March 1884
60 TTLC, Minutes, 13 Aug. 1881. The Toronto Trades Assembly ceased to function after February 1878.
61 The first issue of the *Trades Union Advocate* appeared on 4 May 1882. The masthead of the paper read, 'Non-sectarian – Non-Political.' Donovan's intent in starting the newspaper was to focus on labour reform and steer clear of religious controversy and party politics. The paper was renamed *The Wage-Worker*, on 15 March 1883. At this time, the format was expanded to accommodate the growing number of trade unions and clubs in the city, and an attempt was made meet reader demand for sensationalized literature.
62 The labour platform of the *Trades Union Advocate* was as follows: (1) Reduction of the hours of labour to nine hours per day, (2) the prohibition of children in workshops or factories before age 14, and the enactment of laws for the compulsory education of all under that age, (3) the enactment of uniform apprentice laws, (4) the abolishment of the contract system on all national and municipal work, (5) the abolition of convict labour, (6) the enactment of laws compelling employers to pay their workers weekly, (7) the enactment of laws giving mechanics and labourers a first lien on their work for full wages, (8) to secure for both sexes equal pay for equal work, (9) the establishment of Bureaus of Statistics, (10) the establishment of sanitary inspection of factories and workshops, (11) the abrogation of all laws that do not bear equally upon capital or labour, (12) the doctrine that a public servant is the people's servant, (13) the extension of the franchise so that every taxpayer, a British or naturalized citizen, shall have the vote, and (14) the abolition of property qualifications, or the deposit of money, for candidates for parliamentary or municipal honours. *Trades Union Advocate*, 7 Sept. 1882
63 *Trades Union Advocate*, 21 Sept. 1882
64 Ibid.
65 Ibid.

66 *Trades Union Advocate*, 28 Sept. 1882

67 Ibid.

68 *Trades Union Advocate*, 12 Oct. 1882

69 The question of allowing women to become members of the Knights of Labor was raised formally for the first time at the third session of the General Assembly, held in Chicago in 1879. Phillip Van Patten a leader in the socialist movement and an active Knight, introduced a resolution that working women be permitted to join the Order and form assemblies under the same conditions as men. In accordance with the constitution of the Order, the resolution was referred to the Committee on Laws. The committee reported back favourably. However, a point of order was raised that, since the proposed admission of women represented a fundamental change in the laws of the Order, a two-thirds vote of the General Assembly was necessary to adopt it. Terence V. Powderly, Grand Master Workman, *pro tempore*, concurred, and a vote was taken. The motion failed to secure the necessary majority and the resolution was tabled until the next meeting of the General Assembly.

When the General Assembly met in Pittsburgh the following year, the Pennsylvania District Assembly introduced another additional resolution stipulating that 'for the protection of labor in manufacturing districts ... women should be admitted into this Noble and Holy Order under a provision that they shall have Local Assemblies of their own governed by male officers and that they shall not be entitled to full privileges of this Noble and Holy Order.' The matter was referred to the Committee on Laws, which reported in favour of the admission of women, but on the same terms as men. A modified resolution was eventually adopted that working women be organized under the authority and protection of the Order, but that a committee of five be appointed to prepare the ritual and regulations necessary for the admission of women as members. There is no record of the subcommittee ever meeting. The only formal distinction between men and women institutionalized in the constitution of the Order was that women paid only one-half the initiation fee of men, at 50 cents. Women were also assessed lower rates for the Order's cooperative fund. See Knights of Labor, *Proceedings of the Third Regular Session of the General Assembly*, National Archives, MG 28 I 54, Reel M-3677; Norman J. Ware, *The Labor Movement in the United States 1860–1895: A Study in Democracy* (Gloucester, MA 1959), 347–8; and Terence V. Powderly, *The Path I Trod*, ed. Harry J. Carman, Henry David, and Paul N. Guthrie (New York 1904), 382–3

70 Kealey and Palmer, *Dreaming of What Might Be*, 318

71 Ibid., 97

72 For an in-depth discussion of the strike see Eugene Forsey, 'The Telegraphers' Strike of 1883,' *Transactions of the Royal Society of Canada*, ser. 4, vol. 9 (1971), 245–59.

73 *News*, 18 July 1883

74 TTLC, Minutes, 20 July 1883

75 *Palladium of Labor*, 29 Sept., 6 Oct. 1883. For a biography on Katie McVicar see Gregory S. Kealey, 'Kate McVicar,' in Frances G. Halpenny, ed., *Dictionary of Canadian Biography*, vol. 11 (Toronto 1982), 584. McVicar was a single woman who lived at home, and like most nineteenth-century working women contributed to the household. Unlike most women, however, she remained single and, as Kealey writes, 'her comparative longevity as a factory operative accounts to some degree for her emergence as a prominent leader in the Knights of Labor.' She continued to live at home until her early death on 18 June 1886 at the age of 30.

76 *Palladium of Labor*, 13 Oct. 1883

77 *Palladium of Labor*, 3 Nov. 1883

78 Kealey and Palmer, *Dreaming of What Might Be*, 143–4; Dubinsky, 'The Modern Chivalry,' 47–53

79 Biographical information on Marie Joussaye was compiled from Wayne Roberts, *Honest Womanhood: Feminism, Femininity and Class Consciousness among Toronto Working Women, 1893–1914* (Toronto 1976), 15, 43; and Kealey and Palmer, *Dreaming of What Might Be*, 295, 324. In 1903, Joussaye attempted to organize a union of domestic servants in Toronto. On 9 July 1904 the *Mail and Empire* reported that she had been convicted and sentenced to three months' imprisonment in Dawson City on a charge of obtaining money under false pretences.

80 *Journal of United Labor*, 25 April 1886

81 *Canadian Labor Reformer*, 15 May 1886; Kealey and Palmer, *Dreaming of What Might Be*, 106; Kealey, *Toronto Workers*, 187. The American-born McNab was twice elected Master Workman of LA 2622, a 'mixed' assembly composed of workers employed at Massey's agricultural-implements factory. In 1886, McNab was elected District Master Workman of DA 125. *Canadian Labor Reformer*, 28 Aug. 1886

82 Kealey and Palmer, *Dreaming of What Might Be*, 106

83 Ibid., 102–3, 322

84 *Canadian Labor Reformer*, 12 June 1886; *Palladium of Labor*, 19 June 1886. In December 1885, *The Palladium of Labor* set up a Toronto office and for a short time was published in both Toronto and Hamilton. The Toronto *Palladium* was purchased by Wright, who transformed it into *The Canadian Labor Reformer*. The first issue of *The Canadian Labor Reformer* appeared on 15 May 1886, and was published weekly. Wright departed for the U.S. late in 1887. Wright gained the trust of Master Workman Terence Powderly, and in 1888 was elected to the general executive board of the Knights of Labor, and thereafter replaced D.J. O'Donoghue as Powderly's Canadian adviser. See Christina Burr and Gregory Kealey, 'Alexander Whyte Wright,' *Dictionary of Canadian Biography*, vol. 14 (Toronto 1998); and Kealey and Palmer, *Dreaming of What Might Be*, 248–76.

85 *Palladium of Labor*, 8 May 1886

86 *Canadian Labor Reformer*, 24 July 1886

87 *Palladium of Labor*, 8 May 1886

88 Ibid.

89 Recent historical writing has differed on whether the Knights forged a type of 'labor feminism' or constructed and preserved male patriarchy using an appeal to masculine chivalry. Kealey and Palmer argued that although the Knights admitted women and thereby forged the first truly working-class movement in Canada, they actually reinforced patriarchal relations with appeals to prevailing feminine ideals. In an unpublished MA paper, Kristofferson argued that the Knights in constructing a masculine gender ideology around chivalry perpetuated and preserved patriarchal social relations. Susan Levine, however, argued that the Knights forged a 'labor feminism.' Dubinsky noted that while the Knights opened up a space for women in the labour movement that previously had not existed, the feminist reforms championed by the Knights were not without contradictions. The equal-rights strategy, according to both Levine and Dubinsky, actually represented a meaningful advance for women. See Kealey and Palmer, *Dreaming of What Might Be*, 318; Robert B. Kristofferson, '"True Knights Are We" Unity, Conflict and Masculine Discourse: The Knights of Labor in Hamilton,' Unpublished research paper, Department of History, York University, 1992; Levine, *Labor's True Woman*, chap. 5; and Dubinsky, 'The Modern Chivalry,' 202

90 *Palladium of Labor*, 25 Sept. 1886

91 Martha May has argued that the family-wage ideal worked against the interests of working-class men, women, and families. It reinforced the sexual division of labour in the labour market and gave employers an easy means of undercutting wage rates, thus fostering competition among workers. See Martha May, 'Bread before Roses: American Workingmen, Labor Unions and the Family Wage,' in Ruth Milkman, ed., *Women, Work and Protest: A Century of US Women's Labor History* (London 1985), 7. See also Wally Seccombe, 'Patriarchy Stabilized: The Construction of the Male Breadwinner Wage Norm in Nineteenth-Century Britain,' *Social History* 11:1 (January 1986), 53–76.

92 *Labor Advocate*, 27 Feb. 1891. Ethel Day MacPherson was active in the Toronto women's suffrage movement. She was a member of the Nationalist Club and the Toronto branch of the theosophy society.

93 Ibid.

94 Joan Scott, 'Desconstructing Equality-versus-Difference: Or, the Uses of Poststructuralist Theory for Femininism,' in Marianne Hirsch and Evelyn Fox Keller, eds, *Conflicts in Feminism* (New York and London 1990), 134–48

95 *Palladium of Labor*, 5 July 1884

96 *Palladium of Labor*, 6 Oct. 1883

97 *Palladium of Labor*, 30 May, 20 June 1885

98 *Palladium of Labor*, 26 Jan. 1884

99 *Canadian Labor Reformer*, 1 Jan. 1887

100 Deborah Gorham, 'The Maiden Tribute of Modern Babylon Re-examined: Child Prostitution and the Idea of Childhood in Late-Victorian England,' *Victorian Studies* 21:3 (Spring 1978), 353–80; Judith R. Walkowitz, *City of Dreadful Delight: Narratives of Sexual Danger in Late-Victorian London* (Chicago 1992), 81–134. For a discussion of the McCabe case see Dubinsky, 'The Modern Chivalry,' 170.

101 *Palladium of Labor*, 18 July, 1 Aug., 19 Sept. 1885

102 Dubinsky, 'The Modern Chivalry,' 185; Karen Dubinsky, *Improper Advances: Rape and Heterosexual Conflict in Ontario, 1880–1929* (Chicago 1993), 52; Mariana Valverde, *The Age of Light, Soap, and Water: Moral Reform in English Canada, 1885–1925* (Toronto 1991), 97

103 Knights of Labor, *Proceedings of the Special Session of the General Assembly*, 25 May–3 June 1886

104 At the provincial level, full manhood suffrage was passed by Mowat's Liberal government in 1885. The federal Tory government also passed federal franchise legislation in 1885. This legislation, however, retained property requirements. In cities, owners of properties worth $300, tenants who paid $2 a month or $20 a year rental and had been resident for at least one year, occupants of property worth $300 and resident for at least one year, individual wage earners with a $300 annual income, and sons of owners whose father's property was worth an additional $300 per son gained the vote. It is unclear, however, to what extent Toronto working-class men were actually affected by these franchise restrictions. See Kealey, *Toronto Workers*, 367–8. In November 1876, at the initiative of Dr Emily Howard Stowe, the Toronto Women's Literary Club was established. In 1881 this club organized a deputation to lobby the provincial government for women's suffrage. The club succeeded in 1882 in getting the Ontario legislature to pass a law permitting unmarried women with property qualifications to vote on municipal by-laws. The Toronto Women's Literary Club, renamed the Toronto Women's Suffrage Association in 1884, succeeded that same year in getting full municipal franchise for unmarried women with property qualifications. During the remainder of the decade, the sporadic activities of the Toronto Women's Suffrage Association were largely devoted to the drafting of petitions calling for both municipal franchise for married women and provincial franchise for all. See Catherine Cleverdon, *The Woman Suffrage Movement in Canada*, 2nd ed. (Toronto 1974), 20–1; Dubinsky, 'The Modern Chivalry,' 120–6

105 *Palladium of Labor*, 20 Oct. 1883

106 *Palladium of Labor*, 20 March 1886

107 See Wayne Roberts, '"Rocking the Cradle for the World": The New Woman and

Maternal Feminism, Toronto, 1877–1914,' in Linda Kealey, ed., *A Not Unreasonable Claim: Women and Reform in Canada, 1880s-1920s* (Toronto 1979), 15–45
108 *Palladium of Labor*, 20 March 1886
109 Linda K. Kerber, 'Separate Spheres, Female Worlds, Woman's Place: The Rhetoric of Women's History,' *Journal of American History* 75:1 (June 1988), 30

Chapter 7: 'Bring the Girls into the Fold'

1 *Mail and Empire*, 9 Oct. 1897
2 James A. Schmiechen, *Sweated Industries and Sweated Labor: The London Clothing Trades, 1960–1914* (Urbana and Chicago 1984); Jenny Morris, *Women Workers and the Sweated Trades: The Origins of Minimum Wage Legislation* (Aldershot 1986); Robert McIntosh, 'Sweated Labour: Female Needleworkers in Industrializing Canada,' *Labour / Le Travail* 32 (Fall 1993), 105–38; Christine Stansell, *City of Women: Sex and Class in New York, 1789–1860* (Urbana and Chicago 1987), 104–7; Mercedes Steedman, 'Skill and Gender in the Canadian Clothing Industry, 1890–1940,' in Craig Heron and Robert Storey, eds, *On the Job: Confronting the Labour Process in Canada* (Kingston and Montreal 1986), 152–209; Wayne Roberts, *Honest Womanhood: Feminism, Femininity and Class Consciousness among Toronto Working Women, 1893 to 1914* (Toronto 1976), 37–41. Steedman's article centres on the period after 1900. Only five pages of Wayne Roberts's *Honest Womanhood* were devoted to the militancy of women garment workers in Toronto between 1893 and 1914. Roberts focused on the strike activity of the city's women garment workers and their failed attempts at union organization. McIntosh has compensated for the scholarly neglect of women needleworkers in the Canadian historical writing of the nineteenth-century working-class experience. He argued that the rise of sweating in the Canadian garment industry during the nineteenth century was shaped by the 'structured inequalities of class and gender.' McIntosh's theorizing about patriarchy and capitalism, however, was adopted from his reading of Heidi Hartmann's 1979 essay, which can be criticized for its essentialism and its assumption that patriarchal and capitalist social relations exist separately. See Heidi Hartmann, 'Capitalism, Patriarchy and Job Segregation by Sex,' in Zillah Eisenstein, ed., *Capitalist Patriarchy and the Case for Socialist Feminism* (New York 1979), 206–47.
3 Schmiechen, *Sweated Industries and Sweated Labor*, 42–3, 185
4 Stansell, *City of Women*, 106. Similarly, Jenny Morris found that the majority of homeworkers in the London and Leeds tailoring trades during the nineteenth century were women tied to the home by a gender division of labour that allocated domestic labour to women. See Morris, *Women Workers*, 12.
5 Gregory S. Kealey, *Toronto Workers Respond to Industrial Capitalism, 1867–1892* (Toronto 1980), 307–9; Gerald Tulchinsky, 'Hidden among the Smokestacks:

Toronto's Clothing Industry, 1871–1901,' in David Keane and Colin Read, eds, *Old Ontario: Essays in Honour of J.M.S. Careless* (Toronto 1990), 257–84

6 Mary-Etta Macpherson, *Shopkeepers to a Nation: The Eatons* (Toronto 1963), 24–6, 34–5; George G. Naismith, *Timothy Eaton* (Toronto 1923), 194–6. Eaton's advertised its ready-made clothing line for men in the Spring and Summer Catalogue for 1896 as follows: 'Everyone is reminded of our ability to supply their clothing wants satisfactorily. No need to patronize a merchant tailor at any time. We have all sizes and styles ready for boys, youths, young men, middle-aged men and elderly men. The fact is an argument in itself. The general excellence of our clothing will surprise those who think the ready-made not good enough.' T. Eaton Co., Spring and Summer Catalogue 1896, T. Eaton Collection, F229–162–0–1001, Archives of Ontario

7 Canada, *Census of Canada, 1870–71*, vol. 3, vi–x

8 Steven Fraser, 'Combined and Uneven Development in the Men's Clothing Industry,' *Business History Review* 57 (Winter 1983), 522–47; Edith Abbott, *Women in Industry: A Study in American Economic History* (New York and London 1916), 215–37; Raelene Frances, *The Politics of Work: Gender and Labour in Victoria, 1880–1939* (Cambridge, UK 1993), 26–7; Stansell, *City of Women*, 105–15; Jenny Morris, 'The Characteristics of Sweating: The Late Nineteenth-Century London and Leeds Tailoring Trade,' in Angela V. John, ed., *Unequal Opportunities: Women's Employment in England 1800–1918* (Oxford and New York 1986), 95–121

9 *Globe*, 28 Oct. 1868

10 Martha Eckmann Brent, 'A Stitch in Time: The Sewing Machine Industry of Ontario, 1860–1897,' *Material History Bulletin*, Spring 1980, 3–4; Schmiechen, *Sweated Industries and Sweated Labor*, 26; Robertson and Cook, *Toronto City Directory for 1871* (Toronto 1871), 306; Fisher and Taylor, *Toronto Directory for 1876* (Toronto 1876), 410, 420

11 *News*, 18 Jan. 1888

12 Tulchinsky, 'Hidden among the Smokestacks,' 273; McIntosh, 'Sweated Labour,' 115

13 A.W. Wright, *Report upon the Sweating System in Canada* [hereafter Wright Commission], Canada, *Sessional Papers*, 1896, vol. 29, no. 11 (61, 61A), 13

14 Ibid., 20

15 *Mail and Empire*, 9 Oct. 1897

16 Wright Commission, 13; McIntosh, 'Sweated Labour,' 114

17 Knight of Labour, 'Where Labor Is Not Prayer,' *Walsh's Magazine* (1895–6), repr. in Irving Abella and David Millar, eds, *The Canadian Worker in the Twentieth Century* (Toronto 1978), 155

18 Wright Commission, 23; Stansell, *City of Women*, 106

19 J.M.S. Careless, *Toronto to 1918: An Illustrated History* (Toronto 1984), 134–5; Michael Kluckner, *Toronto the Way It Was* (Toronto 1988), 157

20 Ruth Frager has examined the complex interplay of class, ethnicity, gender, and political ideology in the twentieth-century Jewish labour movement in Toronto. Ethnic factionalism played an important role in the garment trades in the early twentieth century, as non-Jewish garment workers refused to join Jewish workers in strikes. See Ruth A. Frager, *Sweatshop Strife: Class, Ethnicity, and Gender in the Jewish Labour Movement of Toronto 1900–1939* (Toronto 1992)

21 Canada, *Census of Canada 1891*, vol. 1, table iv; Canada, *Census of Canada 1901*, vol. 1, table x; Daniel Joseph Hiebert, 'The Geography of Jewish Immigrants and the Garment Industry in Toronto, 1901–1931: A Study of Ethnic and Class Relations,' Ph.D. thesis, University of Toronto, 1987

22 Stephen A. Speisman, *The Jews of Toronto: A History to 1937* (Toronto 1979), 71–88

23 *Mail and Empire*, 25 Sept. 1897

24 *Mail and Empire*, 9 Oct. 1897

25 Wright Commission, 22, 25–6. In his testimony before the commission Gurofsky revealed that a subcontractor named Fine, located at 14 Front Street West, had appeared before the police court magistrate for non-payment of wages.

26 Knight of Labor, 'Where Labor Is Not Prayer,' 155

27 Wright Commission, 14

28 Ontario Census Returns 1871, City of Toronto, District 46, Schedule 6, Census of 1871, National Archives of Canada, RG 31, vol. 801

29 Joan M. Jensen, 'Needlework as Art, Craft, and Livelihood before 1900,' in J.M. Jensen and Sue Davidson, eds, *A Needle, A Bobbin, A Strike: Women Needleworkers in America* (Philadelphia 1984), 10–11

30 Ava Baron and Susan E. Klepp, ' "If I Didn't Have My Sewing Machine ...": Women and Sewing Machine Technology,' in Jensen and Davidson, eds, *A Needle, A Bobbin, A Strike*, 21

31 My analysis of the 1871 industrial census manuscript for Toronto revealed a total of 16 garment-making establishments where women were listed as proprietors: 11 dressmaking and millinery shops, 1 corset manufactory, 1 millinery and underclothing establishment, 1 shirt factory, 1 underclothing firm, and 1 firm specializing in baby linen and ladies' undergarments.

32 *Industries of Canada: Historical and Commercial Studies of Toronto and Environs* (Toronto 1886), 100, 150

33 *Report of the Royal Commission on the Relations of Labor and Capital* [hereafter *RCRLC*], 1889, Ontario Evidence, 347, 358

34 *Annual Report of the Bureau of Industries, 1889*, 49

35 *RCRLC*, Ontario Evidence, 347, 358

36 Ibid., 349

37 Wright Commission, 10

38 *Annual Report of the Local Board of Health, Including the Annual Report of the Medical Health Officer* (Toronto 1887), 6, City of Toronto Archives, RG 11, Box 167

39 *Mail and Empire*, 9 Oct. 1897

40 *Trades Union Advocate*, 29 June 1882

41 *Trades Union Advocate*, 24 Aug. 1882

42 *News*, 21 Dec. 1882

43 *News*, 3 Jan. 1883

44 *News*, 12 Jan. 1883

45 *News*, 1 Feb. 1883

46 *Trades Union Advocate*, 8 Feb. 1883

47 *News*, 9 Feb., 22 Feb. 1883

48 *News*, 10 Feb., 13 Feb. 1883

49 *Telegram*, 12 March, 15 March; *News*, 13 March, 14 March, 15 March 1883

50 *News*, 13 March 1883

51 *Telegram*, 14 March 1883

52 *Telegram*, 16 March 1883; *News*, 19 March 1883

53 *Telegram*, 25 Nov. 1879

54 *News*, 30 Jan. 1883. The employers' refusal to allow the women to keep a clock in the workroom may also have precipitated the strike. The employers' watch was reportedly notoriously slow in dismissing the women for the noon-hour meal and at the end of the day. See *News*, 7 Dec. 1882, 1 Feb. 1883; and *Trades Union Advocate*, 1 Feb. 1883.

55 *News*, 16 Sept. 1884

56 TTLC, Minutes, 1 Dec. 1882. See also Carolyn Strange, *Toronto's Girl Problem: The Perils and Pleasures of the City, 1880–1939* (Toronto 1995), 21–35

57 *Canadian Labor Reformer*, 15 May, 28 Aug. 1886; Kealey, *Toronto Workers*, 187; Gregory S. Kealey and Bryan D. Palmer, *Dreaming of What Might Be: The Knights of Labor in Ontario, 1880–1900* (Toronto 1987), 106

58 Kealey, *Toronto Workers*, 187; *Canadian Labor Reformer*, 9 Oct., 18 Dec. 1886, 8 Jan. 1887

59 *Canadian Labor Reformer*, 26 June 1886. Wright was prominent in Toronto labour-movement circles in the 1870s and 1880s. He had supported the Tory-Labour alliance that grew out of the nine-hours movement, and was active in the National Policy campaign of 1878–9. During the mid-1880s, Wright was at the forefront of the organization of the Knights of Labor in Ontario, while behind the scenes he remained deeply embedded in Ontario Tory politics. The Toronto edition of *The Palladium of Labor* was purchased by Wright in 1886, and transformed into the *Canadian Labor Reformer*, which he edited. At the 1888 General Assembly of the Knights of Labor, Wright was elected to the General Executive Board. Following

allegations of misuses of funds in 1893–4, Wright became the business agent for American speculators interested in acquiring timber rights in Central America. He was also involved in the Patrons of Industry. During the period immediately before his appointment to the Royal Commission on Sweating, Wright had edited *Industrial Canada*, the journal of the Canadian Manufacturers' Association. During the course of his career, Kealey and Palmer concluded, Wright proved to be 'a blatant opportunist, compulsive factionalist and self-seeking schemer.' For Wright's career in the Knights of Labor, see Kealey and Palmer, *Dreaming of What Might Be*, 248–76. For additional biographical information, see Henry James Morgan, ed., *The Canadian Men and Women of the Time*, 2nd ed. (Toronto 1912), 1188; *Globe*, 13 June 1919; and Christina A. Burr and Gregory S. Kealey, 'Alexander Whyte Wright,' *Dictionary of Canadian Biography*, vol. 14 (Toronto 1998).

60 *News*, 21 March 1887; *Globe*, 21 March 1887
61 *News*, 29 March 1887; Kealey and Palmer, *Dreaming of What Might Be*, 103
62 *Globe*, 21 April 1887; *Canadian Labor Reformer*, 23 April 1887
63 *Globe*, 25 June 1888
64 *News*, 23 June 1888
65 *Globe*, 3 June 1888; *News*, 3 July, 9 July, 10 July 1888; Jean Thomson Scott, *The Conditions of Female Labour in Ontario* (Toronto 1892), 27
66 *News*, 25 July, 26 July 1890; *Globe*, 26 July, 28 July 1890
67 *News*, 26 July 1890; Mariana Valverde, *The Age of Light, Soap, and Water: Moral Reform in English Canada, 1885–1925* (Toronto 1991), 77–9; Carolyn Strange, *Toronto's Girl Problem*, 53–115
68 *News*, 28 July 1890
69 Ibid.; *Globe*, 30 July 1890
70 *News*, 30 July 1890
71 Ibid.
72 Gurofsky to King, 24 Oct. 1897, Mackenzie King Papers, MG 26 J13, mfm C-1901, p. 285–91, National Archives of Canada
73 *Citizen and Country*, 1 April 1899; Roberts, *Honest Womanhood*, 38; Ruth Frager, '"No Proper Deal": Women Workers and the Canadian Labour Movement, 1870–1914,' in Linda Briskin and Lynda Yanz, eds, *Union Sisters: Women in the Labour Movement* (Toronto 1983), 54
74 Alice Kessler-Harris, 'Where Are the Organized Women Workers?' *Feminist Studies* 3 (Fall 1975), 92–110; Frager, 'No Proper Deal,' 44–64; Roberts, *Honest Womanhood*, 43–6
75 *News*, 14 March, 16 March, 23 March, 28 March, 30 March, 1 April 1887
76 *The Tailor* 2:8 (April 1890)
77 *The Tailor* 1:2 (November 1887)
78 Joan Wallach Scott, 'Work Identities for Men and Women: The Politics of Work and

Family in the Parisian Garment Trades in 1848,' in J.W. Scott, *Gender and the Politics of History* (New York 1988), 102; *The Tailor* 1:2 (November 1887)

79 *The Tailor* 1:3 (December 1887), 2:15 (November 1890)

80 *The Tailor* 2:22 (June 1891), 3:25 (August 1893)

81 *Mail and Empire*, 9 Oct. 1897

82 Eugene Forsey, *Trade Unions in Canada, 1812–1902* (Toronto 1982), 465; McIntosh, 'Sweated Labour,' 127

83 Wright Commission, 1–2, 54

84 *The Star*, 11 Jan. 1896

85 Wright Commission, 8, 13

86 Ibid., 17

87 Ibid., 17–19

88 Canada, House of Commons, *Debates*, 1 April 1896

89 *The Tailor* 1:19 (April 1889)

90 *RCRLC*, Ontario Evidence, 167–8

91 *The Tailor* 6:5 (December 1895)

92 The *Star* reported that the dispute between the employers and the journeymen tailors was confined to the King Street West stores, but would probably spread further. The city was divided into districts in which different scales of wages were paid. 'On King street west the scale runs as high as 21 cents an hour and on King street east it goes down to 18 cents, while on Queen street, in some establishments, but 15 cents are paid.' *Star*, 27 Dec. 1985

93 *Star*, 30 Dec. 1895

94 Ibid.

95 *News*, 31 Dec. 1895

96 *The Tailor* 6:7 (February 1896)

97 *Star*, 18 March, 9 April 1896; *Telegram*, 25 March 1896

98 *Telegram*, 22 April, 27 April 1897; *The Tailor* 7:10 (May 1897)

99 King later recalled his response in *Industry and Humanity*: 'On questioning one of the workers as to the remuneration she was receiving for sewing machine and hand work, I found that it came to a very few cents an hour. I shall never forget the feeling of pained surprise and indignation I experienced as I learned of the extent of that woman's toil from early morning till late at night, and figured out the pittance she received. The circumstance that it was Government work, and that the contracting firm was one of high repute in the city, did not lessen the resentment I felt. As I visited other homes and shops, I found the condition of this woman's employment to be in no sense isolated, but all too common.' W.L.M. King, *Industry and Humanity: A Study in the Principles Underlying Industrial Reconstruction* (Boston and New York 1918), 69–70

100 King diaries, 19 Sept. 1897, mfm copy FK 553, University of Toronto. The mid-

1890s were years of uncertainty for young Mackenzie King as he pondered which career – minister, academic political scientist, or politician – would best allow him to lead a 'useful life.' As an undergraduate at the University of Toronto, King was exposed to the political economy of Arnold Toynbee, and he took courses from William James Ashley and James Mavor. From these scholars, King assimilated a view of political economy that ascribed a positive role to the state in the transformation of society, and that also endorsed social-reform movements and trade unionism. 'During his university years,' Paul Craven writes, 'King became imbued with a sense of mission, and much of his involvement with various of the social movements of the day must be put down to his attempts to discover precisely what that mission entailed.' King was active in a variety of social-reform projects. While enrolled as a graduate student at the University of Chicago in 1896, he was involved briefly with the Hull House social settlement. It was during his association with Hull House that King first became aware of the problem of sweated labour. Paul Craven, *'An Impartial Umpire': Industrial Relations and the Canadian State 1900–1911* (Toronto 1980), 59

101 R. MacGregor Dawson, *William Lyon Mackenzie King: A Political Biography, 1874–1923* (Toronto 1958), 101; David Rome, ed., *On Mackenzie King and Jewish Sweated Labour*, part 1, introduction by Saul Hayes (Montreal 1979), iv–v. Hayes writes that King shared a warmth and intimacy with Gurofsky that he rarely enjoyed with others, but this intimacy was expressed with a decided anti-Semitism.

102 Dawson, *William Lyon Mackenzie King*, 68; *Globe*, 30 Sept. 1897

103 W.L. Mackenzie King, *Report of the Honourable the Postmaster General of the Methods adopted in Canada in carrying out of Government Clothing Contracts* (Ottawa 1900), 7–8

104 Ibid., 8

105 Ibid., 30

106 Ibid., 28

107 McIntosh suggested that the two and one-half years' delay meant that Mulock had difficulty convincing his cabinet colleagues to support the resolution. McIntosh, 'Sweated Labour,' 132

108 *Labour Gazette* 1:1 (September 1900), 10–26; Christina Burr and Gregory Kealey, 'Daniel John O'Donoghue,' *Dictionary of Canadian Biography*, vol. 13 (Toronto 1994), 781

Chapter 8: Conclusion

1 *Canadian Labor Reformer*, 23 April 1887

2 Joy Parr, *The Gender of Breadwinners: Women, Men, and Change in Two Industrial Towns, 1880–1950* (Toronto 1990), 245; Ava Baron, 'Gender and Labor History:

Learning from the Past, Looking to the Future,' in A. Baron, ed., *Work Engendered: Toward a New History of American Labor* (Ithaca and London 1991), 29

3 Parr, *The Gender of Breadwinners*, 241; Bettina Bradbury, *Working Families: Age, Gender, and Daily Survival in Industrializing Montreal* (Toronto 1993), 80–117; Michèle Barrett and Mary McIntosh, 'The "Family Wage": Some Problems for Socialists and Feminists,' *Capital & Class* 11 (Summer 1980), 51–72

4 Anne Phillips and Barbara Taylor, 'Sex and Skill: Notes Towards a Feminist Economics,' *Feminist Review* 6 (1980), 82–4; Jane Gaskell, 'The Social Construction of Skill through Schooling: Implications for Women,' *Atlantis* 8:2 (Spring 1983), 13–14; Veronica Beechey, *Unequal Work* (London 1987), 73–88

5 Harry Braverman, *Labor and Monopoly Capital: The Degradation of Work in the Twentieth Century* (New York and London 1974)

6 *News*, 22 Feb. 1883

7 *Ottawa Citizen*, 21 Sept., 12 Dec. 1996; *Toronto Star*, 22 June 1997

Bibliography

This bibliography is a guide to the secondary works that directly contributed to my interpretation of how class, gender, and race informed the politics of work and labour reform in late-nineteenth-century Toronto. The bibliography is by no means complete, however. The foregoing notes provide detailed references to the primary sources consulted for this study and complete references of other secondary works consulted.

Abella, Irving, and David Millar, eds. *The Canadian Worker in the Twentieth Century.* Toronto 1978

Alcoff, Linda. 'Cultural Feminism versus Post-Structuralism: The Identity Crisis in Feminist Theory.' *Signs* 13:3 (1988), 405–36

– 'Feminist Politics and Foucault: The Limits to a Collaboration.' In Arleen B. Dallery and Charles E. Scott, eds, *Crises in Continental Philosophy.* Albany 1990

Alexander, Sally. 'Women's Work in Nineteenth-Century London: A Study of the Years 1820–50.' In Juliet Mitchell and Ann Oakley, eds, *The Rights and Wrongs of Women.* Harmondsworth 1976

– 'Women, Class and Sexual Differences in the 1830s and 1840s: Some Reflections on the Writing of a Feminist History.' *History Workshop* 17 (Spring 1984), 125–35

Allen, Richard. *The Social Passion: Religion and Social Reform in Canada 1914–28.* Toronto 1973

Armstrong, Christopher, and H.V. Nelles. *The Revenge of the Methodist Bicycle Company.* Toronto 1977

Armstrong, Nancy. *Desire and Domestic Fiction: A Political History of the Novel.* New York and Oxford 1987

Armstrong, Pat, and Hugh Armstrong. 'Beyond Sexless Class and Classless Sex: Towards Feminist Marxism.' *Studies in Political Economy* 10 (Winter 1983), 7–43

– *Theorizing Women's Work.* Toronto 1990

Auslander, Leora. 'Feminist Theory and Social History: Explorations in the Politics of
   Identity.' *Radical History Review* 54 (1992), 158–76
– 'Perceptions of Beauty and the Problem of Consciousness: Parisian Furniture Makers.'
   In Lenard R. Berlanstein, ed., *Rethinking Labor History*. Urbana and Chicago 1993
Bailey, Peter. '"Will the Real Bill Banks Please Stand Up?" Towards a Role Analysis of
   Mid-Victorian Working-Class Respectability.' *Journal of Social History* 12:3 (Spring
   1979), 336–53
– 'Ally Sloper's Half-Holiday: Comic Art in the 1880s.' *History Workshop* 16 (Autumn
   1983), 4–31
– 'Parasexuality and Glamour: The Victorian Barmaid as Cultural Prototype.' *Gender
   and History* 2:2 (Summer 1990), 148–72
Baker, Elizabeth Faulkner. *Printers and Technology*. New York 1957
– *Printers and Technology: A History of the International Printing Pressmen and Assis-
   tants Union*. New York 1957
– *Technology and Woman's Work*. New York 1964
Bannerji, Himani. 'Introducing Racism: Notes towards an Anti-Racist Feminism.'
   Resources for Feminist Research 16:1 (March 1987), 10–12
– *Returning the Gaze: Essays on Racism, Feminism and Politics*. Toronto 1993
– *Thinking Through: Essays on Feminism, Marxism and Anti-Racism*. Toronto 1995
Barber, Marilyn. 'The Women Ontario Welcomed: Immigrant Domestics for Ontario
   Homes, 1870–1930.' In Alison Prentice and Susan Mann Trofimenkoff, eds., *The
   Neglected Majority: Essays in Canadian Women's History, Volume 2*. Toronto 1985
Barnett, George E. *Chapters on Machinery and Labor*. Carbondale and Edwardsville, IL
   1969; originally 1926
Baron, Ava. 'Woman's Place in Capitalist Production: A Study of Class Relations in the
   Nineteenth Century Newspaper Printing Industry.' Ph.D. dissertation, New York Uni-
   versity, 1981
– 'Contested Terrain Revisted: Technology and Gender Definitions of Work in the
   Printing Industry, 1850–1920.' In Barbara Drygulski Wright et al., eds, *Women,
   Work, and Technology: Transformations*. Ann Arbor 1987
– 'Questions of Gender, Deskilling and Demasculinization in the U.S. Printing Industry,
   1830–1915.' *Gender and History* 1:2 (Summer 1989), 178–99
Baron, Ava, ed. *Work Engendered: Toward a New History of American Labor*. Ithaca
   and London 1991
Baron, Ava, and Susan E. Klepp. '"If I Didn't Have My Sewing Machine ...": Women
   and Sewing Machine Technology.' In Joan M. Jensen and Sue Davidson, eds, *A Nee-
   dle, A Bobbin, A Strike: Women Needleworkers in America*. Philadelphia 1984
Barrett, Michèle. 'Rethinking Women's Oppression: A Reply to Brenner and Ramas.'
   New Left Review 146 (July–August 1984), 123–8
– 'The Concept of "Difference."' *Feminist Review* 26 (Summer 1987), 29–41

– *The Politics of Truth: From Marx to Foucault.* Stanford 1991

Barrett, Michèle, and Mary McIntosh. 'The "Family Wage": Some Problems for Socialists and Feminists.' *Capital & Class* 11 (Summer 1980), 51–72

Battye, John. 'The Nine Hour Pioneers: The Genesis of the Canadian Labour Movement.' *Labour / Le Travailleur* 4 (1979), 25–56

Beaven, Brian P.N. 'Partisanship, Patronage, and the Press in Ontario, 1880–1914: Myths and Realities.' *Canadian Historical Review* 64:3 (1983), 317–51

Behagg, Clive. 'Masters and Manufacturers: Social Values and the Smaller Unit of Production in Birmingham, 1800–50.' In Geoffrey Crossick and Heinz-Gerhard Haupt, eds, *Shopkeepers and Master Artisans in Nineteenth-Century Europe.* London and New York 1984

Bell, John David. 'The Social and Political Thought of the Labor Advocate.' MA thesis, Queen's University, 1975

Bender, John, and David E. Wellbery. *The Ends of Rhetoric: History, Theory, Practice.* Stanford 1990

Benenson, Harold. 'Victorian Sexual Ideology and Marx's Theory of the Working Class.' *International Labor and Working Class History* 25 (Spring 1984), 1–23

Berger, Carl. *The Sense of Power: Studies in the Ideas of Canadian Imperialism 1867–1914.* Toronto 1970

Berkhofer, Robert F. *Beyond the Great Story: History as Text and Discourse.* Cambridge, MA, and London 1995

Berlanstein, Lenard R., ed. *Rethinking Labor History: Essays on Discourse and Class Analysis.* Urbana and Chicago 1993

Bissell, Claude T. 'Literary Taste in Central Canada during the Late Nineteenth Century.' *Canadian Historical Review* 31:3 (September 1950), 237–51

Blewett, Mary H. *Men, Women, and Work: Class, Gender, and Protest in the New England Shoe Industry, 1780–1910.* Chicago 1988

Bliss, Michael. 'Privatizing the Mind: The Sundering of Canadian History, the Sundering of Canada.' *Journal of Canadian Studies* 26:4 (Winter 1991–2), 5–17

Bock, Gisela. 'Women's History and Gender History: Aspects of an International Debate.' *Gender and History* 1 (1989), 7–30

Boris, Eileen. *Art and Labor: Ruskin, Morris, and the Craftsmen Ideal in America.* Philadelphia 1986

Bradbury, Bettina. 'Women's History and Working-Class History.' *Labour / Le Travail* 19 (Spring 1987), 23–43

– *Working Families: Age, Gender, and Daily Survival in Industrializing Montreal.* Toronto 1993

Bradbury, Bettina, ed. *Canadian Family History: Selected Readings.* Mississauga 1992

Brandt, Gail Cuthbert. 'Postmodern Patchwork: Some Recent Trends in the Writing of Women's History in Canada.' *Canadian Historical Review* 63:4 (1992), 441–70

Braverman, Harry. *Labor and Monopoly Capital: The Degradation of Work in the Twentieth Century.* New York and London 1974

Brenner, Johanna, and Maria Ramas. 'Rethinking Women's Oppression.' *New Left Review* 144 (March–April 1984), 33–71

Brent, Martha Eckmann. 'A Stitch in Time: The Sewing Machine Industry of Ontario, 1860–1867.' *Material History Bulletin,* Spring 1980, 1–30

Brod, Harry, ed. *The Making of Masculinities: The New Men's Studies.* Winchester, MA 1987

Brodie, Alexander H. 'Subscription Publishing and the Booktrade in the Eighties: The Invasion of Ontario.' *Studies in Canadian Literature* 2 (Winter 1977), 95–101

Brooks, Peter. *The Melodramatic Imagination: Balzac, Henry James, Melodrama, and the Mode of Excess.* New Haven and London 1976

Bryson, Norman, Michael Ann Holly, and Keith Moxey, eds. *Images and Visual Culture: Interpretations.* Hanover, NH 1994

Buhle, Mary Jo. 'Gender and Labor History.' In J. Carroll Moody and Alice Kessler-Harris, eds, *Perspectives on American Labor History: The Problems of Synthesis.* DeKalb, IL 1989

Bullen, John. 'Hidden Workers: Child Labour and the Family Economy in Late Nineteenth-Century Urban Ontario.' *Labour / Le Travail* 18 (Fall 1986), 163–87

Burawoy, Michael. *Manufacturing Consent: Changes in the Labor Process under Monopoly Capitalism.* Chicago 1979

Burchell, Graham, Colin Gordon, and Peter Miller, eds. *The Foucault Effect: Studies in Governmentality.* London 1991

Burr, Christina. 'Class and Gender in the Toronto Printing Trades 1870–1914.' Ph.D. dissertation, Memorial University of Newfoundland, 1992

– 'Defending "The Art Preservative": Class and Gender Relations in the Printing Trades Unions, 1850–1914.' *Labour / Le Travail* 31 (Spring 1993), 47–73

– '"That Coming Curse –The Incompetent Compositress": Class and Gender Relations in the Toronto Typographical Union during the Late Nineteenth Century.' *Canadian Historical Review* 74:3 (September 1993), 233–66

Burton, Frank, and Pat Carlen. *Official Discourse: On Discourse Analysis, Government Publications, Ideology and the State.* London 1979

Butler, Judith. *Gender Trouble: Feminism and the Subversion of Identity.* New York and London 1990

Campbell, Marie. 'Sexism in British Columbia Trade Unions, 1900–1920.' In Barbara Latham and Kathy Kess, eds, *In Her Own Right: Selected Essays on Women's History in British Columbia.* Victoria 1980

Campbell, Marie, and Ann Manicom, eds. *Knowledge, Experience and Ruling Relations: Studies in the Social Organization of Knowledge.* Toronto 1995

Canning, Kathleen. 'Feminist History after the Linguistic Turn: Historicizing Discourse and Experience.' *Signs* 19:2 (Winter 1994), 368–404

Careless, J.M.S. *Toronto to 1918: An Illustrated History*. Toronto 1984

Carnes, Mark C., and Clyde Griffen, eds. *Meanings for Manhood: Constructions of Masculinity in Victorian America*. Chicago and London 1990

Chambers, Edward J. 'New Evidence on the Living Standards of Toronto Blue Collar Workers in the Pre–1914 Era.' *Histoire sociale / Social History* 18:36 (November 1985), 285–314

Chapman, Rowena, and Jonathan Rutherford. *Male Order: Unwrapping Masculinity*. London 1988

Christian, Barbara. 'The Race for Theory.' *Cultural Critique* 6 (Spring 1981), 51–63

Clark, Anna. 'The Rhetoric of Chartist Domesticity: Gender, Language, and Class in the 1830s and 1840s.' *Journal of British Studies* 31 (January 1992), 62–88

– *The Struggle for the Breeches: Gender and the Making of the British Working Class*. Berkeley and Los Angeles 1995

Clawson, Mary Ann. *Constructing Brotherhood: Class, Gender, and Fraternalism*. Princeton 1989

Cleverdon, Catherine. *The Woman Suffrage Movement in Canada*. 2nd edition. Toronto 1974

Cockburn, Cynthia. 'The Material of Male Power.' *Feminist Review* 9 (October 1981), 41–58

– *Machinery of Dominance: Women, Men and Technical Know-how*. London 1985

– 'Formations of Masculinity: Introduction.' *Gender and History* 1:2 (Summer 1989), 159–63

– *Brothers: Male Dominance and Technological Change*. London 1983

Colgate, William. *Canadian Art: Its Origin and Development*. Toronto 1943

– *The Toronto Art Students' League, 1886–1904*. Toronto 1954

Connelly, Patricia. 'Women Workers and the Family Wage in Canada.' In Anne Hoiberg, ed., *Women and the World of Work*. New York 1982

– 'On Marxism and Feminism.' *Studies in Political Economy* 12 (Fall 1983), 153–61

Cook, Ramsay. 'The Professor and the Prophet of Unrest.' *Transactions of the Royal Society of Canada*, 4th ser., vol. 13 (1975), 227–50

– 'Henry George and the Poverty of Canadian Progress.' Canadian Historical Association *Historical Papers*, 1977, 143–56

– *The Regenerators: Social Criticism in Late Victorian English Canada*. Toronto 1985

Cook, Ramsay, and Wendy Mitchinson, eds. *The Proper Sphere: Woman's Place in Canadian Society*. Toronto 1976

Cooper, Patricia A. *Once a Cigar Maker: Men, Women, and Work Culture in American Cigar Factories, 1900–1919*. Urbana and Chicago 1987

Cott, Nancy F. *The Bonds of Womanhood: 'Woman's Sphere' in New England, 1780–1835*. New Haven and London 1977

Craven, Paul. *'An Impartial Umpire': Industrial Relations and the Canadian State 1900–1911*. Toronto 1980

Crosby, Christina. 'Dealing with Differences.' In Judith Butler and Joan Scott, eds, *Feminists Theorize the Political*. New York and London 1992

Cross, Michael S., ed. *The Workingman in the Nineteenth Century*. Toronto 1974

Crossick, Geoffrey. 'The Petite Bourgeoisie in Nineteenth-Century Britain: The Urban and Liberal Case.' In Geoffrey Crossick and Heinz-Gerhard Haupt, eds, *Shopkeepers and Master Artisans in Nineteenth-Century Europe*. London and New York 1984

Cumming, Carmen. *Sketches from a Young Country: The Images of Grip Magazine*. Toronto 1997

Curtis, Gerard. 'Ford Madox Brown's "Work": An Iconographic Analysis.' *The Art Bulletin* 74:4 (December 1992), 623–36

Darroch, A. Gordon. 'Early Industrialization and Inequality in Toronto, 1861–1899.' *Labour / Le Travailleur* 11 (Spring 1983), 31–61

– 'Occupational Structure, Assessed Wealth and Homeowning during Toronto's Early Industrialization, 1861–1889.' *Histoire sociale / Social History* 16:32 (November 1983), 381–410

Davidoff, Leonore, and Catherine Hall. *Family Fortunes: Men and Women of the English Middle Class, 1780–1850*. Chicago 1987

Davis, Angela E. 'Art and Work: Frederick Brigden and the History of the Canadian Illustrated Press.' *Journal of Canadian Studies / Revue d'études canadiennes* 27:2 (Summer 1992), 22–36

– *Art and Work: A Social History of Labour in the Canadian Graphic Arts Industry to the 1940s*. Montreal and Kingston 1995

Dawley, Alan. *Class and Community: The Industrial Revolution in Lynn*. Cambridge 1976

Dawson, R. MacGregor. *William Lyon Mackenzie King: A Political Biography, 1874–1923*. Toronto 1958

Dean, Mitchell. *Critical and Effective Histories: Foucault's Methods and Historical Sociology*. London and New York 1994

de Lauretis, Teresa. *Technologies of Gender: Essays on Theory, Film, and Fiction*. Bloomington 1987

– 'Eccentric Subjects: Feminist Theory and Historical Consciousness.' *Feminist Studies* 16:1 (Spring 1990), 115–50

de Lauretis, Teresa, ed. *Feminist Studies / Critical Studies*. Bloomington 1986

Denning, Michael. *Mechanic Accents: Dime Novels and Working-Class Culture in America*. London 1987

Dex, Shirley. 'Issues of Gender and Employment.' *Social History* 13:2 (May 1988), 141–9

Diamond, Irene, and Lee Quinby, eds. *Feminism and Foucault: Reflections on Resistance.* Boston 1988

Downs, Laura Lee. 'If "Woman" Is Just an Empty Category, Then Why Am I Afraid to Walk Alone at Night? Identity Politics Meets the Postmodern Subject.' *Comparative Studies in Society and History* 35:2 (April 1993), 414–37

Dubinsky, Karen. 'The Modern Chivalry: Women and the Knights of Labor in Ontario, 1880–1891.' MA thesis, Carleton University, 1985

– *Improper Advances: Rape and Heterosexual Conflict in Ontario, 1880–1929.* Chicago 1993

Dubinsky, Karen, and Lynne Marks. 'Beyond Purity: A Response to Sangster.' *left history* 3:2 & 4:1 (Fall 1995–Spring 1996), 221–37

DuBois, Ellen, Mari Jo Buhle, Temma Kaplan, Gerda Lerner, and Carroll Smith-Rosenberg. 'Politics and Culture in Women's History: A Symposium.' *Feminist Studies* 6:1 (Spring 1980), 26–64

Eisenstein, Sarah. *Give Us Bread but Give Us Roses: Working Women's Consciousness in the United States, 1890 to the First World War.* London 1983

Faue, Elizabeth. '"The Dynamo of Change": Gender and Solidarity in the American Labour Movement of the 1930s.' *Gender and History* 1 (Summer 1989), 138–58

Ferland, Jacques. '"In Search of the Unbound Promethia": A Comparative View of Women's Activism in Two Quebec Industries, 1869–1908.' *Labour / Le Travail* 24 (Spring 1989), 11–44

Fetherling, Doug. *The Blue Notebook: Reports on Canadian Culture.* Oakville 1985

Fink, Leon. 'The New Labor History and the Powers of Historical Pessimism: Consensus, Hegemony, and the Case of the Knights of Labor.' *Journal of American History* 75 (June 1988), 115–36

Fones-Wolf, Kenneth. *Trade Union Gospel: Christianity and Labor in Industrial Philadelphia, 1865–1915.* Philadelphia 1989

Forsey, Eugene. 'The Telegraphers' Strike of 1883.' *Transactions of the Royal Society of Canada*, ser. 4, vol. 9 (1971), 245–59

– *Trade Unions in Canada, 1812–1902.* Toronto 1982.

Foster, John. 'The Declassing of Language.' *New Left Review* 150 (March/April 1985), 29–45

Foucault, Michel. *Discipline and Punish: The Birth of the Prison.* Translated by Alan Sheridan. New York 1979; originally 1975

– *The History of Sexuality, Volume I: An Introduction.* Translated by Robert Hurley. New York 1978, 1990

– *Power/Knowledge: Selected Interviews and Other Writings 1972–1977.* Edited by Colin Gordon. New York 1980

– *Politics, Philosophy, Culture: Interviews and Other Writings 1977–1984.* Edited by Lawrence D. Kritzman. New York and London 1988

Fowler, Roger. *Language in the News: Discourse and Ideology in the Press.* London and New York 1991

Frader, Laura L. 'Dissent over Discourse: Labor History, Gender, and the Linguistic Turn.' *History and Theory* 34:3 (1995), 213–30

Frader, Laura L., and Sonya O. Rose, eds. *Gender and Class in Modern Europe.* Ithaca and London 1996

Frager, Ruth. '"No Proper Deal": Women Workers and the Canadian Labour Movement, 1870–1940.' In Linda Briskin and Lynda Yanz, eds, *Union Sisters: Women in the Labour Movement.* Toronto 1983

– *Sweatshop Strife: Class, Ethnicity, and Gender in the Jewish Labour Movement of Toronto 1900–1939.* Toronto 1992

Frances, Raelene. *The Politics of Work: Gender and Labour in Victoria, 1880–1939.* Cambridge 1993

Frank, Blye. 'Hegemonic Heterosexual Masculinity.' *Studies in Political Economy* 24 (Autumn 1987), 160–70

Fraser, Steven. 'Combined and Uneven Development in the Men's Clothing Industry.' *Business History Review* 57 (Winter 1983), 522–47

Gallagher, Catherine. *The Industrial Reformation of English Fiction: Social Discourse and Narrative Form 1832–1867.* Chicago 1985

Gaskell, Jane. 'The Social Construction of Skill through Schooling: Implications for Women.' *Atlantis* 8:2 (Spring 1983), 11–25

Gordon, Linda. *Heroes of Their Own Lives: The Politics and History of Family Violence, Boston, 1880–1960.* New York 1988

– 'Response to Scott.' *Signs* 15:4 (Summer 1990), 852–8

Gorham, Deborah. 'The Maiden Tribute of Modern Babylon Re-examined: Child Prostitution and the Idea of Childhood in Late-Victorian England.' *Victorian Studies* 21:3 (Spring 1978), 353–80

Gray, Robert. 'The Deconstruction of the English Working Class.' *Social History* 11:3 (October 1986), 363–73

Griffiths, N.E.S. *The Splendid Vision: Centennial History of the National Council of Women of Canada, 1893–1993.* Ottawa 1993

Grimes, Mary C. *The Knights in Fiction: Two Labor Novels of the 1880s.* Afterword by David Montgomery. Urbana and Chicago 1986

Grimsted, David. 'Melodrama as Echo of the Historically Voiceless.' In Tamara K. Hareven, ed., *Anonymous Americans: Explorations in Nineteenth-Century Social History.* Englewood Cliffs, NJ 1971

Grossberg, Lawrence, Cary Nelson, and Paula A. Treichler, eds. *Cultural Studies.* New York and London 1992

Gutman, Herbert, and Ira Berlin. 'Class Composition and the Development of the American Working Class, 1840–1890.' In Ira Berlin, ed., *Power and Culture: Essays on the American Working Class*. New York 1987

Hagan, J., and C. Fisher. 'Piece Work and Some of Its Consequences in the Printing and Coal Mining Industries in Australia, 1850–1930.' *Labour History* 25 (1973), 19–39

Hall, Catherine. *White, Male and Middle-Class: Explorations in Feminism and History*. New York 1992

Hall, Jacquelyn Dowd. 'Private Eyes, Public Women: Images of Class and Sex in the Urban South, Atlanta, Georgia, 1913–1915.' In Ava Baron, ed., *Work Engendered: Toward a New History of American Labor*. Ithaca and London 1991

Hample, John. 'In the Buzzard's Shadow: Craft Subculture, Working-Class Activism, and Winnipeg's Custom Tailoring Trade, c. 1882–1921.' MA thesis, University of Winnipeg, 1989

– 'Workplace Conflict in Winnipeg's Custom Tailoring Trade, c. 1887–1921.' *Manitoba History* 22 (Autumn 1991), 2–15

Hann, Russell. 'Brainworkers and the Knights of Labor: E.E. Sheppard, Phillips Thompson, and the Toronto News, 1883–1887.' In Gregory S. Kealey and Peter Warrian, eds, *Essays in Canadian Working Class History*. Toronto 1976

– 'An Early Canadian Labour Theorist.' *Bulletin of the Committee on Canadian Labour History* 4 (Autumn 1977), 38–43

Hann, Russell, Gregory S. Kealey, Linda Kealey, and Peter Warrian. *Primary Sources in Canadian Working Class History, 1869–1930*. Kitchener 1976

Hardy, Jack. *The Clothing Workers: A Study of the Conditions and Struggles in the Needle Trades*. New York 1935

Hareven, Tamara. *Family Time and Industrial Time: The Relationship between the Family and Work in a New England Industrial Community*. Cambridge, MA 1982

Harper, J. Russell. *Early Painters and Engravers in Canada*. Toronto 1970

Hartmann, Heidi I. 'Capitalism, Patriarchy, and Job Segregation by Sex.' *Signs* 1:3, part 2 (Spring 1976), 137–69

– 'The Unhappy Marriage of Marxism and Feminism: Towards a More Progressive Union.' *Capital and Class* 8 (Summer 1979), 1–33

Hennessy, Rosemary. *Materialist Feminism and the Politics of Discourse*. London and New York 1993

Heron, Craig. 'The Crisis of the Craftsman: Hamilton's Metal Workers in the Early Twentieth Century.' *Labour / Le Travailleur* 6 (Autumn 1980), 7–48

– 'Towards Synthesis in Canadian Working-Class History: Reflections on Bryan Palmer's Rethinking.' *left history* 1:1 (Spring 1993), 109–21

Heron, Craig, and Robert Storey. 'On the Job in Canada.' In Craig Heron and Robert Storey, eds, *On the Job: Confronting the Labour Process in Canada*. Montreal and Kingston 1988

Hiebert, Daniel Joseph. 'The Geography of Jewish Immigrants and the Garment Industry in Toronto, 1901–1931: A Study of Ethnic and Class Relations.' Ph.D. dissertation, University of Toronto, 1987

Higginbotham, Evelyn Brooks. 'African-American Women's History and the Metalanguage of Race.' *Signs* 17:2 (1992), 251–74

Hobsbawm, Eric. 'Man and Woman in Socialist Iconography.' *History Workshop* 6 (Autumn 1978), 121–38

Homel, Gene Howard. 'James Simpson and the Origins of Canadian Social Democracy.' Ph.D. dissertation, University of Toronto, 1978

– ' "Fading Beams of the Nineteenth Century": Radicalism and Early Socialism in Canada's 1890s.' *Labour / Le Travailleur* 5 (Spring 1980), 7–32

hooks, bell. *Ain't I a Woman? Black Women and Feminism.* Boston 1981

Hulse, Elizabeth. *A Dictionary of Toronto Printers, Publishers, Booksellers and the Allied Trades, 1798–1900.* Toronto 1982

– 'Newspapers Printed on the Co-operative Plan.' *Papers of the Bibliographical Society of Canada* 22 (1983), 81–102

Hunt, Felicity. 'The London Trade in the Printing and Binding of Books: An Experience in Exclusion, Dilution and Deskilling for Women Workers.' *Women's Studies International Forum* 6:5 (1983), 517–24

– 'Opportunities Lost and Gained: Mechanization and Women's Work in the London Bookbinding and Printing Trades.' In Angela V. John, ed., *Unequal Opportunities: Women's Employment in England 1800–1918.* Oxford and New York 1986

Hunt, Lynn. ed. *The New Cultural History.* Berkeley 1989

Iacovetta, Franca. *Such Hardworking People: Italian Immigrants in Postwar Toronto.* Montreal and Kingston 1992

– 'Manly Militants, Cohesive Communities, and Defiant Domestics: Writing about Immigrants in Canadian Historical Scholarship.' *Labour / Le Travail* 36 (Fall 1995), 217–52

Iacovetta, Franca, and Mariana Valverde, eds. *Gender Conflicts: New Essays in Women's History.* Toronto 1992

Irwin, Grace. *Trail-Blazers of American Art.* New York 1971

James, Louis. 'Cruikshank and Early Victorian Caricature.' *History Workshop* 6 (Autumn 1978), 107–20

Jensen, Joan M. 'Needlework as Art, Craft, and Livelihood before 1900.' In Joan M. Jensen and Sue Davidson, eds, *A Needle, A Bobbin, A Strike: Women Needleworkers in America.* Philadelphia 1984

Johnson, Laura C., with Robert E. Johnson. *The Seam Allowance: Industrial Home Sewing in Canada.* Toronto 1982

Jones, Gareth Stedman. *Languages of Class: Studies in English Working Class History 1832–1982.* Cambridge 1983

Joyce, Patrick. *Work, Society and Politics: The Culture of the Factory in Later Victorian England*. Brighton, Sussex 1980

Kallmann, Helmut. 'Canadian Music Publishing.' *Papers of the Bibliographical Society of Canada* 13 (1974), 40–8

Katz, Michael. *The People of Hamilton, Canada West: Family and Class in a Mid-Nineteenth-Century City*. Cambridge, MA 1975

Katz, Michael, Michael J. Doucet, and Mark J. Stern. *The Social Organization of Early Industrial Capitalism*. London 1982

Kaufman, Michael. *Beyond Patriarchy: Essays by Men on Pleasure, Power and Change*. Toronto 1987

Kealey, Gregory S. *Working Class Toronto at the Turn of the Century*. Toronto 1973

– *Toronto Workers Respond to Industrial Capitalism, 1867–1892*. Toronto 1980

– 'Orangemen and the Corporation: The Politics of Class during the Union of the Canadas.' In Victor L. Russell, ed., *Forging a Consensus: Historical Essays on Toronto*. Toronto 1984

– 'The Writing of Social History in English Canada, 1970–1984.' *Social History* 10:3 (1985), 247–66

– 'Work Control, the Labour Process, and Nineteenth-Century Canadian Printers.' In Craig Heron and Robert Storey, eds, *On the Job: Confronting the Labour Process in Canada*. Kingston and Montreal 1986

– 'Class in English-Canadian Historical Writing: Neither Privatizing, Nor Sundering.' *Journal of Canadian Studies* 27:2 (Summer 1992), 123–9

Kealey, Gregory S., ed. *Canada Investigates Industrialism*. Toronto 1973

Kealey, Gregory S., and Bryan D. Palmer. *Dreaming of What Might Be: The Knights of Labor in Ontario, 1880–1900*. Toronto 1987; originally 1982

Kealey, Gregory S., and Peter Warrian, eds, *Essays in Canadian Working-Class History*. Toronto 1976

Kealey, Linda, Ruth Pierson, Joan Sangster, and Veronica Strong-Boag. 'Teaching Canadian History in the 1990s: Whose "National" History Are We Lamenting?' *Journal of Canadian Studies* 27:2 (Summer 1992), 129–31

Keller, Morton. *The Art and Politics of Thomas Nast*. New York 1968

Kerber, Linda K. 'Separate Spheres, Female Worlds, Woman's Place: The Rhetoric of Women's History.' *Journal of American History* 75:1 (June 1988), 9–39

Kessler-Harris, Alice. 'Where Are the Organized Women Workers?' *Feminist Studies* 3 (Fall 1975), 92–110

– 'Gender Ideology in Historical Reconstruction: A Case Study from the 1930s.' *Gender and History* 1:1 (Spring 1989), 31–49

Klein, Alice, and Wayne Roberts, 'Besieged Innocence: The "Problem" and Problems of Working Women –Toronto, 1896–1914.' In Janice Acton et al., eds, *Women at Work, 1850–1930*. Toronto 1974

Klink, Carl F., ed. *Literary History of Canada: Canadian Literature in English*. Toronto 1973; originally 1965

Kluckner, Michael. *Toronto the Way It Was*. Toronto 1988

Kutcher, Stanley Paul. 'John Wilson Bengough: Artist of Righteousness.' MA thesis, McMaster University, 1975

Lacombe, Michele. 'Theosophy and the Canadian Idealist Tradition: A Preliminary Exploration.' *Journal of Canadian Studies / Revue d'études canadiennes* 17:2 (Summer 1982), 100–17

Land, Hilary. 'The Family Wage.' *Feminist Review* 6 (1980), 55–77

Landry, Donna, and Gerald MacLean. *Materialist Feminisms*. Cambridge and Oxford 1993

Lawson-Peebles, Bob. 'Henry George the Prophet.' *Journal of American Studies* 10:1 (April 1976), 37–51

Leach, William. *True Love and Perfect Union: The Feminist Reform of Sex and Society*. New York 1980

Levine, Susan. *Labor's True Woman: Carpet Weavers, Industrialization, and Labor Reform in the Gilded Age*. Philadelphia 1984

– 'Class and Gender: Herbert Gutman and the Women of "Shoe City."' *Labor History* 29 (Summer 1988), 344–55

Lewis, Jane. 'The Debate on Sex and Class.' *New Left Review* 149 (January–February 1985), 108–18

Lipset, Seymour Martin, Martin A. Trow, and James S. Coleman. *Union Democracy: The Internal Politics of the International Typographical Union*. New York 1956

Lipsig-Mummé, Carla. 'Organizing Women in the Clothing Trades: Homework and the 1983 Garment Strike in Canada.' *Studies in Political Economy* 22 (Spring 1987), 41–71

Logan, Harold A. *The History of Trade-Union Organization in Canada*. Chicago 1928

Lord, Barry. *Painting in Canada: Toward A People's Art*. Toronto 1974

Lowe, Graham. 'Class, Job and Gender in the Canadian Office.' *Labour / Le Travailleur* 10 (1982), 11–37

– 'Mechanization, Feminization and Managerial Control in the Early Twentieth-Century Canadian Office.' In Craig Heron and Robert Storey, eds, *On the Job: Confronting the Labour Process in Canada*. Montreal and Kingston 1986

Macdonell, Diane. *Theories of Discourse: An Introduction*. Oxford and New York 1986

Macpherson, Mary-Etta. *Shopkeepers to the Nation: The Eatons*. Toronto 1963

MacTavish, Newton. *The Fine Arts in Canada*. Toronto 1925

Mailloux, Steven. *Rhetorical Power*. Ithaca and London 1989

Malson, Micheline R., Jean F. O'Barr, Sarah Westphal-Wihl, and Mary Wyer, eds. *Feminist Theory in Practice and Process*. Chicago and London 1989

Mangan, J.A., and James Walvin, eds. *Manliness and Morality: Middle-Class Masculinity in Britain and America 1800–1940*. New York 1987

Mark-Lawson, Jane, and Anne Witz. 'From "Family Labour" to "Family Wage?" The Case of Women's Labour in Nineteenth-Century Coalmining.' *Social History* 13:2 (May 1988), 151–74

Marks, Lynne. *Revivals and Roller Rinks: Religion, Leisure and Identity in Late-Nineteenth-Century Small-Town Ontario.* Toronto 1996

May, Martha. 'Bread before Roses: American Workingmen, Labor Unions and the Family Wage.' In Ruth Milkman, ed., *Women, Work and Protest: A Century of US Women's Labor History.* London 1985

Maynard, Steven. 'Rough Work and Rugged Men: The Social Construction of Masculinity in Working-Class History.' *Labour / Le Travail* 23 (Spring 1989), 159–69

McCallum, Margaret E. 'Separate Spheres: The Organization of Work in a Confectionery Factory: Ganong Bros., St. Stephen, New Brunswick.' *Labour / Le Travail* 24 (Fall 1989), 69–90

McClelland, Keith. 'Some Thoughts on Masculinity and the "Representative Artisan" in Britain, 1850–1880.' *Gender and History* 1:2 (Summer 1989), 164–77

McIntosh, Robert. 'Sweated Labour: Female Needleworkers in Industrializing Canada.' *Labour / Le Travail* 32 (Fall 1993), 105–38

McKay, Ian. 'Capital and Labour in the Halifax Baking and Confectionery Industry during the Last Half of the Nineteenth Century.' *Labour / Le Travailleur* 3 (1978), 63–108

McKillop, A.B. *Contours of Canadian Thought.* Toronto 1987

McLaren, Angus. *Our Own Master Race: Eugenics in Canada, 1885–1945.* Toronto 1990

Mellen, Peter. *The Group of Seven.* Toronto 1970

Middleton, Bernard C. *A History of English Craft Bookbinding Technique.* New York and London 1963

Middleton, J.E. *Canadian Landscape as Pictured by F.H. Brigden.* Toronto 1944

Milkman, Ruth. 'Organizing the Sexual Division of Labour: Historical Perspectives on "Women's Work" and the American Labor Movement.' *Socialist Review* 49 (January–February 1980), 95–149

Mitchinson, Wendy. 'The YWCA and Reform in the Nineteenth Century.' *Histoire sociale / Social History* 12:24 (November 1979), 368–84

Mohanty, Chandra. 'Under Western Eyes: Feminist Scholarship and Colonial Discourses.' *Feminist Review* 30 (Autumn 1988), 60–88

Montgomery, David. *Beyond Equality: Labor and the Radical Republicans 1862–1872.* New York 1967

Morgan, Cecilia. *Public Men and Virtuous Women: The Gendered Languages of Religion and Politics in Upper Canada, 1791–1850.* Toronto 1996

Morris, Jenny. *Women Workers and the Sweated Trades: The Origins of Minimum Wage Legislation.* Aldershot 1986

- 'The Characteristics of Sweating: The Late Nineteenth-Century London and Leeds Tailoring Trade.' In Angela V. John, eds, *Unequal Opportunities: Women's Employment in England 1800–1918*. Oxford and New York 1986
Morris, May. *William Morris: Artist, Writer, Socialist*. Volume I. New York 1966
Morton, Desmond. *Mayor Howland: The Citizens' Candidate*. Toronto 1973
Morton, Suzanne. 'Separate Spheres in a Separate World: African–Nova Scotian Women in Late-19th-Century Halifax County.' *Acadiensis* 22:2 (Spring 1993), 61–83
Mosse, George L. *Nationalism and Sexuality: Respectability and Abnormal Sexuality in Modern Europe*. New York 1985
Moxey, Keith P.F. 'Semiotics and the Social History of Art.' *New Literary History* 22 (1991), 985–99
- *The Practice of Theory: Poststructuralism, Cultural Politics and Art History*. Ithaca and London 1994
Moxon, Joseph. *Mechanick Exercises of the Whole Art of Printing*. Edited by Herbert Davis and Harry Carter. New York 1962; originally 1683
Naismith, George G. *Timothy Eaton*. Toronto 1923
Nash, Kate. 'The Feminist Production of Knowledge: Is Deconstruction a Practice for Women?' *Feminist Review* 47 (Summer 1994), 65–75
Newman, Louise M. 'Critical Theory and the History of Women: What's at Stake in Deconstructing Women's History.' *Journal of Women's History* 2:3 (Winter 1991), 58–68
Newton, Judith. 'History as Usual? Feminism and the "New Historicism."' In H. Aram Veeser, ed., *The New Historicism*. New York and London 1989
- ''Family Fortunes': "New History" and "New Historicism."' *Radical History Review* 43 (1989), 5–22
- 'Historicisms New and Old: "Charles Dickens" Meets Marxism, Feminism and West Coast Foucault.' *Feminist Studies* 16:3 (Fall 1990), 449–70
Nicholson, Linda. 'Interpreting Gender.' *Signs* 20:11 (1994), 79–105
Offen, Karen. 'Defining Feminism: A Comparative Historical Approach.' *Signs* 14:1 (1988), 119–57
Osterud, Nancy Grey. 'Gender Divisions and the Organization of Work in the Leicester Hosiery Industry.' In Angela V. John, ed., *Unequal Opportunities: Women's Employment in England 1800–1918*. Oxford and London 1986
Ostry, Bernard. 'Conservatives, Liberals, and Labour in the 1870s's.' *Canadian Historical Review* 41 (1960), 93–127
Palmer, Bryan D. *A Culture in Conflict: Skilled Workers and Industrial Capitalism in Hamilton, Ontario, 1860–1914*. Montreal 1979
- 'Response to Joan Scott.' *International Labor and Working-Class History* 31 (Spring 1987), 14–23

- *Descent into Discourse: The Reification of Language and the Writing of Social History*. Philadelphia 1990
- *Working-Class Experience: Rethinking the History of Canadian Labour, 1800–1991*. 2nd edition. Toronto 1992

Parker, George L. 'A History of a Canadian Publishing House: A Study of the Relation between Publishing and the Profession of Writing, 1890–1914.' Ph.D. dissertation, University of Toronto, 1969
- 'The Canadian Copyright Question in the 1890s.' *Journal of Canadian Studies / Revue d'études canadiennes* 11:2 (May 1976), 43–55
- *The Beginnings of the Book Trade in Canada*. Toronto 1985

Parr, Joy. 'Disaggregating the Sexual Division of Labour: A Transatlantic Case Study.' *Comparative Studies in Society and History* 30:3 (July 1988), 511–33
- *The Gender of Breadwinners: Women, Men, and Change in Two Industrial Towns, 1880–1950*. Toronto 1990
- 'Gender History and Historical Practice.' *Canadian Historical Review* 76:3 (September 1995), 354–76

Pedersen, Diana. '"Keeping Our Good Girls Good": The YWCA and the "Girl Problem," 1870–1930.' *Canadian Women's Studies* 7:4 (1986), 20–4

Peiss, Kathy. *Cheap Amusements: Working Women and Leisure in Turn-of-the-Century New York*. Philadelphia 1986

Perlman, Selig, and Philip Taft. *History of Labor in the United States, 1896–1932. Volume IV, Labor Movements*. New York 1966; originally 1935
- *A Theory of the Labor Movement*. New York 1970; originally 1928

Peterson, William S. *The Ideal Book: Essays and Lectures on the Arts of the Book by William Morris*. Berkeley and Los Angeles 1982

Phelan, Shane. 'Foucault and Feminism.' *American Journal of Political Science* 34:2 (May 1990), 421–40

Phillips, Anne. *Divided Loyalties: Dilemmas of Sex and Class*. London 1987

Pierson, Ruth Roach. 'Experience, Difference, Dominance and Voice in the Writing of Canadian Women's History.' In Karen Offen, Ruth Roach Pierson, and Jane Rendall, eds, *Writing Women's History: International Perspectives*. Bloomington and Indianapolis 1991
- 'Colonization and Canadian Women's History.' *Journal of Women's History* 4:2 (Fall 1992), 134–56

Piva, Michael J. *Condition of the Working Class in Toronto, 1900–1921*. Ottawa 1979

Pollock, Griselda. '"With My Own Eyes": Fetishism, the Labouring Body and the Colour of Its Sex.' *Art History* 17:3 (September 1992), 342–82
- 'Feminism/Foucault –Surveillance/Sexuality.' In Norman Bryon, Michael Ann Holly, and Keith Moxey, eds, *Images and Visual Culture: Interpretations*. Hanover and London 1994

Poovey, Mary. 'Feminism and Deconstruction.' *Feminist Studies* 14:1 (Spring 1988), 51–65
– *Uneven Developments: The Ideological Work of Gender in Mid-Victorian England.* New York 1988
Powell, Leona M. *The History of the United Typothetae of America.* Chicago 1926
Pretzer, William Stanley. 'The Printers of Washington, D.C., 1800–1880: Work Culture, Technology, and Trade Unionism.' Ph.D. dissertation, Northern Illinois University, 1985
Ramazanoglu, Caroline, ed. *Up Against Foucault: Explorations of Some Tensions between Foucault and Feminism.* London and New York 1993
Reynolds, Siân. *Britannica's Typesetters: Women Compositors in Edwardian Edinburgh.* Edinburgh 1989
Riley, Denise. *'Am I That Name?' Feminism and the Category of 'Women' in History.* Minneapolis 1988
Roberts, Elizabeth A.M. 'Women's Strategies, 1890–1940.' In Jane Lewis, ed., *Labour and Love: Women's Experience of Home and Family.* Oxford and New York 1986
Roberts, Wayne. 'The Last Artisans: Toronto Printers, 1896–1914.' In Gregory S. Kealey and Peter Warrian, eds, *Essays in Canadian Working Class History.* Toronto 1976
– *Honest Womanhood: Feminism, Femininity and Class Consciousness among Toronto Working Women, 1893 to 1914.* Toronto 1976
– 'Studies in the Toronto Labour Movement, 1896–1914.' Ph.D dissertation, University of Toronto, 1978
– '"Rocking the Cradle for the World": The New Woman and Maternal Feminism, Toronto, 1877–1914.' In Linda Kealey, ed., *A Not Unreasonable Claim: Women and Reform in Canada, 1880s–1920s.* Toronto 1979
Roediger, David R. *The Wages of Whiteness: Race and the Making of the American Working Class.* London and New York 1991
Rome, David, ed. *On Mackenzie King and Jewish Sweated Labour, 2 Parts.* Introduction by Saul Hayes. Toronto 1979
Roper, Michael, and John Tosh, eds. *Manful Assertions: Masculinities in Britain since 1800.* London and New York 1991
Rose, Sonya O. '"Gender at Work": Sex, Class and Industrial Capitalism.' *History Workshop* 21 (Spring 1986), 113–31
– 'Gender Antagonism and Class Conflict: Exclusionary Strategies of Male Unionists in Nineteenth-Century Britain.' *Social History* 13:2 (May 1988), 191–208
– *Limited Livelihoods: Gender and Class in Nineteenth-Century England.* Berkeley and Los Angeles 1992
– 'Gender History / Women's History: Is Feminist Scholarship Losing Its Critical Edge?' *Journal of Women's History* 5:1 (Spring 1993), 89–128

Rosenberg, John D. *The Darkening Glass: A Portrait of Ruskin's Genius*. London 1963

Rosenfeld, Mark. '"She Was a Hard Life": Work, Family, and Community Politics, and Ideology in the Railway Ward of a Central Ontario Town, 1900–1960.' Ph.D. dissertation, York University, 1989

Ross, Ellen. 'Survival Networks: Women's Neighbourhood Sharing in London.' *History Workshop* 15 (1983), 67–96

Roy, Catherine. 'The Tailoring Trade 1800–1920.' MA thesis, University of Alberta, 1990

Russell, Victor L., ed. *Forging a Consensus: Historical Essays on Toronto*. Toronto 1984

Rutherford, Paul. 'The People's Press: The Emergence of the New Journalism in Canada, 1869–99.' *Canadian Historical Review* 66:2 (June 1975), 169–91

– *The Making of the Canadian Media*. Toronto 1978

– *A Victorian Authority*. Toronto 1981

Ryan, Mary P. *Cradle of the Middle Class: The Family in Oneida County, New York, 1790–1865*. Cambridge, UK 1981

Samuel, Raphael. 'Workshop of the World: Steam Power and Hand Technology in Mid-Victorian Britain.' *History Workshop* 3 (Spring 1977), 6–72

– 'Art, Politics, and Ideology.' *History Workshop* 6 (Autumn 1978), 101–6

Sangster, Joan. 'Beyond Dichotomies: Re-assessing Gender History and Women's History in Canada.' *left history* 3:1 (Spring/Summer 1995), 114–17

Sawicki, Jana. *Disciplining Foucault: Feminism, Power, and the Body*. New York and London 1991

Schmiechen, James A. *Sweated Industries and Sweated Labor: The London Clothing Trades, 1960–1914*. Urbana and Chicago 1984

Schultz, John, ed. *Writing about Canada: A Handbook for Modern Canadian History*. Scarborough 1990

Scott, F.R., and H.M. Cassidy. *Labour Conditions in the Men's Clothing Industry*. Toronto 1935

Scott, Joan W. 'On Language, Gender, and Working-Class History.' *International Labor and Working-Class History* 31 (Spring 1987), 1–13

– 'Deconstructing Equality-versus-Difference or The Uses of Poststructuralist Theory for Feminism.' In Marianne Hirsch and Evelyn Fox Keller, eds, *Conflicts in Feminism*. New York and London 1990

– *Gender and the Politics of History*. New York 1988

– 'Review of *Heroes of Their Own Lives: The Politics and History of Family Violence*.' *Signs* 15:4 (Summer 1990), 848–52

– 'Response to Gordon.' *Signs* 15:4 (Summer 1990), 859–60

– 'The Evidence of Experience.' *Critical Inquiry* 17 (Summer 1991), 773–97

Seaton, Beverly. 'Considering the Lilies: Ruskin's "Proserpina" and Other Victorian Flower Books.' *Victorian Studies* 28:2 (Winter 1985), 255–82

Seccombe, Wally. 'Domestic Labour – A Reply to Critics.' *New Left Review* 94 (1975), 89
– 'Patriarchy Stablized: The Construction of the Male Breadwinner Wage Norm in Nineteenth-Century Britain.' *Social History* 11:1 (January 1986), 53–76
Segal, Lynne. *Slow Motion: Changing Masculinities, Changing Men.* New Brunswick, NJ 1990
Shikes, Ralph E. *The Indignant Eye: The Artist as Social Critic in Prints and Drawings from the Fifteenth Century to Picasso.* Boston 1969
Silverman, Eliane Leslau. 'Writing Canadian Women's History, 1970–82: An Historiographical Analysis.' *Canadian Historical Review* 63:4 (1982), 513–33
Smith, Dorothy. *The Conceptual Practices of Power: A Feminist Sociology of Knowledge.* Toronto 1990
Smith, F.B. *Radical Artisan: William James Linton 1812–97.* Manchester 1973
Smith-Rosenberg, Carol. *Disorderly Conduct: Visions of Gender in Victorian America.* New York and Oxford 1985
Soffer, Benson. 'The Role of the Union Foremen in the Evolution of the International Typographical Union.' *Labor History* 2:1 (Winter 1961), 62–81
Somers, Margaret R. 'Narrativity, Narrative Identity, and Social Action: Rethinking English Working-Class Formation.' *Social Science History* 16:4 (Winter 1992), 591–630
Speisman, Stephen A. *The Jews of Toronto: A History to 1937.* Toronto 1979
Stansell, Christine. 'A Response to Joan Scott.' *International Labor and Working-Class History* 31 (Spring 1987), 24–9
– *City of Women: Sex and Class in New York, 1789–1860.* Urbana and Chicago 1987
Steedman, Carolyn. 'The Price of Experience: Women and the Making of the English Working Class.' *Radical History Review* 59 (1994), 108–19
Steedman, Mercedes. 'Skill and Gender in the Canadian Clothing Industry, 1890–1940.' In Craig Heron and Robert Storey, eds, *On the Job: Confronting the Labour Process in Canada.* Kingston and Montreal 1986
Strange, Carolyn. *Toronto's Girl Problem: The Perils and Pleasures of the City, 1880–1930.* Toronto 1995
Strong-Boag, Veronica. *The Parliament of Women: The National Council of Women of Canada 1893–1929.* Ottawa 1976
Strong-Boag, Veronica, and Anita Clair Fellman, eds. *Rethinking Canada: The Promise of Women's History.* 2nd ed. Toronto 1991
Sutherland, Fraser. *The Monthly Epic: A History of Canadian Magazines.* Markham, Ont. 1989
Sykes, A.J.M. 'Trade-Union Workshop Organization in the Printing Industry –The Chapel.' *Human Relations* 13 (1960), 49–65
Thomas, John L. *Alternative America: Henry George, Edward Bellamy, Henry Demarest Lloyd and the Adversary Tradition.* London 1983

Thompson, E.P. *William Morris: Romantic to Revolutionary.* London 1955
– *The Making of the English Working Class.* Harmondsworth 1966; originally 1963
Tillotson, Shirley. 'We May All Soon Be "First Class Men": Gender and Skill in
  Canada's Early Twentieth Century Urban Telegraph Industry.' *Labour / Le Travail* 27
  (Spring 1987), 97–125
Tilly, Louise A. 'Gender, Women's History, and Social History.' *Social Science History*
  13:4 (Winter 1989), 439–82
Toews, John E. 'Intellectual History after the Linguistic Turn: The Autonomy of Mean-
  ing and the Irreducibility of Experience.' *American Historical Review* 92:4 (October
  1987), 879–907
Tolson, Andrew. *The Limits of Masculinity.* London 1977
Tracy, George A. *History of Typographical Union.* Indianapolis 1913
Trofimenkoff, Susan Mann. 'One Hundred and Two Muffled Voices: Canada's Indus-
  trial Women in the 1800's.' *Atlantis* 3:1 (Fall 1977), 66–84
Tucker, Eric. *Administering Danger in the Workplace: The Law and Politics of Occupa-
  tional Health and Safety Regulation in Ontario, 1850–1914.* Toronto 1990
Tulchinsky, Gerald. 'Hidden among the Smokestacks: Toronto's Clothing Industry,
  1871–1901.' In David Keane and Colin Read, eds, *Old Ontario: Essays in Honour of
  J.M.S. Careless.* Toronto 1990
Valverde, Mariana. '"Giving the Female a Domestic Turn:" The Social, Legal and
  Moral Regulation of Women's Work in British Cotton Mills, 1820–1850.' *Journal of
  Social History* 21:4 (1988), 619–34
– 'The Love of Finery: Fashion and the Fallen Woman in Nineteenth-Century Social
  Discourse.' *Victorian Studies* 32:2 (Winter 1989), 169–88
– *The Age of Light, Soap, and Water: Moral Reform in English Canada, 1885–1925.*
  Toronto 1991
– 'As If Subjects Existed: Analysing Social Discourses.' *Canadian Review of Sociology
  and Anthropology* 28:2 (1991), 173–87
– 'The Rhetoric of Reform: Tropes and the Moral Subject.' *International Journal of the
  Sociology of Law* 18 (1991), 61–73
Veruh, Ron. *Radical Rag: The Pioneer Labour Press in Canada.* Ottawa 1988
Vicinus, Martha. *The Industrial Muse: A Study of Nineteenth Century British Working-
  Class Literature.* New York 1974
– '"Helpless and Unfriended": Nineteenth-Century Domestic Melodrama.' *New Liter-
  ary History* 1 (Autumn 1981), 127–43
Vipond, Mary. 'Blessed Are the Peacemakers: The Labour Question in Canadian Social
  Gospel Fiction.' *Journal of Canadian Studies / Revue d'études canadiennes* 10:3
  (August 1975), 32–43
Waite, P.B. *Canada 1874–1896: Arduous Destiny.* Toronto 1971
Walby, Sylvia. *Patriarchy at Work.* Minneapolis 1986

Walkom, Thomas L. 'The Daily Newspaper in Ontario's Developing Capitalist Economy: Toronto and Ottawa, 1871–1911.' Ph.D. dissertation, University of Toronto, 1983

Walkowitz, Judith R., Myra Jehlen, and Bell Chevigny. 'Patrolling the Borders: Feminist Historiography and the New Historicism.' *Radical History Review* 43 (1989), 23–43

– *City of Dreadful Delight: Narratives of Sexual Danger in Late-Victorian London.* Chicago 1992

Walsh, Margaret. 'The Democratization of Fashion: The Emergence of the Women's Dress Pattern Industry.' *Journal of American History* 66:2 (September 1979), 297–313

Ware, Norman J. *The Labor Movement in the United States 1860–1895: A Study in Democracy.* Gloucester, MA 1959

Watt, Frank William. 'Radicalism in English-Canadian Literature since Confederation.' Ph.D. dissertation, University of Toronto, 1957

– 'The National Policy, the Workingman, and Proletarian Ideas in Victorian Canada.' *Canadian Historical Review* 40 (1959), 1–26

Weedon, Chris. *Feminist Practice and Poststructuralist Theory.* Cambridge, MA, and Oxford 1987

Weeks, Jeffrey. 'Foucault for Historians.' *History Workshop* 14 (Autumn 1982), 106–19

Weir, Angela, and Elizabeth Wilson. 'The British Women's Movement.' *New Left Review* 148 (November–December 1984), 74–103

White, Hayden. *Tropics of Discourse: Essays in Cultural Criticism.* Baltimore 1978

White, Randall. *Ontario 1610–1985: A Political and Economic History.* Toronto and London 1985

Wilentz, Sean. *Chants Democratic: New York City and the Rise of the American Working Class, 1788–1850.* New York 1984

Williams, Raymond. *Politics and Letters: Interviews with New Left Review.* Thetford, UK 1979

– *Culture.* Glasgow 1981

– *Culture and Society 1780–1950.* New York 1983; originally 1958

– *Problems in Materialism and Culture.* London 1987

Wilson, Alan. *John Northway: A Blue Serge Canadian.* Toronto 1965

Wright, Cynthia. '"Feminine Trifles of Vast Importance": Writing Gender into the History of Consumption.' In Franca Iacovetta and Mariana Valverde, eds, *Gender Conflicts: New Essays in Women's History.* Toronto 1992

Young, Iris. 'Socialist Feminism and the Limits of Dual Systems Theory.' *Socialist Review* 10:2/3 (March–June 1980), 169–88

Zeitlin, Jonathan Hart. 'Craft Regulation and the Division of Labour: Engineers and Compositors in Britain, 1890–1914.' Ph.D. dissertation, University of Warwick, 1983

Zerker, Sally. *The Rise and Fall of the Toronto Typographical Union, 1832–1972: A Case Study of Foreign Domination.* Toronto 1982

Index

Abbott, J.G. 15
Adair, Maggie 110
Aitken, Margaret 111
Albion Hotel 17
Ally Sloper's Half-Holiday 64
American Pressman 111, 113
Anthony, Susan B. 104
Anti-Poverty Society 9, 41, 84
apprenticeship 99, 178; and bookbinding
    117–18; 'devil' 123; and masculinity
    123; and typesetting machines 108–9,
    124, 206n42
Armstrong, John 137, 140
Arnold, Mathew 38
art workman 120–1. *See also* craftsman
    ideal
Astor, Jacob 21

Bailey, Peter 64, 92, 191n37
Baker, Elizabeth 111
Barnaby Rudge 58
Baron, Ava 98, 122
Beale, Charles 100
Beale, Henry 100–1
Beaty, James 58, 87
Beaty, Sam 58
Beaverback 71

Beecher, Thomas K. 90
Bengough, John Wilson 8, 10–11, 180;
    childhood and early career 56–7;
    'chalk talks' 56, 82–3, 89, 92; and
    Henry George 57; and John A. Mac-
    donald 64–5; and independence 66–7;
    and National Policy 69–78; and single
    tax 78, 80, 84; and free trade 78, 80,
    82; and landlordism 81–2; president,
    Single Tax Association 84; alderman
    84; and prohibition 90–4. See also
    Grip
Berger, Carl 44
Bindery Women's Union No. 34 116–17
Blake, Edward 59
Blewett, Mary 136
Bock, Gisela 6
bookbinding 113, 115–18; and middle-
    class women 120
Bradbury, Bettina 4
brainworkers 9, 32, 35, 54, 181
Braverman, Harry 183
breadwinner ideology 31, 106, 113,
    124–5, 146–7, 180
Brigden, Frederick 121
Brigden, Frederick H. (the elder) 11,
    100–1, 120–2

Briggs, Jimuel D.B. 33, 59. *See also* T. Phillips Thompson
Brotherhood of Telegraphers 143
Brown, George 5, 15–18, 22, 33, 59–61
Bryant, Grace 156
Buchanan, Isaac 70
Burnett, J.H. 160

Canada Cotton Company 48
Canada First 33
Canada Presbyterian 110
Canada Temperance Act 94
Canadian historiography 3–4, 185n4
Canadian Labor Protection and Mutual Improvement Association 22
Canadian Labor Reformer 146–7, 167
Canadian Methodist Magazine 96
Canadian Pacific Railway 18, 47
Canadian Printer and Publisher 108, 116, 120–1
Central Press Agency 104
Charlesworth, J.W. 171
Charlesworth, W.G. 140
Charlton, John: and seduction bill 44, 148–9
Childs, Charlesworth & Co. 136
Christian Guardian 108
Christianity 42, 56, 180; and community 74, 129; and craftsman 21, 62, 64, 121
Christie Street Anglican Church 85
Christopherson, E.S. 176
Clark, Anna 4
Clarke, E.F. 109
Cobden-Sanderson, T.J. 120, 209n97
Cockburn, Cynthia 4
colonialism 17, 66, 180
compositor 102–3
Cook, Ramsay 10, 42
Cooper, Thomas 16
cooperative commonwealth 125

Coopers International Union 7, 23; Local 3 7, 14
Cooper's Shoe Factory 135–6, 138, 140
craftsman ideal 11, 118, 120–1. *See also* Christianity
craftsmanship 26
Crawford, John 61
Currency Reform League 70

Damer, King & Co. 135
Dance, John 14
Daughters of St Crispin 12, 135
Denison, George Taylor 44, 156
Dickens, Charles 58, 199n10
diphtheria 162
Donovan, Eugene 137, 139, 141–3, 162, 164
domestic-labour debate 133
domesticity 25, 31, 106, 117–18, 124, 126, 146, 151, 180; and middle-class 147; and motherhood 129–31, 133, 164, 179; and working men 131–3
Dominion Alliance for the Total Suppression of the Liquor Traffic 92
Dudley & Burns 104
Dunlop, Stewart L. 105–6, 123

East Market Square 17
Eaton, Timothy 153
Eckert, Thomas 143
Elwin, Malcolm 24
Empire 108, 168
Enjolras 9, 38, 148. *See also* T. Phillips Thompson

Fair Wages Resolution 178
family 127, 152, 158, 171, 177–8, 184. *See also* separate spheres
Fax, James 180
Female Operatives' Union 139–41

femininity 29, 128, 133, 137, 142, 145, 180; and fashion 133, 160; and middle-class women 133
Fenian Raids 32–3
Financial Reform League of Canada 70
fireside 131. *See also* domesticity
flaneur 87
Flapdoodle: A Political Encyclopedia and Manual for Public Men 62
'For Lillie's Sake' 131–2
Foran, Martin 14, 23–4, 192n52
Foster, Miss 138
Foster, William 33
Foucault, Michel 191
fraternity 103, 125
Freed, A.T. 105
Friendly, A., & Company 165
Frogham, Miss 140

garment industry 11, 152–3; contracting 156–7; custom tailoring 154; outwork 152–3, 157; ready-made trade 154, 156, 173; sweating 11, 152–3, 172, 176
Gazette (Whitby) 57
Geary, W.H. 167, 171
George, Henry 11, 34, 37, 39, 180, 194n29
Giblin, John 138
Globe, The 15–17, 22, 27, 87, 100, 108–9, 137, 168
Glockling, Robert 116–17, 169
Glockling, William 116
Goldsmith, Charles 117
Gooch, E.S. 14
government clothing contracts 176–7
Gowan, Ogle 94
Grant, George Munro 44, 85–6
Grierson, Donald 167–8
Grip 8, 11, 69, 180; origins 56–8; plat-form 97

Grip Printing and Publishing Company 99–100
Gurnett, Helen 161
Gurofsky, Louis 157, 159, 170, 173, 176
Gutenberg, Johannes 101

Hall, Catherine 66
Hall, George 156
Ham, George H. 57
Hamilton, W.B. 140
Hann, Russell 10
Heakes, Samuel R. 48, 161
Hewitt, John 14, 189, 197n61
Hocken, H.C. 109
Hogarth, William 89
Home Rule 50
House of Lords Select Committee on Sweating 173
Howland, William 33, 49–50, 174
Hughes, Thomas 120
Hugo, Victor 38, 194n21
Hunter, Rose & Co. 100

immigrant: living conditions 152, 176
immigration: British 8, 17; Chinese 8, 18, 42, 71–4, 162, 180, 184, 195n43; Eastern European Jews 158; and garment workers 172; Irish 158; Irish-Catholics 9, 89; Italians 157
Imperial Federation 44–5
imperialism 180
'In the Reign of Justice' 13
independent democracy 43, 46
industrial capitalism: development of 3–4; and craftsman ideal 118; and employers 27; labour theory of value 19; and slavery 81
International Brotherhood of Bookbinders (IBB) 116–17; and Toronto Local 28 116

International Printing Pressmen's Union of North America (IPPU) 112
International Typographical Union (ITU) 98, 104
Iok, Mei 184
Irish Land League 34, 40
Irving, A.S. 58

Johnson, Charles 121
Journal of United Labor 144
Journeymen Tailors' Union of America (JTU) 171, 173–5, 176, 178
Joussaye, Marie 144, 215n79
Judge, James 14
Jury, Alfred 40, 50, 167, 173, 197n61

Kealey, Gregory 10, 34
Kelmscott Press 120
Kerber, Linda 12, 150
King, J.D. 137
King, William Lyon Mackenzie 152, 157, 157–8, 172, 233n99
Kingsley, Charles 16
Kingston Military College 45
Knights of Labor 3, 7, 9–10, 166; and women workers 12, 143, 214n69; organization 34; Uriah Stephens 34; and Christianity 41; assisted immigration 45; Terence Powderly 70; and women bindery workers 116; District Assembly 125 116, 145; and domesticity 127; Pioneer Assembly 136; Morse Assembly 143, 146; District Assembly 45 143; Excelsior Assembly 144; Hope Assembly 145, 167–8; Silver Fleece Assembly 145; Hand-in-Hand Assembly 116, 146; and equal rights 151, 180; Golden Fleece Assembly 168; Silver Fleece Assembly 168
Knights of St Crispin (KOSC) 135

Labor Advocate, The 84–5, 95, 147
Labor Reform Songster, The 35
labour reform: education 9, 22, 34–7, 127–8, 180; politics 47
landlordism: Irish Land Question 38, 40, 194n23
Laurier, Wilfrid 62
Leader, The 100
Lennon, John B. 175
Les Misérables (Hugo) 38
Linton, William J. 100, 120, 122
literature: conduct literature 128; melodrama 24–5, 29–30; poetry 17–18
liquor trade 92
Lowell, James Russell 38
Lumsden, John 105
Lynne, Marks 7

McCabe, Maria 148
McCormick, John 20, 191n26
Macdonald, John A. 14–15, 47, 64; and *Ontario Workman* 14–15; and Pacific Scandal 59–61; and National Policy 69, 71, 75–6
MacDonald, J. Ramsay 115
McGee, D'Arcy 32
Machinists' and Blacksmiths' Union 21
McInnis, Donald 48–9
Mackenzie, Alexander 59–64
Maclean, John 69
McLean, J.B. Publishing Co. 108
McMillan, Joseph C. 15
McNab, Samuel 145, 167
MacPherson, Ethel Day 120, 147, 216n92
McVicar, Katie 144, 215n75
Mail, The 48–50, 87, 108
Mail and Empire, The 158, 176
male suffrage 45, 190n20; and Natives 45–6
March, Charles 50, 198n76
masculinity 8, 17, 128, 178, 180, 202n75;

and chivalry 148; and Christianity 21;
and printing trades 99, 103, 123; and
respectability 20; and self-elevation
20–1; and self-help 20–1
Massey's agricultural implements 145, 167
Master Printers' Association 15–16
Master Tailors' Association 176
maternal feminism 150
Merchant Tailors' Association 171
Mergenthaler, Otto 107
Merritt, William 175
Methodist Book and Publishing House
116–17, 207n43
militarism 45
Milliken, A.J. 64
Miller, Mrs A.W. 160
Ministerial Association 85
Morgan, Cecilia 7
Morris, William 11, 119–20, 125
Mosse, George 66
Mowat, Oliver 50, 59–60
Mullock, William 176
Murray Printing Co. 108

Nast, Thomas 57, 69
National, The 33, 69–70
National Club 9, 33
National Council of Women 12
National Labor Union 16
National Policy 11, 48, 180
National Typographical Union 104
nationalism 66–9
News, The 9, 35, 37, 44, 46, 49–51, 54,
136, 165, 169, 183
News Printing Company 109
nine-hours movement 7, 16, 22, 30, 127
Northwest Rebellion 40

O'Donoghue, Daniel J. 40, 137, 173, 178,
197n61
Oliver, Rev. William 85

'Only a Labouring Man' 180
'Only the Working Class' 144–5
Ontario Bureau of Industries 115
Ontario Factories Act 115
Ontario Ministry of Labour, 184
Ontario Society of Artists 58
Ontario Stereotype Co. 109–10
Ontario Workman 14–15, 19, 22–3,
126–35, 150, 180; 'Grains of Gold'
128; 'The Home Circle' 128, 133
Orange Order 188n28, 189n2
Other Side, The 23–4
'Our Social Club' 37, 42–3, 47, 149

Pacific Scandal 59–60
Palladium of Labor, The 9, 35, 37, 46,
54, 144, 146–7, 196n53
Pall Mall Gazette 148, 196n49
Palmer, Bryan D. 34
Parker, Sir George Munro 44
Parnell, Charles 50
partyism 46–7
patriotism 18, 44
Patrons of Industry 9
Pennington, George 172
Phillips, Anne 4
Phillips, Wendell 38
Phipps, R.W. 69
'Political Economist and the Tramp, The'
53–4
political economy: capital 39; monopoly 39
Politics of Labor, The 3, 9, 38, 42, 52–3
Poovey, Mary 131
post-structuralism 6–7
Poverty and Progress 11, 34, 37, 39
press feeders 112–13
pressmen 111–12
printers' chapel 205n25
Printers' Miscellany 107
printing industry 11, 99, 101; and women
workers 11

private sphere 12, 118
public sphere 12, 31, 117–18

race: Anglo-Saxon 11, 44; and racism 18
rag-baby 71
Reade, Charles 24, 192n45
Richmond Hall 167, 170, 173, 176
Riel, Louis 40
Riordan, Charles 109
Robertson, John Ross 33
Robinson, C.B. 110
Roney, John 50, 198n76
Rose, Sonya 12
Roy, Allie 110
Royal Commission on the Relations of
    Labour and Capital 105, 161
Royal Templars 90
Ruskin, John 11, 118–20, 125
Ruskin Literary Society 120
Ryan, Mary 131

sabbatarianism 94–5
St Andrew's Hall 167
St James Square Presbyterian Church
    169
St John's Ward 158
St Simon's Church 85
Score, R.J. 175
Scott, Andrew 21
Scott, Joan 4, 171
seduction: 'Maiden Tribute' 148, 196n49
separate spheres 12, 126–7, 137, 149–50,
    171, 180, 210–11n2. See also private
    sphere; public sphere
sewing machine 156
sexuality 29, 106–7, 126, 142, 174, 179
Sheppard, Edmund E. 9, 35, 50
Simmons, George Richard 121
Simpson, James 120
single tax 10, 41, 80–1, 84–5

Single Tax Association 9, 41, 86; and
    labour reform 85
Sleeth, David 15
Smallpiece, H.R. 33
smallpox 162
Smith, Adam 38
Smith, Frank 94–5
Smith, Goldwin 33
Smith-Rosenberg, Carroll 131
Social Darwinism 51
socialism 43, 125
Sons of Temperance 90
Spectator (Hamilton), 105
Spencer, Herbert 38, 51, 53
'Spread the Light' 35–6
Stansell, Christine 153
statesmanship 69
Stevens, W.H. 142
Stones of Venice, The 119
Stowe, Emily Howard 46, 120, 217n104
Stowe, Harriet Beecher 38
Stowe-Gullen, Augusta 120
Street, Rev. Charles 85
street railway 94–6, 203n90; Kiely-
    Everett syndicate 96
strikes: printers 109–11; shoemakers
    135–41; telegraphers 143; women gar-
    ment workers 166–9
Swinburne, A.D. 38

Tailor, The 171–2
tailoresses 162, 167–8, 174
Taylor, Barbara 4
Taylor, H.A. 171
Telegram, The 165–6
Telegraph, The 33, 100
Telfer, Andrew 169
Telfer & Harold 166
Telfer Manufacturing Company 168
Temperance Hall 139

Tenniel, John 58
Theosophical Society 9, 120
theosophy 41, 120
Thompson, Edward 4
Thompson, T. Phillips 3, 9, 69, 120, 147,
    180; childhood and early career 32–3,
    193n4; and *The Palladium of Labor*
    37; and Toronto Nationalist Associa-
    tion 84
Thoreau, Henry 38
Timms, Moore and Co. 104
Titus, F.E. 120
Tom Brown's School Days 120
Toronto Art Students' League 121
Toronto Board of Trade 76–7
Toronto Bookbinders' Benevolent Soci-
    ety 116
Toronto Nationalist Association 84,
    120
Toronto News Company 58
Toronto Printing Press Assistants' and
    Feeders' Union 112
Toronto Printing Pressman's Union,
    Local 10 112
Toronto Secular Society 41
Toronto Trades Assembly (TTA) 7, 14
Toronto Trades and Labor Council (TTLC)
    34, 49, 73, 137, 141, 166–7, 169, 170,
    181; and assisted immigration 45; and
    the National Policy 77–8; and single tax
    85
Toronto Typographical Union, Local 91
    98, 105, 108, 123, 137
Toronto Women's Literary Club 46
Toronto Women's Suffrage Association
    9, 41, 46, 120, 217n104
Trades and Labor Congress of Canada
    (TLCC), 172
Trades Union Advocate 137, 139–42,
    162, 213nn61, 62

Treble, J.M. 162
Trevellick, Richard 16
Truth, The 104
Tweed, William Marcy 57
typesetting machines 107–10; linotype
    107–8; Rogers Typograph 108
Typographical Journal, The 123

union label 172
United Empire Loyalists 44
United Garment Workers of America
    (UGWA) 170
Up-to-Date Primer, The 79

Wage Worker, The 137
Walker and Hutchinson 156
Walkowitz, Judith 64
Warwick Bros. and Rutter 120–1
Watson, M.J. 161
Weir, William 69
Western Union Telegraph Co. 143
Whitman, Walt 38
Wholesale Boot and Shoemakers' Union
    136, 138
Williams, James S. 14, 127
wire stitchers 115
Withrow, J.J. 47
Withrow, Rev. W.W. 96
Woman's Christian Temperance Union
    90, 167
women: Amazon 139, 164; dressmakers
    160; and equal pay 141–3, 147, 180;
    garment workers 154, 157, 163; living
    conditions of 165; as press feeders
    112–13, 115–18; and printers 104–7,
    110–11; warrior allegories 131
Women at Work, Ontario 1850–1930 4
Women's Art Association 120
women's suffrage 46, 149; and prohibi-
    tion 93–4

Women's Typographical Union, No. 1
  104
Woods, Bert 152
Workingmen's College 120, 122
Workingmen's Liberal Conservative
  Union (WLCU) 69, 71
Working Women's Association 104
Workingwomen's Protective Association
  144
World, The 104

Wright, Alexander Whyte 40, 60, 146,
  157, 161, 167, 172, 221n59; editor of
  The National 70; and Knights of Labor
  70; Wright Commission 157, 159,
  172–4
Wynne, Captain 71

YWCA 12
York Hotel 101
York Typographical Society 101, 122

STUDIES IN GENDER AND HISTORY

General editors: Franca Iacovetta and Karen Dubinsky

1 Suzanne Morton, *Ideal Surroundings: Domestic Life in a Working-Class Suburb in the 1920s*

2 Joan Sangster, *Earning Respect: The Lives of Working Women in Small-Town Ontario, 1920–1960*

3 Carolyn Strange, *Toronto's Girl Problem: The Perils and Pleasures of the City, 1880–1930*

4 Sara Z. Burke, *Seeking the Highest Good: Social Service and Gender at the University of Toronto, 1888–1937*

5 Lynne Marks, *Revivals and Roller Rinks: Religion, Leisure, and Identity in Late-Nineteenth-Century Small-Town Ontario*

6 Cecilia Morgan, *Public Men and Virtuous Women: The Gendered Languages of Religion and Politics in Upper Canada, 1791–1850*

7 Mary Louise Adams, *The Trouble with Normal: Postwar Youth and the Making of Heterosexuality*

8 Linda Kealey, *Enlisting Women for the Cause: Women, Labour, and the Left in Canada, 1890–1920*

9 Christina Burr, *Spreading the Light: Work and Labour Reform in Late-Nineteenth-Century Toronto*